More . . .

Fifty-four strikingly evocative photographs unveil the private sides of the best and brightest men of stage and screen.

CAUGHT IN THE ACT
New York Actors
Face to Face

Photographs by Susan Shacter
Interviews by Don Shewey

They are America's leading men: glamorous, attractive, talented, famous. The envy—and fantasy—of millions worldwide. Their names glitter from marquees twenty feet above us. Names like William Hurt, Kevin Kline, Christopher Reeve, Raul Julia, Gregory Hines, Sam Waterston, and more. Known as New York actors, they are today's most gifted performers, who came from all over to study, to struggle, to succeed in the toughest town in show business. Now they share their talents and secrets, with exclusive interviews—in this stunning, surprisingly candid, beautifully illustrated book.

Neile McQueen Toffel

MY HUSBAND, MY FRIEND

Ⓢ
A SIGNET BOOK

NEW AMERICAN LIBRARY

PUBLISHED BY
THE NEW AMERICAN LIBRARY
OF CANADA LIMITED

This is an authorized reprint of a hardcover edition published by
Atheneum Publishers and published simultaneously in Canada
by Collier Macmillan Canada, Inc.

First Signet Printing, December, 1986

2 3   4   5   6   7   8   9

For my daughter,
TERRY MCQUEEN-FLATTERY,
and for my son,
CHAD MCQUEEN

FOR HIS extraordinary understanding in an extremely unusual and difficult situation, I thank my husband, Al Toffel. This book would not have been possible without his active support.

WORLDS of gratitude to Suzanne Reynolds Merrill, who listened and listened and listened! And to Ann Lonergan Smith, who urged me to write in the first place.

Preface

THIS BOOK is the story of a young girl and a young man who meet, fall in love, marry, and through his talents and her instincts, scale the heights of the movie kingdom.

I never had the least notion of writing for public consumption the intricacies and the intimacies of a marriage that Steve and I had been so successful in protecting from the world at large.

I feel compelled to do so to dispel the myths that have been written about us by people who never knew us and by people who claim that they were Steve's best friend and that Steve's life story could not be told properly without them. Their audacity startles me.

I write this also as a legacy for my children. I hope they will understand that love must be tended very carefully and gently, for once the bough breaks, the cradle does fall and all hell breaks loose.

Finally, for anybody who might be interested, my marriage to Steve did not end due to his predisposition for cars, as has so often been reported. That reasoning is absurd. One would have to be either stupid or a little touched in the head, neither of which I am, to leave a husband because of his love of machinery.

So here then is our story. It is written in my own hand, over a period of many months at odd moments in a usually busy schedule, at my kitchen counter.

Prologue

IT WAS JUNE of 1976, and the day was unseasonably warm and humid. A storm had been hovering off the California coast for days, unable to decide whether to come in or blow away. I was to meet with Steve at noon in the suite he kept at the Beverly Wilshire Hotel. Alone. For the very first time since our divorce in 1972. It had been drizzling on and off all morning and the rain would make valet parking unavoidable. (All those years with Steve had taught me to park and lock my own car whenever possible. Steve always steered clear of parking attendants; he was convinced that the dings on his vehicles appeared only when his car was parked by strangers.) Being dampened by the rain would not be conducive to keeping my wits about me. I also didn't want my teeth chattering away. I was already nervous and I wanted to have a clear head. I wanted to be ready for whatever was going to go down.

"Hi," I muttered shyly as we stood facing each other. He had opened the door and he, too, was unsure of himself. "Hello, baby," he said as he gave me a kiss on the cheek. As he led me into the suite, where lunch was waiting on the coffee table, we exchanged self-conscious small talk to level out the uneasiness we felt being in each other's presence once again. On this day, after too long, he wanted us to talk without having anyone else spying on us or even observing us.

By the time we had finished our lunch and gone through our life histories since our parting, it seemed like old times.

"You're comfortable here, aren't you?" He was amused by the idea that the interim years seemingly had wiped the slate clean, enabling me to relax and communicate with him like the old days.

I thought for a second and said, "Well, why not? Do you realize we've spent more time with each other than with anybody else in this whole world? And we're not enemies, are we? At least ... not anymore, I hope!" I smiled and he laughed.

There was a pause and then he sighed. "No, I guess not."

But I could feel the relaxed and easy banter was now coming to an end. The blue eyes were now suddenly staring at me unwaveringly. I began to feel uneasy, but I was determined to play it cool. My mind nervously shot back to the last time we had been together. It had been an angry encounter and it had been at the last house we had shared together, on Oakmont Drive in Brentwood, when he had come to pick out what he had wanted for himself. We had already been divorced, although that particular part of the settlement had had to wait until the completion of *The Getaway*. I had become bullish and determined to keep a piece of furniture, for no reason other than to annoy him, and had told him a quickly concocted story about a matinee idol and me. Even though Steve was supposedly in love with someone else, I knew it would provoke him. He stormed out of the house.

That was roughly four years ago. He was now married to Ali MacGraw and I was involved with somebody else on a more or less impermanent basis. However, we had never been out of touch with each other for longer than a few days at a time, although our conversations centered mostly around our children, Terry and Chad. Our divorce had not been easy on them. Terry was not quite thirteen and Chad was eleven—impressionable ages—and problems continually arose. We tried as best we could to keep one step ahead of them.

Once in a while Steve would solicit my advice on other matters. I guess habits, once established—especially when my tastes and judgments had proved right in the past—never die. One of those matters concerned a new movie that had been offered him called *The Towering Inferno*. He had been offered the leading role of the architect, but he wasn't too keen on the part. He was more intrigued by the role of the fire chief that had been penciled in for Ernest Borgnine. "But it's a smaller part," he said.

"Smaller, how? Are you saying it's a cameo role?"

"No, no. But he doesn't come in until halfway through the film. What do you think about that?"

If Steve was considering a smaller role I knew the part had to be of heroic proportions. So, what was being asked of me was a little reassurance. A little stroking, as he used to say. Every once in a while he needed that from me. I suppose because I had been there for him since the beginning and he knew that, no matter what, I could be counted on to support him.

Now, in this quiet room, my uneasiness shifted to controlled hysteria as he leaned over to speak. He looked at me intensely and I thought, He's married. What am I doing here? This is exactly the sort of thing he pulled on me when we were married! But just as quickly I told myself, Hell, that's not my problem! I have other things to worry about. Like, please, God, let this be a good meeting. Don't let it get out of hand. I wanted more than anything finally to lay to rest the pain and sorrow we had inflicted on each other.

He started speaking—very slowly—which was sometimes an ominous sign. (Steve when wounded reacted like an animal in the jungle. He would become still as his eyes fixed on his prey, and then he'd pounce without warning.) I was on my guard.

"I never expected you to file for divorce," he said. "Why did you do that?"

I was speechless. Words refused to form in my mouth. Then he continued, "I never expected you to connect with somebody else so soon ... I wish you had given me time. I needed that time ... I needed it, goddamn it! I couldn't cope with ... things as easily as other men!"

I sensed the anger rising in him and almost by reflex I started checking out the exits and the telephones. Oh, God! Is this going to start all over again after all these years? How did I allow myself to get in this situation? I should have known better! If he goes berserk it's going to be all over the papers!

But to my surprise and relief he continued talking and revealed to me for the very first time that he wished I had stayed at the Oakmont house until he was able to exorcise the demons that had plagued him.

It was wishful thinking on his part. I had tried to wait him out, but God, his behavior had made it humiliating and impossible. For me, a clean break had been the only answer. I had to get my life back in order and my self-esteem back, or I would have been lost.

He studied me for what seemed a long while then asked if he could hold me. I slipped into his arms ever so gently. And then he asked, "Do you suppose we could try again?"

When I didn't answer he blurted out, "*Christ! What the fuck did I do?*"

I don't remember how long I slept, but when I opened my eyes, I panicked before I realized I was still in the Don Quixote Suite. With him. I turned my head and saw the familiar face still sleeping. I reached for a cigarette, lit it, and stared at the man who had given me so much happiness and so much pain. How could something so right have gone so wrong? Was it possible, as he had asked me earlier, to start over again? I leaned against the headboard and agonized over the question.

I still loved him with all my heart. And I expected I always would.

But there was a difference this time around.

I knew I was no longer in love with him, and somehow I felt stronger for that knowledge.

Yet I believed, and always will, that I owe much of what I am today to him. Our strong history together was unerasable. He had introduced me to the world of "life." Before him, my entire universe revolved solely around dancing and the theater and my need to make that theatrical world work for me. Naturally, that meant classes to keep my body and mind in tune with one another so when my brain commanded, my body responded. It also meant auditions for yet other shows, so that a new set of eight performances a week could replace a used set of eight performances a week.

He had taught me how to drive and handle a car well.

He had taught me about guns.

He had even taught me about fashion by introducing me to *Vogue* and *Harper's Bazaar*—his knowledge of which he'd picked up from models he had dated.

He had shown me many of the simple pleasures in life, country walks and motorcycle riding, which I had shut my eyes to because of my compulsiveness.

He also had taken me to my first opera. In an effort to enlarge our appreciation for an art form we were not conversant with but were willing to experience, we went to the Metropolitan Opera to see *Aida*. Steve had said, "I never heard *Aida* and I want to take a shot at it." Unfortunely, we discovered we had no affinity for the medium. We both had dozed off.

His Hollywood celebrity had made us welcome to palaces all over the world. The leaders of foreign countries could not have been warmer to us. And we had exulted in that glory. Together we had reaped an enormous harvest.

We had grown up together and as far as we were concerned we had always been alone except for each other. Although both our mothers were alive and well at that time, our relationship with them had had no bearing on our relationship with one another. There had been no family to cushion us or give us support or advice.

We had children together.

Together we had built his phenomenally success-ful career.

And now here we were, having just made love, in the Don Quixote Suite of the Beverly Wilshire Hotel.

I blew a smoke ring and watched it float silently up toward the ceiling. God, the irony of it all, I thought. Are we a cliché or are we not a cliché?

It was twenty years after it had all begun and four years after our divorce. The way it was would never be again. We simply were not the same people any-more. If we tried again, might not the results be more devastating the second time around? Both of us had gone to psychiatrists to work out our prob-lems and mine had told me, "It takes two to tango." I had been a willing partner to the destruction of our marriage although I had conveniently blamed it all on Steve. Like it or not, I had also been guilty. So then what guarantees could we possibly extract from each other that would prevent us from grinding down our togetherness the next time around?

This much I was certain of: I could never again be a complacent partner. I was now wiser and I had also rediscovered my strength. He, on the other hand, seemed to be more troubled than ever before. The spirit that had personified Steve was gone. This man who had radiated magic had let his physical being crumble. He looked unkempt and his body had ballooned to un-movie star proportions. The intensive amount of time spent with his psychiatrist seemed to have been for naught.

So what, then? What kind of relationship are we to develop here?

As I put my cigarette out, I knew instinctively that the only successful kind of relationship I could have with him was to be his friend. And if we tumbled into bed occasionally, well, that was all right, too. Then I was assured of having the best of him without having to contend with the worst of him.

I checked my watch and slid silently out of bed and left him a note that simply said, "I love you." I dressed, left the suite, and went downstairs to retrieve my car. The weather, in the few hours I had been inside, had changed. The rain had stopped and in its place were big, soft, lazy, billowy clouds. To the west a rainbow had started to form. Within a few minutes, as I stepped into my car, I heard the whistle that time had made so familiar and the "Hey, Nellie!" that inevitably accompanied it. I looked up to find him on the balcony of his hotel suite. I laughed, shook my head, and said, "It's Neile, as in kneel down, you creep!"

A wide grin spread over his face. "I love you, baby."

Our eyes locked for a few seconds and I understood that he meant it. "I love you, too, honey. See you soon."

I got in my car and headed west toward the rainbow on Wilshire Boulevard. I had to pick up our daughter, Terry. She and I had a date to go to dinner and catch a movie.

I

The Beginning: 1930-1969

1

IN A VERY unusual way our lives paralleled each other's in texture if not in content.

Steve was an only child. I was an only child.

Both our mothers were young girls who had been appalled at having found themselves pregnant. Motherhood had been thrust upon them and neither was ready for it.

Steve's father abandoned him when he was barely six months old. I never knew my father.

He was raised in the midwest by his great-granduncle while his mother worked and pursued other things in life. I was raised in the Philippine Islands by a kind old man (who had also raised my mother) while she continued a dancing career in the Far East and pursued avenues more pleasant than motherhood, which she found dreary.

He was in reform school. I was in a Japanese concentration camp.

As a teenager, he joined the Merchant Marine and embarked upon an education in life's ways that would become the formative influence on the public persona of Steve McQueen. At fourteen, I was sent to the mainland to boarding school, which broadened my horizon as far as seeing what the Western world was like. It was there at Rosemary Hall that I recognized my artistic bent.

Later, he enlisted in the Marine Corps. My Parris

3

Island, or basic training camp, was the Katherine Dunham School of Dance.

By yet another amazing coincidence, Steve's mother and my mother, during approximately the same years, met and fell in love with men named Victor. Each man became the love of each woman's life.

Our shared backgrounds notwithstanding, emotionally we were poles apart. He was volatile, while I had inherited from my background the Oriental's compliant nature. But our differences seemed minimal. When we met we felt we had already known each other a very long time. That, and eventually our children, would bind us together forever.

Terrence William McQueen left his wife, Julian Crawford McQueen, almost as soon as baby Steven Terrence was born to them on March 24, 1930, in Beech Grove, Indiana.

Young and beautiful Julian, unable to cope with what life had dealt her, left little Steve with his great-granduncle, Claude Thompson.

Uncle Claude had a working farm in Slater, Missouri, and the young boy spent a big chunk of his early life learning the rules and virtues of a God-fearing society. It was an austere and lonely place, and Steve learned to love the horses and the pigs and the chickens and the cows and whatever other animals inhabited the land. He told me that sometimes, during especially cold mornings, he would curl up with the cows as soon as he had finished milking them. Then if time allowed he would let sleep overtake him.

His routine rarely varied. Usually, he awoke early, performed his chores, walked two miles to school, walked back the same two miles, performed a few more chores, did his homework, had dinner, and then went to bed.

Invariably, he dreamt about his mother. He wondered where she might be and what she might be doing.

Julian, in fact, was busy getting married and forming alliances with men which never seemed to last. We never did get an accurate count of how many times she married. Reports varied and Julian kept silent. Always.

She occasionally wrote letters to Uncle Claude and Steve to inform them of how things were going.

She came back once to see her son and, on a whim, took him back to Indianapolis to live with her. But this proved too cumbersome for her life-style as a swinging single woman who also held down a job during the day. What sort of job is unclear, since Julian, at this time, was totally unskilled. Consequently, their togetherness was short-lived. Back he went to Uncle Claude for a few more years.

In his own quiet way Uncle Claude loved Steve, and their relationship formed the foundation on which our own children would someday be raised (a lot of love and a lot of discipline). He was a quiet man not given to displaying emotions, but nevertheless one sensed they ran deep. Steve was very fond of him.

Indeed, soon after our marriage, Steve picked me up in a rented car at the Starlite Theatre in Kansas City where I had been working. Together we drove to Slater. He wished desperately to see the old man one more time before Uncle Claude passed on. He longed to tell him that although they hadn't communicated much over the last few years, Uncle Claude was never very far from his heart. He also wanted very much for the old man to see that he had grown to be a respectable young man. That he had married and had chosen a craft and was on his way to becoming a responsible citizen. The misfit was now light-years away.

Most of all, he yearned to show me where his roots were and for me to meet the man who had nurtured him. He wanted me to understand the loneliness that had surrounded him as a young boy.

When we arrived at the farm, dusk hadn't settled

yet and the late afternoon light was throwing velvety shadows around the rural landscape. I had never been to a working farm before, and I was awed by the beauty and serenity of the landscape. Quite literally, the only sounds to be heard were those of the animals, which terrified me because of their unfamiliarity.

Then quietly the porch door opened and, ever so slowly, out came Uncle Claude, followed by his much younger wife. Standing beside Steve, I could see the old man aching to, but unable to hug or touch this great-grandnephew, whom he obviously had a deep affection for.

Instead he just thrust out his hand and said, "Hello, boy! How ya been?"

Steve grabbed his leathery hand and said shyly, "Fine, Uncle Claude. I want you to meet my wife, Neile."

When Steve was twelve years old, Julian dislodged her son from this stable environment by taking him with her to her new apartment in Beech Grove, where she had returned to live. Very quickly, the sullen and quiet boy who was unwise to the ways of the world slipped into undisciplined unruliness. School became a sometime thing and his street-smart education began.

One day Julian, who had started to drink rather heavily, arrived home and informed her son that they would soon be three, for she was getting married that very night.

Steve's new stepfather, a man named Berri (Steve couldn't remember his first name), took a dislike to his new stepson upon their first meeting. He then proceeded to prove it by frequently giving the boy a thrashing. As much as she may have wanted to, Julian was powerless to protect her son from the physical abuse that he was suffering. To her, the obvious solution of sending Steve back to Slater was unthinkable. What would Uncle Claude say? She wanted the old man to believe that after all those years Julian was finally able to provide for her son, albeit through marriage. More and more alcohol became her escape from the unhappy life she had made for herself.

Not long after the wedding, Berri decided that moving west to California was the way to improve their lot. The war was in progress and fortunes were being made in California through war-related industries. He meant to ride the wave.

Almost immediately upon their arrival in Los Angeles, Julian started showing signs of disillusionment with her husband. As the marriage became increasingly volatile, Steve began spending his days with the various gangs in the neighborhood so as not to make the situation at home worse. To him, Los Angeles was at once fascinating, confusing, and turbulent. For the first time in his life he found himself with an ambition. He desired to be the "leader of the pack." To do so, he determined he had to win the other kids' respect by becoming the "baddest ass" of them all.

If the gang leader decreed that ten hubcaps were to be stolen today by each gang member, Steve would bring back twenty. If the order of the day was for each to steal two bottles of wine, then he would just work harder and return with four. Fear of being caught just simply had to be conquered or one would miss out on what life was all about. Looking through my mountain of scrapbooks (fifty, more or less, of our life together), I see old interviews and I am struck by the correlation between the life of the boy Steve and the man Steve. For instance, he once tried to explain his interest in auto racing as part of an effort to find out about himself, to find out who Steve McQueen was and to establish that identity. "Then of course the element of danger enters into it," he said. "As in bullfighting, not only is there danger, but there's that same kind of magnificent drama, including the matter of style."

Stealing was basic and racing was sophisticated, but it was the old song with a new melody.

Later, while filming *Le Mans* in 1970, someone repeated to him something that Karl Wallenda of the Flying Wallendas had said: "Life is walking on the wire; the rest is waiting in the wings." It might have been Steve talking. Indeed, the eloquence of that simple statement touched him almost mystically. Steve had basically been saying the same thing for a long time. In any case he immediately instructed his writers to incorporate Mr. Wallenda's words into the script.

But for now, the stage was set. The little bandit was caught for a second time in the process of stealing hubcaps off a Cadillac. Julian, beside herself over her son's behavior, compounded by her failing marriage, opted to send him to the California Junior Boys' Republic in Chino, a home for wayward boys. She felt that at the very least she was protecting her only son by keeping him out of the reaches of a cruel stepfather. Steve never saw it that way, though. It was just one more rejection from a mother who had rejected him all his life.

One day, in a quiet moment during one of my visits with the children to Julian in San Francisco, where she finally settled, she turned to me and asked, "What was I supposed to do? I had lost control of Steve, I had a very hostile husband, and I had to work. I had no other recourse but to sign that court order that sent him to the Boys' Republic."

She continued, as if asking for my approval, "It did have the effect of improving the oppressive atmosphere in my house. But the pain and guilt I felt were not worth it. Drinking just made the world a little saner."

And then, tearfully, she asked whether I thought her son had ever forgiven her. As I looked into her eyes I understood for the first time how this woman had suffered.

"Yes, of course," I replied, knowing full well that he hadn't and never would. He hated her and yet he couldn't turn her out of his life entirely. She was, after all, his mother. Yet he would get even with her by making her feel his childhood loneliness, that is, by limiting her access to us—her only family. It was distressing to see this unforgiving side of him, and I hoped that someday I could reconcile the mother and the son.

The California Junior Boys' Republic in Chino was a despairing and wretched place for #3188 aka Steve (Buddy) Berri aka Steve McQueen. Ultimately the persistent staff and the belligerent young boy would come to terms with each other.

Before this came to be, however, his undisciplined and rebellious behavior had to be gently steered. For an angry young man the difficulty lay in his unwillingness to abide by the laws that governed the school. The institution ran on an honor system based on trust, and the by-laws were dictated by the boys themselves. Yet trust was the very thing Steve lacked. Trust in anybody or anything. He attributed this to Julian's neglectful behavior. It was what he referred to, during some of his quiet and reflective moments with me, as his "bottomless pit," meaning a hole in his soul that no one could ever fill.

Twice, in fits of anger and frustration and loneliness, he escaped and was quickly apprehended and taken back to the school. He was told, "Decide to leave the school and the courts will be forced to put you in jail. Stay in school and all you have to learn is to function in a give-and-take society."

Still he persisted in skipping out. Punitive measures only strengthened his disaffection and his resolve to "don't trust no one. Do unto them before it's done unto you."

He was often ostracized by the group for various other infractions, like creating disturbances and refusing to do his chores. For the more serious of these, the butter paddle was applied to his backside many a time.

"It sure did hurt!" was his good-natured assessment many years later when the bitterness over the Boys' Republic was a thing of the past. Steve also told me of times too numerous to count when he would have to run around the track for God knows how many laps, while the rest of the boys were loaded into buses waiting to take them to the picture show.

Eventually, Steve came around, thanks to Mr. Panter, the school superintendent, who had taken an interest in him. Mr. Panter, with his kindly ways, reminded Steve of Uncle Claude. He was able to relate to this gentle, caring man whose ministrations helped solidify Steve's fragile feeling of self-worth. More important he was able to channel Steve's ferocious energy constructively and give him the self-respect he so badly needed.

The one discordant note during this period was again Julian. His mother never visited and very seldom wrote. During holiday periods when the boys were allowed to go home, Steve would invariably be the only boy left at school. There he would wander the grounds alone, barely able to contain the pain that tore his heart.

Unbeknownst to Steve, Julian was preparing herself for the divorce that now seemed inevitable. Immediately upon his confinement to the Boys' Republic, Julian determined to master a trade. She wished not to have to depend on another possibly disastrous relationship for her survival. To her credit, she became a draftsman and eventually wound up working for North American Aviation.

One day, quite unexpectedly and quite happily for her, Julian Crawford McQueen Berri became a widow. Although she did not wish her husband ill, she nevertheless was perversely grateful for his heart attack and subsequent demise. She sent word to Steve of his stepfather's untimely death and informed the school that she was moving to New York. She promised to send for her son just as soon as her affairs were in order.

Although her knowledge of New York was nil, Julian's sixth sense somehow guided her to the one place in the city that would accept her unquestioningly. The Village. Feeling free at last and ready for adventure, she melded with the local color as if she had been there all her life. Nobody bothered her and she was able to indulge an inclination for a bohemian way of life which had been denied her in Indianapolis. She found herself a cold-water flat and was able to transform the "dump," as she called it, into a very livable, very artsy home with very little money. She drank and smoked in public when it pleased her, she entertained her gentlemen friends in her flat when she found it convenient, and she worked when it was necessary.

One day she ran into a Los Angeles acquaintance, Victor Lukens, a cinematographer she had met at a party. While sparks had not ignited then, they apparently arced now. Pretty soon Julian abandoned her cold-water flat and the two set up housekeeping in Victor's nearby one-bedroom apartment. Julian said to me that this period had been the happiest in her life.

Several months after her arrival in New York, when she felt secure enough in her relationship with Victor Lukens, Julian impulsively sent for Steve. It was April of 1946, and Steve was sixteen years old. He had not yet completed the ninth grade, but he was itching to move on. The unexpected opportunity provided by Julian to go to New York was an exciting prospect. He made a quick determination to forgo his high school education. True, he had grown attached to the school and true, he had been elected to the Boys' Council, the most prestigious group in the school; but it was also true that confinement had not been easy on him. He had adjusted well over these last eighteen months, but now at this tender age he wanted to chart his own course—wherever it might take him. Julian would have nothing to say about it.

If he entertained any hopes of establishing a seminormal relationship with his mother, they vanished when he stepped off the Greyhound bus on 42nd Street. As soon as he gave his mother an awkward kiss on the cheek he realized she was inebriated. But she was in control of herself. She immediately launched into a nervous chatter about New York, her new life, and her new man. (Later Julian would say that she had been a nervous wreck over this reunion and had needed to fortify herself.)

As soon as they arrived in the Village, she laughingly told Steve she had to get him out of the stiff new denims he had arrived in. He looked out of place in New York, like a comic-strip character. She bought him some new clothes that made him look like a "native," introduced him to Victor, gave him some money to tide him over for the week, and showed him his new lodgings. That last part confused him; he had expected to stay with his mother. But then Julian explained to her son that her relationship with this man was new and important to her, and she did not wish to make waves by bringing him into their small quarters. She hoped he understood. Steve stared at her and said, "Sure." Nothing she did surprised him anymore. With her one could never assume anything.

The room she had rented for him was one in a three-bedroom apartment that belonged to an actor friend of Julian's who happened to be gay. In her haste, she forgot to apprise Steve of the situation. How she could have been so remiss is astonishing, given the fact that her young son was not wise to the ways of the world.

In any case, Steve came home one night and, to his horror, discovered his landlord in the arms of another man on the couch in the living room.

As far as he was concerned, Julian had done it again.

Following the unpleasant discovery in his rooming house in the Village, Steve became disinclined to use his room unless absolutely necessary. He did not have the means to move out. His unfamiliarity with his surroundings made it difficult to function independent of Julian's largesse. But now, more often than not, he began spending the night with girls he would befriend during the day.

Ultimately, he met two rather exotic-looking characters named Ford and Tinker. Ship's mates they were. They regaled him with tales of romantic adventures on various Caribbean islands. It sounded intriguing to the young man, and the next thing he knew Steve was on board the tanker *Alpha* bound for Cuba and the Dominican Republic with a fake ablebodied seaman's card his new friends had acquired for him.

To his dismay he discovered that the workload was only this side of slavery. When the tanker docked at Santo Domingo in the Dominican Republic (Steve always referred to this country as the "Dominion Republic"), he decided to jump ship. He found work in a brothel as a towel boy. His blond, blue-eyed looks made him a favorite of the house staff, whose clientele was usually dark-haired and dark-eyed. The perks that came Steve's way were plentiful. He said to me with a twinkle in his eyes, "I was one happy fella!"

After an idyllic eight weeks, he worked his way back to the United States and wound up at Port Arthur, Texas, at another brothel. This time he was a waiter. This was followed by a series of odd jobs. He became a "grunt" (laborer) in Waco oilfields, a hi-jacker in a lumber town, and a carnival huckster selling pen-and-pencil sets. Finally, he found himself in Myrtle Beach, South Carolina, where his exhausted soul confronted the loneliness, the rejection, and the desperation that lay beneath his nomadic life. He was tired of running. He was only seventeen years old and already he felt old.

He decided to enlist in the Marine Corps. At least he would know where home was for the next three years.

It took a few minor adjustments in the Marine Corps—like two twenty-one-day stints in the brig—finally to get Steve McQueen, PFC, in line. He liked Myrtle Beach and he liked two girls he had met there even more. As soon as he was given his first weekend pass, he headed for the house of one of the girls and extended the weekend to a week. The Marine Corps called his absence from the base going AWOL. Steve called it taking it easy after the strenuous boot camp training. He was thrown in the brig. On his very next weekend pass, he did the very same thing that had gotten him into trouble. Only this time, as soon as he arrived in Myrtle Beach, he went looking for the other girl and, to be fair, spent a week with her too. Not surprisingly, the shore patrol was waiting for him, and this time, in addition to the usual brig stint, he was confined to the base until further notice.

If Steve was determined to outfox the Marine Corps, the Corps was just as determined to outfox Steve until ultimately he realized that being part of the team was what was required of him.

When Steve got into the swing of things, he positively reveled in it. His enlistment in the Marine Corps turned out to be the best decision he had made in his young life. He loved the physical aspects of marine life, the physical discipline the Corps instilled, which, throughout our time together, never left Steve. Though wiry at five ten and a half, he was proud of the way his body looked and he insisted that I, as his wife, keep fit. In fact, he would insist on inspecting my body in the harsh light and making suggestions on how improvements might be made. Being the good wife that I was, I complied. It never occurred to me to tell him to go to hell.

Another aspect of the Marines that he loved was their faith in his mechanical skills, which were minimal. Nevertheless, he was able to wing it. What he didn't know, he invented. And then they assigned him a tank. It was his to drive! Now the Marine Corps became not only his surrogate mother and father, it was Santa Claus, too. He drove and took care of this tank with the fervor of a child who has received his first bicycle. He also tried to soup up the engine, which did not work. It didn't matter. He was delighted with his new toy.

Minor mishaps were common occurrences with PFC McQueen. His favorite escapade took place during a maneuver in Labrador. A case of pork and beans somehow managed to find its way into Steve's tank. He and two buddies, tired of cold K rations, devised a way to warm up the cans. One would rev up the engine, another would hold the can of beans over the exhaust pipe, and the third would keep watch for unfriendly persons or officers who might happen to stumble upon this little operation. After success with several cans, lo and behold, the unforeseen happened. A twenty-four-ounce can of pork and beans exploded under the intense heat, spraying its contents far and wide. For days and weeks later, beans could be seen stuck on tanks, jeeps, helmets, caps. Nothing and no one had been spared a bean or two. Steve always recounted this espisode with glee.

Being a tank driver with the Second Marine Division of the Fleet Marine Force was not all pranks and hijinks. There were always dangerous exercises and training maneuvers to perform under simulated wartime conditions. During one of the division's cold-water amphibious exercises off Labrador, a transport struck a sandbank and flung several tanks with their crews into the frigid ocean. Quite a few men drowned. Steve unthinkingly jumped in the water when he saw a marine barely clinging to a turret that jutted out of the water. His fearless execution of a heroic act saved the marine's life and earned him a citation from his unit commander.

One of his proudest moments was being chosen as part of the honor guard protecting President Harry Truman's yacht. The honor was most likely a reward for his bravery on that cold day in the North Atlantic.

Twenty-one days before the outbreak of the Korean War, PFC Steven T. McQueen was honorably discharged from the Marine Corps. Months later he learned that his whole outfit had been wiped out in the Korean conflict.

Afterward, he would remember his Marine experience with affection and gratitude. He felt it had shaped him up and had given him the discipline that comes from living in close quarters with other men. Otherwise "I would have ended up in jail or something. I was a wild kid."

Once more he found himself in a lonely situation. He felt like a ship without a sail. He missed the Corps. He missed the camaraderie. And most of all he missed his home.

He returned to Myrtle Beach, where at least he knew a few people. This time around, he took a good, hard look at how "civilians" conducted their lives and thought that maybe he might like some of that for himself someday. But how? His money was almost gone, he had no job, he had no formal education, and he didn't even have a trade. The only thing he knew how to do well was drive a tank and, as yet, there was no call for tanks on the streets of America. He didn't need much to survive. As he said, "When you're poor, you work for the basics. You can't be choosy." But he was not going to look for work in Myrtle Beach. There they had known him as a leatherneck, and he was going to make his exit as a leatherneck.

Following a brief detour in Washington, D.C., where he picked up some money driving cabs, Steve decided to give New York another try. He had been away three years. He found himself a $19-a-month cold-water flat and began working a dizzying variety of jobs. In rapid succession, he delivered television sets (not profitable yet), he made sandals, he made artificial flowers, he bartended, he drove trucks, he worked at the post office, he sold encyclopedias door to door—and he stole. He developed a scheme whereby he would pick up a piece of merchandise in a store, then look as if he had bought said piece of merchandise and was in the process of maybe exchanging it for something else, when suddenly he would change his mind and say rather innocently, "No, thank you. I think I'll just take my money back." In fact, he used this same technique at Schwab's Drugstore in Los Angeles as late as 1959, the night our daughter, Terry, was born. Our good friend Suzanne Pleshette was fixing him dinner that night. They wanted to toast the baby's birth, but there was nothing to toast with. Steve immediately got on his motorcycle and zoomed off to Schwab's, only a few blocks away. There he went through his routine. He picked up a bottle of wine, pretended it was his, and asked to exchange it for something better. This time, though, the charade really was a game to him. He was already starring in "Wanted—Dead or Alive" and had just started work on the film *Never So Few.* He was not in any real need of money—although he had the most irritating lifelong habit of not carrying any cash—and he certainly could afford a bottle of wine. He just wanted to see whether he could still do it. Then he returned to Suzanne's house, toasted his wife and his new daughter, had dinner, and got smashed.

In 1951, while contemplating whether he should go to tile-setting school with his GI Bill, a girl he was seeing convinced him to accompany her to the Neighborhood Playhouse, where she was taking acting classes. He was introduced to Sandy Meisner, who was the director and teacher *extraordinaire*. He was impressed with Steve's quality and in no time at all Steve was in the school. He worked hard; in fact, he worked much the same way as he had when he was a young gang member in Los Angeles, doubling everything that was asked of him. One day, his enthusiasm and lack of acting technique got the better of him. He was asked to do an improvisational scene with a girl. In the middle of the improvisation, the girl slapped him, which caught Steve by surprise, and he in turn knocked her cold, which took everybody by surprise.

Two years later he became a scholarship student at the Uta Hagen–Herbert Berghof School and got his first acting job doing Yiddish theater with Molly Picon. He had one line and was paid $40 a week. This was followed by a play in upstate New York summer stock in which he played an English fop opposite Margaret O'Brien. George Englund, who directed the play and who later became a good friend, came backstage as soon as the curtain went down on opening night and said, "Steve, I want you to know you were embarrassing." Criticism of his acting then did not bother Steve McQueen one bit. He liked what he was doing. He just had to find a way to make acting like him. He decided that technique was the answer.

Technique, at this point, meant to Steve feeling comfortable with the author's words and feeling comfortable with his body on stage. (Later on, as a movie star, he would conclude that his personality, projected onto the screen, was the most important element in his acting technique.) As a means to an end, he went on every casting call that Equity posted.

A few months later he was cast in a touring company of *Member of the Wedding*, starring Ethel Waters. When the tour finished, he found himself in Chicago with *Time Out for Ginger*, starring Melvyn Douglas. In 1955, after a brief "rest" period, Steve showed up in Maine with Gary Merrill in *The Gep*, hoping the play would get to Broadway. It didn't.

At the conclusion of that ill-fated play, Steve returned to New York and the unemployment line and auditioned for the Actors Studio. He knew that the Studio was churning out a very special breed of actors. Plus the Studio had the additional cachet of being an exclusive club. He wanted in.

He auditioned for Lee Strasberg, doing the park scene from *Golden Boy*. He was one of five out of hundreds who made it.

Almost immediately he began to do television shows here and there. Not big roles, but big enough so that he had his foot in the door.

In the early spring of 1956, along came a movie titled *Somebody Up There Likes Me*. It was to be directed by Robert Wise and it was to star Paul Newman. Paul was also from the Actors Studio. He was also older and more of a seasoned performer than Steve.

When the film was released late that year, Paul Newman became the talk of the movie world. He had been wonderfully brilliant in the film, while Steve had been absolutely dreadful in a minor part. Steve's competitiveness with Paul started way back then. He quietly vowed to himself that he would catch up with Paul Newman someday. And he would—but it would take him eighteen years to do it.

This competition with Paul Newman had its beginnings in the chip on Steve's shoulder. It was irrational, he knew, but Paul grated on him. He was handsome, talented, and came from a middle-class family in Cleveland. Steve felt that Paul hadn't come by his "rebel" status honestly. Steve used to say that, most probably, Paul was in college while he, the *true* rebel, was busy stealing hubcaps. Paul, being the older of the two, had the added edge of maturity. He was also a working actor, with an impressive list of television and Broadway credits. And now Paul had become an honest-to-goodness film star.

In the meantime, the year 1955 found Steve involved with an assortment of women. Among them were an older acting teacher, a dancer from the Latin Quarter, a daughter of an army officer, and a scattering of actresses and models who inhabited the clubs and coffeehouses of New York City. He was just twenty-five years old. Life was for the taking. But by early 1956 he had slowed down. He concentrated a bit more on his career, although the womenfolk were still a very visible part of his life.

His path was about to collide with that of a petite, dark-haired twenty-two-year-old successful Broadway dancer.

2

MY MOTHER was a hugely successful Manila-based dancing star in the Far East known as "Miami." At age thirteen she had entered a dancing contest and shortly after surprised herself and her mother by earning more money than anyone else in the family. Her father had died a few years earlier and it had been rough going. Being totally untrained and in a country where the formal dance was unheard of, Miami adopted movements she had seen performed by the varied ethnic groups in the islands and created her own dance form. She borrowed from the Malaysians, from the Polynesians, and threw in a bit of the Spanish flamenco. Eventually, the hula from Hawaii became her signature dance.

At twenty, she met a tall, dark, handsome stranger who appeared at the stage door one night and fell madly in love. Miami was of Spanish and German descent, while the man was of unknown origins. As I was growing up, my mother alternately described my father to me as a plantation owner, a soldier of fortune, and sometimes as somebody who was attached to the diplomatic corps stationed in Hong Kong or Singapore or Thailand. She never went into any great detail. A few sentences sufficed and her manner invited no questions. The only thing I was able to ascertain was that the man was a mixture of English, Chinese, and Filipino blood. Thus, I was a "mestiza," as anybody with mixed blood is referred to in the islands. A half-caste, which my mother was loathe to acknowledge since prejudices with regard to one's origins abound in the Philippines. When she became pregnant, Miami and the man married. Unfortunately, she soon discovered an unhappy fact.

The man was already somebody else's husband.

From this unlikely, illegal union in the mid-thirties and in this unlikely country, on a blistering tenth of July, was born a female child named Ruby Neilam Salvador Adams, to be nicknamed Neile. She would one day become a renowned dancer in her own right, and she would also become the wife of an American movie star.

My mother never "married" again, although her life was populated with men. She was a staunch Catholic who was nevertheless able to separate her emotional life from her devotion to the Church.

In order to maintain her popularity in the Far East, it was essential for her to make nightclub and theatrical appearances throughout that part of the world. Although Miami barely made enough to keep her in her sparkling costumes, she always made sure her dependents never wanted in their basic needs. My care was entrusted to a kind, sweet man named Binoy, who had been with our family since the days when my grandfather had been stationed in Manila during the Spanish-American War. When my grandparents died of illnesses, it was part of the natural order that Binoy, by then a member of the family, would stay with my mother and her brother. Then when I was born, Binoy helped raise me. With her heavy travel schedule I saw very little of Miami in those early days and when I did, her needs as a woman came in direct conflict with my need for a mother. It seemed that I was always an afterthought.

One of her gentlemen friends I remember well was impressive. He was introduced to me as the General. He strutted about like a proud peacock and smoked a funny-looking pipe. His presence in the neighborhood was an anomaly. We lived in a poor section of Manila with unpaved streets where cars were rarely seen. The popular mode of transportation was a horse-drawn carriage called a calesa. But the General was always driven to our house, chauffeured by a man in uniform. And always at his departure, the car would leave trails of dust. When the novelty of his beautiful automobile wore off, the people who lived around us found his visits irksome.

My mother had been introduced to the General by my godmother, Fanny Lewin. Aunt Fanny and her husband, Ted, owned and operated various private gambling casinos. They were an important couple in the American community of Manila.

I have no idea to what extent my mother was involved with General Douglas MacArthur; I was not at that time in tune with the complicated state of human relationships. However, I liked him even though I was always commanded "to go outside and play" during his visits. He was always nice to me and he always brought me my favorite candy. Hershey bars.

December 8 is a Catholic holiday. The Philippines, being a Catholic country, was observing the day. It meant that all its children were out of school when all hell broke loose. "The day of infamy," as President Roosevelt christened it, began in Manila almost simultaneously with Pearl Harbor. The recorded day's difference between December 7 and December 8, 1941, has to do with the international date line.

I was still a small child, yet I found myself smack in the middle of "infamy." The sounds and smells and horrors of war became a way of life for four years. In a minute my child's world turned upside down.

Where there had been bicycles, lightning bugs, ABC's to learn, and games to play, suddenly there were strafing planes, burning houses, dead horses, and fear in the streets. By January 2, 1942, the city was crowded with fierce-looking Japanese soldiers made more fierce by the sound of their long bayonets dragging the ground as they walked. Search and seizure became a way of life and hunger was a constant companion.

Approximately six months after the Japanese occupation began, the convent schools around the city of Manila reopened their doors under the watchful eyes of the Japanese authorities. Learning the katakana (the Japanese alphabet) was the first priority, and learning Japanese history was a close second.

I was elected to play a little marching song on the school's dilapidated piano as the schoolchildren filed out of the building in the mornings. It was the only activity I looked forward to. It somehow seemed a special moment in time that had nothing to do with the war and it delighted me. In a perverse way, it also gave me, for the very first time, my little place in the sun. This little marching song was short and simple, so my little hands had to pound it out repeatedly until everyone was outside. Then I would run to join the entire group to pay respect to the flag of the Rising Sun and sing "Kimigayo," the Japanese national anthem.

Each day the progress of the war and the Japanese victories were announced in the classrooms. The intent was to imprint upon our young minds the might and awesomeness of the Japanese Armed Forces. It did.

My mother's deep involvement with the guerrillas became her undoing. She was thrown into Bilibid prison and was made to stand and stare at the sun for several hours, blinding her temporarily. She could very easily have been executed, but some quirk of fate spared her life. She was transferred to Santo Tomas prisoner-of-war camp after a brief period and, by the grace of God, was granted the opportunity to take me along with her.

Before the war, Santo Tomas had been a university situated on forty acres of land. Now the Japanese had turned it into a concentration camp. Yet except possibly for the total loss of freedom and the very real shortage of food, life inside Santo Tomas's high stone walls was no worse than outside. Both were equally miserable.

Wake up call was always at 7:00 AM. Breakfast was a watery gruel; lunch and dinner consisted of a cup of rice and one leafy vegetable. The food line was always two blocks long and portions were small. There were no second helpings. A few of us were either brave or hungry enough to attempt to creepy-crawl around garbage cans for cooked camote (native sweet potato) skins. Whenever one of us was caught, however, food would be withheld from the culprit for one or two days depending on the guard.

My imagination ran rampant in camp. As a first grader just before the war, I had spent my Saturday and Sunday afternoons at the movies, totally captivated by Shirley Temple and Sheena, Queen of the Jungle. Now my fantasies took over. I danced and sang with Shirley and cavorted all over those jungles with Sheena! It helped alleviate the boredom of camp life. I learned how to be as unobtrusive as possible. No use in being noticed. It could only spell trouble in the long run.

Then, in October of 1944, B-24 bombers began making daily appearances in the skies of Manila. Their methodical annihilation of Japanese installations gave hope to everyone in the camp that the war was being won by the good guys.

By January 1945 we heard that explosives had been strung around the camp's perimeter and that the Japanese High Command had ordered the campsite leveled at the start of the expected American landing. The Japanese were expecting the invasion to come from the bay side and accordingly had left a skeleton crew to man our part of Manila, while mobilizing the rest of their armies into the expected battleground.

To everyone's surprise, at approximately six o'clock in the evening of February 3, two tanks of the 44th Tank Battalion and several units of the 1st Cavalry Division came roaring toward camp—from the inland side. Racing aainst time, they had one specific purpose. Occupy Santo Tomas. The tanks crashed through the gates and quickly and efficiently secured the buildings and surrounded the grounds. It took several days for all fighting to cease in the camp, however, for there were many Japanese soldiers who were determined to die for their country. A remaining few surrendered on the condition they be granted safe conduct, at least to the main gate. The Americans agreed and released them to the waiting Filipinos just outside. Apparently these Japanese soldiers fell into the hands of an angry mob.

The Japanese guns that had been pointed toward Manila Bay in anticipation of the American landing had now been turned around. They began an almost total annihilation of our part of the city. The days, nights, weeks, and months that followed were dominated by death, maiming, and hunger.

I was wounded by shrapnel on my right leg and swooped up and rushed to the emergency section by a tank driver named Tony Denauro. I never had a chance to thank him for saving my life. Years later, after I had become a professional dancer and was touring the United States as part of a nightclub act, I tried to track him down to thank him. Sadly, I never found a listing for him. I hoped and prayed that the fates had been kind to him.

The war years had been brutal, but we had survived. I had learned to steal garbage to stay alive, endure hunger and not complain. I felt immortal, as most children do.

My aunt Fanny Lewin had also survived Santo Tomas; and her husband, Ted, had miraculously managed to endure the Bataan Death March and four years in a POW camp in Japan.

As soon as Uncle Ted returned to Manila, he started to rebuild the family fortune, wheeling and dealing in record time to reopen his Alcazar Club to the officers of the armed forces and other assorted foreigners. Almost anyone who had a good line of credit and wanted a little gambling action was welcome.

To tide us over, my mother went to work for Uncle Ted as a dealer, enabling her to get us out of the corrugated tin shack Binoy had fashioned for us after our release from Santo Tomas. We had had a tearful reunion with Binoy, his wife, and his two young children, who were born during the war. Binoy and his family, my mother and I, moved into a one-bedroom apartment shared with four other families.

My mother was now twenty-nine years of age. Her dancing days were over. Theatrical shows as they had been before the war were nonexistent. It was time for a new beginning. That came in the person of Victor Rodgers, a lawyer from New York City, whom my mother met at the Alcazar Club.

Victor had a line of credit a mile long and when it became obvious to him that my mother had the contacts to get things rolling, they then became business partners. They bought and sold war surplus commodities such as tanks, guns, jeeps, etc., and soon they began making enormous profits. Their partnership operated only on a professional level for a while; then the two became enamored of each other. Unfortunately, my mother's Victor, too, was married, with children and grandchildren to boot. I never came to like him and neither did any of my mother's friends.

In 1947, as soon as Miami's financial picture improved, she bought Binoy and family a little house, and I was sent to the Maryknoll Convent in Hong Kong. The following year, in the summer of 1948, an unlikely three short years from Santo Tomas, I set sail on the SS *President Wilson* bound for the Rosemary Hall boarding school in Greenwich, Connecticut, and culture shock!

For a while I didn't know where my mother's residence was, although I received cards and checks from her. She and Victor were conducting business all over the Far East. Once or twice she surprised me by making a personal appearance at the school—with Victor. Whereas her nomadic existence prior to the war had little or no effect on me, I now resented her absences from my life. There was much I needed to know about growing up, and there was nobody to guide me. I was jealous of all the attention she lavished on Victor while none was forthcoming to me. And so I withdrew from her and harbored a resentment toward her and him that never really disappeared. When eventually her focus became riveted on me, it was too late. The years of separation had done their job. She and I never had an easy time communicating with each other, although we both tried. I will always be grateful to her for getting me out of the Philippines. She had incredible courage and indestructible spirit.

The first time I visited her at a house she had rented in Englewood, New Jersey, I told her that I had enjoyed participating in the school plays.

"Maybe I'll be an actress!" I announced.

"Don't be silly, Neile. You're too shy! You should forget such thoughts, darling. And besides . . . look, you're not beautiful . . . it's true you could develop your personality, but it's tough, you know? I want you to take a secretarial course so you can be self-sufficient."

It was then that I promised myself that somehow I would make it in the way she never had. I didn't know how I would go about it, but I would find a way.

But first I had to graduate from Rosemary Hall.

My days at Rosemary Hall over and done with, I pacified my mother by completing an intense course in typing. To my surprise, as a reward for being "a good girl," she consented to let me spend eight weeks working in an upstate New York summer stock theater. For a fee (which my mother grumbled about but paid anyway) I was allowed to do some set painting, some set decorating, and a little acting. I worked hard and I enjoyed the ambience of the theater, but I was not as enchanted as I had imagined I would be.

After my servitude in stock, I came back to New York City a little older and a little more independent. I became determined to pursue a career in acting as well as to get out from under my mother's watchful eye. I also wanted to get away from Victor's smirking scrutiny. My mother was beside herself. I was seventeen and she was sure I was doomed. She was angry and reluctant to support me in my pursuit of an impossible dream. But I persisted and finally she agreed to advance me the funds to enroll in acting classes provided I repay her. Agreed!

I enrolled at both the American Theatre Wing and the American President School of Acting and set about finding an apartment and acquiring a roommate. I settled in and tried to connect with the missing element in my life, that magical world to which I knew I belonged.

I threw myself into classes hoping that something would rub off on me. When the President Theater decided to stage *A Connecticut Yankee* I was awarded the dancing lead simply because none of the other student actresses would touch the part. Dancing was foreign to them, they claimed. Well, it wasn't exactly second nature to me, but I was not uneasy with the demands of the role, so I thought, well why not.

The search to fill the void in my life was about to end.

During rehearsals, I discovered the exhilaration of singing and dancing on stage. For me, it was infinitely more satisfying than just plain acting. It felt comfortable and warm. I felt positive I could master this musical dance form that I had chanced upon.

But where could I go to learn? I started asking around and would invariably be pointed in the direction of ballet schools, which I knew were not for me. I found it impossible to articulate what it was I was desperate to find. My ignorance contributed to my frustration.

Then in the spring of 1952 I went to see *The King and I*. To my astonishment I saw what seemed to me a hundred dancers doing movements I felt familiar with, dances I had culturally absorbed in the Far East. My heart started to pound rapidly. I could hardly catch my breath. "My God, I can do that!" I was so excited that after the first act I stood in the back of the theater to watch the rest of the show.

By the time *The King and I* ended, I knew I had found my calling.

I was going to dance, by golly! My mother could have the Far East. Broadway was going to be mine!

I was in luck. As soon as I returned to my apartment I called the theater where *The King and I* was running and asked to speak to the "boss." The one who hires girl dancers, I said. The operator connected me to the stage manager, and with the temerity of the ignorant, I plunged in.

"Ah . . . excuse me . . . ah . . . but how does one go about getting a job with the show? Ah, you know, as one of those dancers? I can, ah, do what they do."

He immediately detected from my manner that I

was a total amateur. However, he was a very nice and very patient man.

"Where were you trained and what are your credits?"

"I beg your pardon?" I had no idea what he was talking about. He might as well have spoken in a foreign language. My mind was unable to grasp the words "trained" and "credits." Finally, in a most gentle way, he suggested that maybe I should go to a dancing school if I wanted to pursue this as a career.

Dancing school. There it was again. Visions of ballet. My age was not compatible with ballet training. Those kids start at age six. I was eighteen, for God's sake. Besides, ballet did not seem to be *the* dance form on Broadway. How do I get this across to him?

The man was insistent. Look in the phone book and go down the list, he said.

I did.

When I dialed the Katherine Dunham School of Dance on West 43rd Street, I knew I had hit the jackpot. Over the phone I could sense the difference. This was no ordinary dancing school. I did not hear a tinkling piano. What I heard made me stand straight up. Those were drums I was hearing!

This was an Afro-dance school I was told, and as luck would have it, scholarship auditions were being held this week. I had no idea what Afro dancing was, but the commotion on the other end of the phone warranted investigation. Bright and early the next day, I hopped on a bus, got off at 44th Street and Broadway, galloped to 43rd Street, and ran up the narrow staircase to my new *home*. Never mind that the place was jammed with would-be dancers. Never mind that the powers that be were lined against the wall, seated at a long table, taking us in with their eyes. Never mind that notations were being made as we made our way across the floor led by an instructor. Never mind that I suddenly realized at this audition how stupidly naive I was to have thought that I was ready for *The King and I*. I had this overwhelming confidence that the people who held my future in their hands could see that inside this untrained body was a dancer dying to come out.

And see they did. I was awarded a scholarship. In order to subsidize myself and not have to go to my mother, I became a photographers' model for detective and crime magazine stories. Although it was an honest way to make a living, my mother was scandalized and quickly stopped talking to me. It was impossible to convince her that these pictures were outrageously innocent. Generally the work consisted of nothing more than acting out for the still camera scenes that depicted prostitutes being carted away by policemen. Of course, to titillate the magazine buyer we would be attired in nothing but panties and bras. Sometimes nightgowns would do. Everything depended on the stories.

In truth, a whole world of unemployed actors' and actresses' lives was made a little pleasanter by these photographers. The pay was decent, the hours flexible, and the photographers' studos were always bustling with new faces. The turnover was terrific since the young men and women worked only when in need of funds.

Steve and I often used to wonder whether we might have seen each other during one of those many photo sessions. He was also one of the many nameless faces who came "to pick up a few bucks" whenever necessary. Although I never made the cover of any of those crime magazines, Steve did. It showed him hiding behind a curtain, obviously up to no good, while a girl in a flimsy negligee lay innocently sleeping on the bed.

Dance classes became my church and my faith. I worked hard at it and very slowly I saw improvement. Then one day the following spring I was invited to join a new nightclub act, Nita Bieber and Her Dancers.

Nita Bieber, formerly under contract to MGM, had been a member of the elite Jack Cole dance group. The Cole jazz-Oriental technique, I discovered, was right up my alley. The pay was not much but it would be good experience. I would join the ranks of professional dancers and travel cross-country in the bargain! While playing an engagement in Los Angeles at the Coconut Grove as Lena Horne's opening act, I stumbled upon a copy of the *Hollywood Reporter,* the trade paper of the entertainment industry. How neat, I thought. I had never seen one before. While leafing through the pages something caught my eye. A Broadway-bound show was advertising for singers and dancers. The choreographer's name was Jack Cole! For a moment I froze. My thinking didn't take me that far. Finally it clicked! How could I let this opportunity pass me by. What if by some miracle I get it? Will Nita think me ungrateful? Probably *yes!* I don't care. I'm going!

The next morning found me dancing behind Jack Cole as he demonstrated his choreography. As I looked around at the hundreds of other dancers I became hopeful. I was the right type and I was intimate with his technique.

Sure enough, I made the chorus of the new musical called *Kismet.* The book was somewhat weak, compared to the music, sets, costumes, and choreography. As in any show with a not particularly strong book but a very strong choreographer, new dances were thrown in to cover the weak spots. Only another dancer knows what dancers go through during the mounting of a new Broadway show. I do not exaggerate when I say that the physical and mental abuse that was meted out to the dancers was Olympian. Most of the time I'd go back to my hotel room, take a shower in my underwear so I would be spared the extra effort of removing it from my body and washing it. It was much easier to wash myself and my underwear in one fell swoop. I was only nineteen but in the morning I would literally have to roll out of bed and ever so slowly and gingerly work out my aching muscles so that finally I could stand and move about. While each minute ticked away, each muscle would loosen up so that by 10:00 AM I would be ready to go. But those days of pain were worth it. If I only could, I would do it all over again.

We spent six weeks in Los Angeles, six weeks in San Francisco, four weeks in Boston, and four weeks in Philadelphia performing and perfecting our show for its New York opening. All in all, it took us six months to get to Broadway, traveling in our own private train. Six months of dancing for hours and hours and hours.

I joined *Kismet* as a chorus dancer. By the time we opened in New York I was a featured dancer, and four months later, Jack Cole picked me to replace Reiko Sato as *the* lead dancer when she decided to leave the show to spend some time with Marlon Brando instead.

Kismet, starring Alfred Drake, Doretta Morrow, Richard Kiley, and Joan Diener, opened on December 3, 1953, to no reviews. There was a newspaper strike going on, which actually worked to our advantage since the majority of the critics hated the show. But by the time publication resumed, the show had become a runaway hit. Word of mouth had triumphed over the printed word. That, and the producers' decision to bombard the airwaves with their own sensational reviews, more than paid off the heavily indebted show. *Kismet* had cost a then astronomical $600,000 to bring into New York. We heard that half of that amount had been invested by Marion Davies as a show of faith in her nephew, Charles Lederer, who had written the show with Luther Davis. The beautiful Ziegfeld Theatre stood on the corner of 54th Street and Sixth Avenue. What a treat it was when early the next morning I stuck my head out of my nearby new studio apartment to see ticket buyers lined around the corner. They actually were standing there, in the cold, waiting patiently for the box office to open. I jumped up and down and whooped and yelled to my walls, "Hot damn! We're in!"

And so the exciting days of my new life on Broadway began. I determined to take every advantage of what appeared to be a long period of employment and put every minute to good use. I had a lot of catching up to do. My good fortune wouldn't last if I did not persevere. So I added speech and singing lessons to my already crowded schedule. I had to rid myself of my Spanish, Philippine, and Hong Kong inflections. I was exotic looking enough without having to sound exotic, too. My long hair would also have to go, although for now it was absolutely essential for the show. I was already looking ahead to when *Kismet* would close. If I were to proceed to where I wanted to proceed, a change in image was definitely in order. I needed a more all-American image.

Finally, in April of 1955, almost two years after it had begun rehearsals in Los Angeles, *Kismet* said good night to Broadway. I felt sad but I was also looking forward to new beginnings.

A month later, Henry Weiss, my theatrical agent, had me booked into a number of different summer theaters. Neile Adams was no longer "only a dancer." She was now in a different category. Suddenly I had achieved the rank of a singing and dancing comedienne and my billing kept moving up closer to the title of the shows. I was having a wonderful time.

Under Rodgers and Hammerstein's sponsorship I did *Me and Juliet* at the Pittsburgh Civic Light Opera that summer. They wanted to test my range in the hope they could use me in *Pipe Dream*, their new show opening the following spring. I felt I was on my way to defining for myself the personality I would someday be on stage and in films.

When I returned to New York at summer's end, my name was added to the client roster of Hillard Elkins. His first job for me was to negotiate a major agreement with the Versailles Club in New York. I was to be featured with Jack Cassidy in a new revue opening in November of 1955.

The Rodgers and Hammerstein show fell through; they sat in the theater with their mouths agape as I performed their songs for them. The theater giants were finicky about their scores. They did not tolerate deviations—which I didn't know. No matter that my reviews had been sensational. They wanted everything sung as written.

Thank goodness, the Versailles guaranteed me six months of steady employment.

By May 1956, I was sitting on top of the world. So much had happened. My reviews had been terrific and *Life* magazine had just run a four-page spread on me when director George Abbott, one of Broadway's legends, selected me to replace Gwen Verdon in *Damn Yankees* and the Versailles Club would not let me go. Nick Prounis, owner of the club, had an enormous blow-up made of the first page of the article and displayed it in the lobby. It showed me just having stepped out of a gown in the middle of my song, leaving me in a very skimpy, lacy black leotard. The title of the piece in big, bold letters was *What Neile Wants Neile Can't Get*, which was a parody on the hit song from *Damn Yankees*, "Whatever Lola Wants Lola Gets." It was Nick Prounis's way of thumbing his nose at George Abbott.

Mr. Abbott immediately decreed that as soon as my contract was up, I would go into the Carol Haney role in *The Pajama Game*, the other show he directed, in the same part that had already launched Shirley MacLaine, who was now on her way to becoming a big star. The show was still playing at the St. James Theatre to packed houses. The St. James held a special magic for me. It was the very same theater that had housed *The King and I* in 1952 when I first realized that dancing was where it was at for me. That was just four short years ago. Could a young performer ask for anything better?

And then, in just a matter of weeks, two young people, born on the opposite sides of the sea, would catch a glimpse of each other and, like moths to a flame, would be drawn inextricably to each other.

3

HE LOVED dancers and musicians, so it was not surprising that he first crept into my consciousness on a hot May day in 1956, between dance and singing classes.

Dance classes in those days at Carnegie Hall were electrically charged, with dancers like Chita Rivera, Matt Mattox, Neile Adams, Julie Newmar, DeeDee Wood, Marc Breaux, David Winters, and Ron Field inhabiting the studios, and four, five, six drummers working the congo drums to accompany the gyrating dancers just for the sheer joy of it. Some days—although not this day—Marlon Brando would join the drummers; this would pump our adrenaline to such a point that some of us would actually vomit after a long, arduous class. It was wild discipline at its very best, and as such attracted sightseers from the neighboring ballet classes eager to catch a high pitch of excitement unmatched anywhere!

I was on 57th Street, through with my first dance class and on my way to singing class. I was wearing my favorite red dress, Empire style, with a crinoline under it as was the fashion of the day.

As I turned the corner on Sixth Avenue toward 56th Street, I saw several groups of people coming toward me. Some I knew and some I didn't know.

Sigyn Lund was one I knew. She was very blond and very beautiful. A dancer, who at the moment was unemployed. She had been in the chorus of *Me and Juliet* on Broadway, the same musical I had starred in with Jo Sullivan, Swen Swenson, and John Reardon at the Pittsburgh Civic Light Opera the previous summer. Rumor had it that Sigyn was the heiress to a Swedish shipping fortune. She certainly seemed to be living better than any of us. I mean, what gypsy had a dog? A *big* dog at that?

I was in my own world. Tomorrow I would go into rehearsals for *The Pajama Game*, which meant performing nights at the Versailles and working days learning the new show. Hot doggie! I couldn't wait!

As I walked toward them, I became vaguely aware of a blond fella-with-dog who seemed to have materialized from out of nowhere, and who fell in with Sigyn's group. Suddenly, blond fella-with-dog caught my eye.

"Hi!" he said as he looked me over.

I stared. Hmmm. Nice-looking I thought. As the groups passed by me, he stood directly in my path.

"You're pretty."

"Oh, thank you. So are you." (God, Neile, are you corny!)

"What's your name?"

And before I could answer, I heard Sigyn's voice call *"Steve!"*

"See ya."

"See ya."

I did not see him again till late one afternoon a few weeks later when I walked into Downey's Restaurant on Eighth Avenue, and there he was sitting at the front table with Frank Corsaro, who had directed *A Hatful of Rain,* and Ben Gazzara, who was starring in it.

I had already opened in *The Pajama Game* and had been three weeks into it when a clean-up rehearsal had been called. Since I was planning to have an early snack and a shower before the show, I decided to barrel into Downey's, across the street, for a quick bite. I was still in my rehearsal outfit, which consisted of white sailor pants (in those days a good majority of dancers utilized war surplus stores for inexpensive clothing), a bare midriff, and a turtleneck shirt tied at the bottom of the bra line.

Obviously I impressed blond-fella at the front table because he wound up with a bowl of spaghetti in his lap.

"Hey—good one, kid," I remarked. He had an adorable smile and wonderfully piercing blue, blue eyes which were now simultaneously crinkled in laughter and embarrassment *and* quite unexpectedly taking me to someplace I had never been.

For a brief, confusing moment.

At my table, the wandering, scrutinizing eyes of my fellow gypsies were quick to pick up on the little comedic exchange that had just occurred.

"He's cute but stay away from him. He fucks anything that moves."

"He's bad news."

Me: "Why? Who is he? What's his name?"

They: "Steven McQueen. He's currently in rehearsal to replace Ben Gazzara in *Hatful.*"

Me: "Yeah?"

They: "Yeah." "Yes, pass, kid. He's not so hot anyway from what I hear. At least not as hot as he thinks he is."

Me: "Oh."

After a brief dissection of blond-fella, who now had a complete name, we went back to business. Zoya Leporska, who was our dance captain and who had taught me the dance routines, had a message from George Abbott: "You are the best Gladys the show has ever had." I don't know whether she was telling the truth or not. I didn't care. I was flattered. My name was now up on the marquee along with John Raitt, Julie Wilson, and Eddie Foy, Jr. True, theirs were above the title while mine was directly below. But then mine was by its little ole self. In any case the technical whys and wherefores were of no consequence to me. I was not only singing and dancing "Steam Heat" and "Hernando's Hideaway," but acting opposite those greats of the American theater. Eddie Foy, Jr., was most especially sweet and helpful. I idolized him as did everyone in the cast.

Steve McQueen hovered around me for the next few days (on the streets, on the way to the theater, after theater, after classes) without making his move—which I felt he would just as soon as he had opened in *Hatful* and had gotten that under his belt and out of the way. Replacing Ben Gazzara in *A Hatful of Rain,* after all, was a big break. He would have been mad to have allowed any romantic entanglement to break his concentration.

D day for him as Benny's replacement was July 2, 1956. I had made it a point to find out. The game had become intriguing to me. I saw him at Downey's two or three times having a bite with Sigyn. Obviously, they were a "thing." Whether this "thing" had just started or was just ending, I couldn't tell. I just hoped my heart would be still when we connected. The excitement this flirtation was generating in my person was threatening to blur the importance of the exciting things that were unfolding in my professional life.

Joe Pasternak, the MGM producer, had just made good the promise he'd made me during my *Kismet* days that he would use me in something. He had come backstage after the show, had introduced himself, and said, "You're too young now but someday I'll have a part for you in one of my movies. I'm doing two or three down the road."

Now, out of the blue, he had called my manager and told him that *This Could Be the Night,* his new movie, would start filming around October 1. There was a wonderful featured part in it for me and could I be sprung from the show? Of course, said Hilly, whose motto it was always to answer in the affirmative and then to work it out later.

Also, my *Pajama Game* producer, Hal Prince, had informed me at the theater one matinee day that *Life* magazine was going to do another story on me. A follow-up from the previous story of three months ago. Hal said, "I can't believe it. They keep coming to you." In a way he was right. It seemed everytime I picked up a magazine, there I'd be. My God, I was hot!

The end of the first week in July had come and gone and blond-fella still hadn't come forward and I was getting annoyed. Damn him anyway!

Finally July 10 was here and I had a date with Mark Rydell, then a fairly successful actor and jazz pianist. It was my twenty-second birthday and I was joining Mark at Downey's after the evening's performance. Mark was the only man I was dating at the time. Not because of any arrangement or understanding between us; I just found it simpler and less complicated to deal with one man at a time.

I walked into Downey's that night after the show. There *he* was again at the front table with Ben and Frank and Mike Gazzo, the author of *A Hatful of Rain*. This time I knew exactly who he was and I gave him my most dazzling smile. (I had practiced it enough, God knows.) I felt his eyes boring right through me. "Hi" was all I said to the table as I walked past.

It was only a matter of a few minutes, just enough to be able to extricate himself nonchalantly from his friends so he wouldn't appear too anxious, before Mark Rydell formally introduced Neile Adams to Steve McQueen. It would be four years, soon after our son, Chad's birth, before he would see Mark again after that fateful night.

The following evening in the alley adjacent to the theater, on my way to the stage door, I heard a loud, crass whistle. I stopped for a brief second, totally annoyed at this assault on my sensibilities. I whirled around ready to do battle, confident as I was that the whistle was meant for me. I was right. The whistler surprised me, though, since we had made a date for two days hence. It was *him,* which irritated me even more, for as I came face to face with him he said, "Hey, Nellie!" We had been introduced, we had made a date, and he had stalked me for days. Surely somebody somewhere must have said my name loud enough for him to hear how it was pronounced! Asshole! So in my most high-and-mighty voice I hissed, "It's Neile as in heel or kneel, as in kneel down."

Again that crinkly embarrassed smile. God, how am I going to resist this?

"Okay. Neile. Sorry." He put his hand to his heart as if he'd been shot. He proceeded while I now stared, mesmerized.

"You're, ah, not going to see Mark tonight, right?"

"Right. How'd you know?"

"Well—one just knows those things, you know?"

I nodded in agreement as if I did know—when in truth I didn't know what the hell he was talking about.

He forged ahead, "Since you're—ah—well—ah— free tonight, why don't I pick you up after the show and we'll have a bite to eat." It was impossible to decline and since I had just come from class and would require little warm-up this evening, I invited him to my dressing room. He was impressed with the size and the cheeriness of the room. He was also impressed that I had my very own wardrobe lady, who was getting my things ready for the evening's performance. Unconsciously I must have wanted to establish the fact that I was a successful and independent individual. That I felt that I was somethin' —much as he felt he was the cat's ass!

Years later, I found out Steve had simply told

Mark Rydell, the evening we were introduced, that he was moving in. As in, "Sorry, buddy, but all's fair in love, etc., etc."

I suppose at the table Mark could see the inevitability of the situation, although I hadn't yet. I assumed he had decided I wasn't worth haggling over!

Someday, though, the two would work together—Mark as a guest star and Steve as star of his own television series.

And years later, in an ironic twist of fate, Mark would be directing Steve just as our marriage frayed at the seams.

Mark Rydell by then would be a much respected director and Steve would be at the very zenith of his stardom and starting a very imperceptible decline, brought about by the power that world-renown brings and his natural tendency toward self-destructiveness.

If my life as a budding star performer was a whirlwind of activities, Hurricane Steve blew winds that swept me along with such intensity that everything else prior to his arrival paled by comparison.

On our first date the night he had surprised me at the St. James Theater alley, I had been heavily encumbered with crinolines. He propped me on his motorcycle—sidesaddle—and told me he was taking me home. Before I could protest, he said clearly and forcefully, "Put your left arm around my waist, hold your skirt down with your right hand, and hold on to your heels! Now, where do you live? You've got to change into something more comfortable. We're going down to the Village."

That seemingly simple command obviously touched something deep inside me. I had been directed and told what to do all my life—from my mother, to the nuns, to Binoy, to the Japanese, to the choreographers and directors I had worked for—but Steve, with those innocuous words, somehow immediately made me feel comfortable and at home. At that moment any reservations I might have had about this wild man vanished.

Going to the Village was a new experience. Going to the Village on a motorcycle was a new and exhilarating experience. We went to a few coffeehouses, exploring and talking, talking and exploring, until the wee small hours of the morning. Then we went back to my apartment. We never said good night, for by the time the sun came up we had already discovered the secret chart to each other's heart.

Fortunately, I was young enough that even with our late, late dates I was never at a loss for energy. Nothing and no one could possibly deter me from accomplishing what I had set out to do. My dance classes, my singing classes, and my acting classes were all-important and were never missed, no matter how exhausting the previous day or night had been. And of course, *The Pajama Game* was my first priority. The show was spawning all sorts of offers for me. MGM had already beckoned, and I awaited their command. The Tropicana Hotel, a new luxury establishment in Las Vegas, was hoping to lure me with an extravaganza that would inaugurate the opening of their showroom. An immediate answer was required. How available was I? Not at all. I had no intention of leaving Broadway—at least not yet.

A Hatful of Rain was beginning to show signs of fatigue. Plans were being made regarding a road tour, and rumor had it that producer Jay Julien wanted to replace Steve. His reviews had been lukewarm with the exception of *Variety*'s. *Variety* had called his performance of addict Johnny Pope "effective" and, unlike the rest of the press, had acknowledged the role would be difficult for the most experienced actor to play, let alone a young performer making his Broadway debut. In fact, I think, the biggest drawback to his performance was his youth. Vivian Blaine, who had replaced Shelley Winters as his wife, was too mature for him to play opposite. Steve still had a baby face, while Vivian looked like a sophisticated woman.

Nonetheless, in spite of the rumors, in spite of the notices, he had to carry on. And finally, Mark Richman, also of the Actors Studio, started showing up at the Lyceum Theatre to catch the performances, and Steve knew of course that his number was up.

He would last until September 22, and by remarkable coincidence that would also be my last night with my show. The big difference was that I would then be on my way to the coast with a seven-year contract in my pocket with MGM, my dream studio, while Steve would join the ranks of the unemployed.

I was grateful that we saw each other's show on Labor Day weekend, when the St. James and the Lyceum theaters were dark on alternate nights. I was impressed with the raw energy behind his performance, but could see that it hadn't yet been channeled properly. It seemed to me all visible technique and no personality. I hoped that somebody somewhere could help him with that missing element. I had no idea that, with very minor suggestions, the somebody would be me.

All through September he was depressed with his present situation although he handled it well. He would say, "Ain't no big never mind," when in fact I knew it was a big never mind. In the interim he showed me a whole new world—mostly by night. Every night he would pick me up at my St. James dressing room and sit there and shoot the breeze while I removed my makeup and while Julie Wilson, whose dressing room adjoined mine, teased him about his motorcycle and me about my crinolines and high heels. Usually we left the dividing door between the rooms open unless some privacy was needed. The flowers that were ever present in our rooms were a marked contrast to Steve's dressing room at the Lyceum, which was a typical dramatic actor's room. Dreary.

Without ever mentioning it, I felt he equated the decor of our dressing rooms with the level of success we'd each reached. His was fair, for he had no immediate prospects. My cheery dressing room was indicative of where I was going.

He was proud of who I was. He enjoyed showing me off and loved the fact that my Sundays, which had always been spent in restful seclusion from the rest of the world, now belonged to him.

His appearance in my life was expanding my world. Now there was Birdland and jazz musicians. Now there was Fire Island. Now there were motorcycle rides to the country. Now there were late-night double features on 42nd Street after our Saturday performances. James Cagney (his all-time favorite) and Humphrey Bogart and Cary Grant and Gary Cooper were never missed. Now there was the Village, with its colorful assortment of characters. His world, I soon discovered, was inhabited by people who operated just this side of the law. That remained constant throughout our marriage. He also introduced me to people like John Altoon, Bob Fortier, and Miles Davis and B. J. Brownjohn. For the first time I saw, felt, and understood the beatniks. Who they were and what they were about. I could never have been one—I was much too square—but at least my exposure to their world gave me a real appreciation for their way of life. They embraced me because I was the "bandido's" girl, as Steve was known around the Village.

Little did I know that he would always want me to remain the way I was—naive, successful, young, adoring, and always at his bidding. "Nellie" (which he always called me when he was especially loving) must never be allowed to grow up. She could deal with her show world and his show world, but the real world Steve would handle.

Except, of course, he couldn't.

At the end of our first week together, which had been spent in my apartment, Steve asked me why not move in together.

"Either your place or mine," he offered magnanimously.

I asked him to describe his apartment, since I had not been to it and he had seemed in no hurry to take me there. "It's a fifth-floor walk-up and it's a cold-water flat. I don't think you'll like it," he said, grinning.

After that brief description, there was no doubt that his apartment was not exactly my ideal. So my place it would be. I had gone beyond cold-water flats a while ago and I had no intention of going back. I also knew his moving in with me was going to create a scene with my mother. I knew her reaction to the fact that her daughter was "shacked up" with a man would be hurt disbelief. She would go into a tirade, which was a joke, considering her own history. It's odd that my mother, who had otherwise always led an exemplary life, could be burdened with the inability to pick a man she could call her own. In any event, I made the decision not to confront the issue until absolutely necessary. There was no reason why I shouldn't live with this man if I so desired. I was an independent, self-supporting girl and whether she'd appreciate my reasoning or not, I was my mother's daughter. Steve was someone I wanted to share the here-and-now with. We certainly wouldn't be ostracized by our peers. So why not? And if so, it wouldn't have mattered anyway. Steve came up with the idea of telling her that I had a new roommate. She would assume it was a girl and all would be well. He was right.

He arrived on moving day with very little. A suitcase with his clothes, his motorcycle gear, and a bus-stop sign that he had swiped from a Village street and now used as a barbell. The man was obviously used to traveling light. He found a garage to house his beloved BSA motorcycle, which he had bought when he sold an MG sports car he had won in a poker game. As any New Yorker knows, the streets of Manhattan can be hazardous when one isn't paying particular attention to one's driving. Steve and car fell into an excavation hole on Sixth Avenue, inflicting heavy damage on the MG. Repair costs had been prohibitive and he had decided on a motorcycle as his next mode of transportation.

Also in that same garage was a beautiful Bugatti. One day he was overcome by an overwhelming desire to feel its engine hum with him at the wheel. He "borrowed" the car while the attendant was looking someplace else, quickly drove it down the block until he spotted a phone booth, jumped out, and called me to say that he had a big surprise for me.

"Meet me downstairs right away. I'll be there in a minute."

Around the corner came Steve in this gorgeous car. As it came toward me my mind started racing. Was this the same car I had been seeing in the garage? Could Steve have possibly exchanged his motorcycle for this car? No. It couldn't possibly be, could it? Was this the surprise? Oh, I know. He bought the car. No! He couldn't have. That car must cost thousands. No, I know. The owner lent it to him. No! He stole it. *Oh, my God!* I think he stole it!

"Quick, jump in. We're going for a ride around the park, baby!" I was horrified because now I was sure he had stolen the damn thing. He quickly saw the expression on my face and told me not to worry. "I just borrowed it for a little while," he said. The owner would never find out.

"Oh, God. I'll wind up in jail for this!"

"Relax, honey. Nobody'll throw us in jail. Let's just have us a g-o-o-o-d time!" His boyish enthusiasm was so infectious it was hard not to respond. He continued talking excitedly until I calmed down, and suddenly, there I was, a willing accomplice in this clandestine adventure.

Some time later, the garage attendant was stupefied to have a grinning Steve quietly hand him the key to the Bugatti. I was petrified. I thought there might be a confrontation, but the man was so stunned that Steve was able to finesse himself out of the situation without a problem. Having finally satisfied his curiosity about this beautiful car, Steve was able to pass it every day and feel that he and it were buddies sharing a private joke.

4

SO WE SETTLED down happily on West 55th Street.

I had much to teach him about housekeeping. Dirty he wasn't by any means, but my God, was he sloppy.

Eventually, though, I dropped my housekeeping lessons. All he had to do was smile and I would simply find it easier to pick up after him than to nag him. I did have one small success. Because he was clean and neat about his person, he responded well to a sweater-folding session. There was something endearing about his pride in his newfound ability to put his sweaters away neatly and be reasonably certain that when he took one out to wear it would not be wrinkled.

What Steve did on non-matinee days was a mystery to me. I knew he would attend classes at the Actors Studio, although he would not do scenes. Years later I realized that he disliked stage performing. Classes were a means to an end. While he was on Broadway, he saw no reason why he should do double duty. He had enough to worry about with his role in *Hatful*. Preparing scenes while one was out of work was entirely different from doing them on stage while one was being paid. As much as he admired Lee Strasberg, the old man had a way of dissecting and criticizing an actor's work that Steve found intimidating and frightening at the same time.

"I would rather take my chances with the paying public."

He also had just discovered film. The small part he had had in the Paul Newman movie had whetted his appetite. He liked this medium better than the others. However, when I saw the movie, I had to tell him just how awful he was. At that point, he was not sure whether he was Marlon Brando or James Dean, so he wound up imitating both and showed absolutely nothing of himself.

But he would learn. He could accept constructive criticism, especially when he knew we were on the same team. Although I was not inclined to criticize directly what was wrong with his acting *technique*, I could see clearly and impart to him what was missing from the man I saw on the screen in contrast to the man I knew off screen.

I instinctively knew there were other girls lurking around. He didn't strike me as the monogamous type. But I didn't ask and he didn't volunteer anything. I figured what I didn't know wouldn't hurt me.

I did notice, though, little quirks in his personality that I had never seen in any person before. For instance, he'd come home and have a laughing jag over some innocuous remark either one of us would make. He would eat voraciously and systematically empty out the refrigerator of the eggs, raw meat, and milk and candy bars (normal staples for a dancer) I would stock it with. Then there would be days when he'd be so hyper he could hardly sit down, and these would generally be his snappy days, when he would pick an argument with me. One such argument took place over my lack of a suntan. He liked me dark so he could really see my white teeth. During the times when I acquired a deep tan he would refer to me as his Brown Baby. However, once in my desire to please Steve I was dressed down at the theater by Hal Prince. I had allowed myself to get too dark, which prompted Hal to tell me to stop going into the sun immediately. My role as the factory worker Gladys was not compatible with a deep tan. Ours was not an interracial cast, I was told. Sheepishly, I apologized and promised to de-tan.

I refused to cook from the very beginning. I had no affinity for it and it wasted too much of my time. Besides, I had a studio apartment with a little kitchen. So after my last dance class, I'd run home, shower, and then we'd have a snack at the health food store. Our dinners were almost always taken at Downey's after our performances. The restaurant walls were covered with pictures taken back then. It was a remarkable reminder of the faces that were around during that remarkable era on Broadway. Steve and I were up there in a picture taken in Central Park before we were married. It showed two young people with happy baby faces.

I liked a quiet and leisurely warm-up and getting to the St. James no later than seven o'clock for an eight-thirty curtain afforded me that luxury. I particularly liked having the empty stage, with only a work light, to myself. I had fallen into this habit very early in the game and I had found it prepared me well for the night's work ahead. The curtain was always up at this time and looking out into the auditorium while I stretched on stage never failed to stir me. It was a trip to know that in an hour and a half's time people from all over the country would fill up the entire place and watch me perform. I also could see the various people performing their various tasks to keep the theater in beautiful shape. Some would be dusting, some would be polishing the brass or chrome, some would be vacuuming, some would be going around the theater with long feather dusters against high walls and corners to make sure there weren't any cobwebs to be seen, while others would be changing light bulbs. Finally the usherettes would come, pile their stacks of programs against the walls, and I would know that it was time to put my makeup on. When I was in *Kismet* at the Ziegfeld Theatre, the last order of the day before the doors were opened to the public was to spray the theater with rose mist. It was Billy Rose's signature.

While slow and easy was my style, Steve's was just the opposite. As soon as he had walked me to the St. James, he would double back to the apartment, pick up his motorcycle, and park it in the alley of the Lyceum for easy access after the show. Then he would pick me up and away we'd go. It didn't matter where. We would always have a terrific time.

Once on a Sunday afternoon, on our way to a birthday party for Julie Wilson, George Abbott and Hal Prince, my bosses, were mortified to see their dancing star riding in back of this madman's motor-cycle, weaving in and out of traffic in what seemed to them a maniacal manner. When we all arrived at the party, Mr. Abbott gently requested that I stop riding around on motorcycles. Specifically, Steve McQueen's motorcycle.

Unaware as I was that love had already touched me, I had acquiesced but soon discovered that George Abbott's request had to be denied. Since I couldn't tell him that, I just went about my business as quietly as possible.

It's amazing what happens when love rears its lovely head.

Finally, September 22 was here. Our final perform-ances with our respective shows were over and we were on to a new phase. I was expected on the West Coast for tests and wardrobe fittings and for meet-ings with Robert Wise, the director of *This Could Be the Night*. I had to leave immediately, and indeed I was already packed for the Monday flight. I calcu-lated that I would be back home in New York in a week to ten days' time, which would give me about ten free days with Steve before I had to turn around and fly back to Hollywood. Actually the starting date of the film depended on Jean Simmons, the star of the movie. She had just had a baby and was still recuperating. I suspect she also must have had to lose some weight. I frankly didn't mind the time off. I had been employed steadily for the last three years and my body needed a little rest.

Steve, who hadn't liked the thought of being left behind and unemployed, gathered a group of motorcycle buddies and organized a trip to Cuba. He thought he might catch up with Lionel Olay, a journalist friend who was writing a series of articles on Fidel Castro. Steve figured that all he would have to do was follow Castro's scent and he would find Lionel. I worried about him. It was a dangerous time to travel to Cuba. Batista would soon be overrun by Castro and his rebels. The whole country was in an upheaval. But Steve was determined. He figured the trip back and forth would take them two weeks.

Lionel lived above us on 55th Street. The apartment belonged to Rod Steiger, who let Lionel use it whenever he was away, which was often. Rod Steiger was a very busy man. He was one of the most successful actors around.

It was at Lionel's one night that I first heard the word "marijuana" and saw how it was consumed. "First you roll it, then you smoke it," Steve said. There I plainly saw the cause of his sometimes erratic behavior. The highs and the lows. Clearly, Steve's familiarity with this substance was of long standing. He was an experienced hand at it. And just as clearly, he liked it a lot.

On October 3, 1956, two days before my scheduled departure from Hollywood for New York, I received a cable from Havana. It said:

I LOVE YOU HONEY SEND ME MONEY LET ME KNOW

HOW WHATS HAPPENING IN CARE OF WESTERN UNION
CON AMOR

ESTEBAN

On the right-hand corner of the cablegram, it said:
Sender Waiting Answer By Wire
I sat down and carefully assessed the situation. I
didn't want to act on instincts alone. I was concerned
for his safety—true. And yet I knew he wouldn't be
careless. He'd been around the block more than once.
I wondered if he'd found Lionel Olay. I wondered if
he'd had any problems with his motorbike. I wondered why he needed money. Could he be in jail? I
doubted that. I think I would have heard from somebody. If not me, surely Julian, his mother, would
have. And she most certainly would have notified
me. I wondered if the motorcycle buddies had remained together. Was Steve alone? Did they all split
and go their separate ways?
After a while, I made my decision and sent him
this wire:

I LOVE YOU TOO HONEY NO MONEY HOME DAY AFTER
TOMORROW

NELLIE

I wondered how that would go over. I thought if I
wired him money, it would only delay his return.
Knowing him as I did, I felt he would continue his
adventure until his supply ran low. At that point he
would either wire me for more money or he would
come on home. So I said to myself, don't send him
any money. Obviously his supply is low and he must
come home. Now! At least we'd have some time
together before I started the movie. Who knew how
long it would take him to wend his way back? Cuba is
a long way from New York City on a motorcycle.
That done, I thought I had best call Julian. Just in

case. After so many heartbreaking years, mother and son had finally arrived at an uneasy truce—partly because of her unhappy personal situation and partly because of me. Julian's relationship with Victor Lukens, for whatever reason, had come to an abrupt end. Her emotional connection with this man had lasted longer than it had with any other person, and their breakup had devastated her. Steve had accidentally run into her at a bar in the Village, literally unable to get off the bar stool because she had had one too many, and had seen her safely home. Once, and then twice, he had had to get her out of Bellevue Hospital after the authorities had called to tell him they were treating her for acute alcoholism. Although Steve had been mortified, there was no way he could turn his back on her. Not now. He did not want her in his life, but he felt an obligation to see her through this particularly miserable period. He wanted her to be aware of his presence in the neighborhood. He hoped that might keep her sober and off the streets. Apparently this logic worked, because Julian was able to curb her craving for alcohol, at least publicly. Many years after Julian's death and four years after Steve's death, I learned that Victor Lukens had had a wife somewhere in Florida and that he had died sometime in the 1970s.

When I came into the picture, Victor had already been gone from Julian's life for over a year. When Steve introduced me to her she was delighted. Not with me necessarily—it was because Steve had brought her a girl, a total stranger, and he had brought me to her of his own volition. And as for me, having expected the worst from all that Steve had told me, I was shocked to find Julian charming, bright, and friendly. She may have been trying to impress me and she may have been looking for an ally to help her regain Steve's trust in her. It didn't matter. I liked her. But Steve always kept her at arm's length. He didn't want her unhappiness to spill onto us.

Now I was on the phone with her asking her for any information she might have about her son and Cuba. She was surprised. She had no idea that Steve was on a motorcycle odyssey. And no, she had not heard anything from anyone, so all must be going well. I thanked her and said I'd be home within two days.

I was a little apprehensive about Steve's return home. First, I was worried about how angry he might be about my apparent lack of concern for him. At least, that's how I would have felt if I had asked the person I was living with to send money and he hadn't complied. Second, after only three months together, I didn't know what new emotions might have evolved, if any, during our first time apart. We had already survived the personality clashes that two people bring to a new relationship. I hoped with all my heart that there would be no surprises. I wanted to start work on my first movie in a happy frame of mind. And that led to reason number three. I was working. Would Steve come to resent that?

While I had been in Beverly Hills during my ten-day period of tests and meetings at MGM, I had written Steve every night to share with him the exciting events of the day. The front gate of the studio was awesome to me. Upon my arrival, Kenny Hollywood, the legendary studio guard, directed me to my dressing room on the lot. This dressing room contained a bathroom and a kitchenette, and a bed. I was chomping at the bit to get started. MGM musicals were fast becoming extinct. Louis B. Mayer was no longer at the helm of MGM and my idols, June Allyson, Van Johnson, Gene Kelly, and Esther Williams had all moved on to nonmusical films. I never saw any of them while I was on the lot.

The movie I had signed for was a fluffy comedy. The role of Jean Simmons's love interest in the film had been given to Tony Franciosa, making his movie debut. He had been plucked out of *A Hatful of Rain* on Broadway—a bit of information not lost on Steve. Then I found out that Julie Wilson, my *Pajama Game* cast mate, was going to be joining us. I was thrilled. This would be our third show together.

My role in the film was that of a young stripper who would rather cook than strip. The film's choreographer, Jack Baker, devised a strip number for me that became the prototype for other strip numbers. My costume was made out of bits and pieces of newspapers, and while I sang and danced, my costume progressively got skimpier. Jack had me ripping off those pieces of paper until there were almost none left. It was risqué for that time, but it was cute.

I flew home to wait for Steve and to pack my bags for the long stay in California. Because I sensed Steve wouldn't be gone too much longer, I made sure to come home directly after each class. On my fourth day home at about five in the evening, I spotted a motorcycle parked on the curb as I rounded the corner on 55th Street. My heart skipped a beat and I started walking faster to see whether it was the one I knew. Oh, yes it was! Not only that, the trail of miscellaneous items sprinkled from the curb all the way up to our apartment was unmistakably Steve's. As I flew up the stairs—two, three at a time—I became aware that I had missed this man enormously. This sudden revelation broke my stride momentarily. I was seized by the wonder of it all. Never had I missed anyone. Could this be it? Could this be love? He opened the door just in time for me to fling myself at him. If this was love, so be it! I liked this man! God Almighty, I might as well admit it—I LOVED this man! I liked the way he made me feel. I danced to his music. Together we burned brightly. I thought, "This is the man who'll take me through the years."

He was filthy and looked tired from the long ride but he was happy to be back. I quickly apologized for not sending him the money and I hoped he understood.

He looked at me tenderly. "It's all right, baby. I admire your spunk. But I gotta tell you it was tough traveling without any bread (money) in my pocket—especially through the South! But when you have a tough ole lady [me] you have to be resourceful or you're dead!"

My worrying had been a wasted effort. He had sold his gear as the need arose. Little by little.

He plopped into the living room chair and sat me on his lap while he recounted some of his adventures. Then quite suddenly he put his arms around me and said, "I love you, baby. It sure is nice to be home."

In apartment 4A on West 55th Street, as night settled on New York City, all was well with the world.

Before my return to Los Angeles, Steve and I had talked of his coming to join me, although we did not define the time. I had wanted two weeks to myself so I could see what my routine and the schedule would be. I did not want to be encumbered with having to worry about somebody else. I had two dance numbers and a song to learn and rehearse, and a role to play. When I wasn't facing the cameras, I'd be in rehearsal hall. When I wasn't doing either, they'd have me in wardrobe. When the wardrobe fittings were finally over, I would be left to concentrate on the dance rehearsals and the day's shooting schedule. It was tiring, naturally, but I was blissfully happy.

Steve and I spoke to each other two or three times a day. I would call him just as soon as I woke up and then again just before I went to bed. In between he would call me at the studio. I knew my phone bills would be enormous, but I didn't care. I could afford it. I was in the Big Time! I was making what seemed like an enormous salary. Every time my salary went up I thought of my mother, who had worried about my ability to support myself and had tried to discourage me from embarking on a dancing career. My mother was actually now taking credit for her wisdom in having sent me to dancing school! I felt acutely grateful to her for having the good sense to get me out of Manila and into the world. We would have gotten on terrifically except for one thing. Steve. She just couldn't bear him. She used to pick away at his manners. You'll never get invited to the best houses if he eats like that, she would say. Why don't you teach him how to eat properly if he's going to be hanging around you?

Unfortunately, their first meeting had been a disaster. I had never properly identified my roommate's gender to her. There just never seemed to be the right moment. So she had always assumed that my roommate was a she. I had been rehearsing some new songs for upcoming auditions and I had told her to drop in if she felt like it—anytime. One day she did. And a little while later, in came Steve. Gorgeous (which didn't count with her) and shirtless. He was also very much in need of a shower, having been in Central Park playing baseball with the *Hatful of Rain* team. My mouth dropped. The moment of truth had descended on me and there was no escape. Especially when Steve came over to give me a kiss.

"Mother—I would like you to meet my—ah—roommate." I said it as softly as I could. But she heard it loud and clear. My words and her brain connected immediately. Her eyes narrowed as she glanced at me, and with a painful grimace she shook hands with him. That done, she turned to me and said, "I'm going. I'll talk to you later." I worried about the telephone call. Steve said not to worry, "I'll protect you. She can't do nuthin' to you." As a peace offering we sent her flowers and took her out to dinner. I had hoped this would soften the blow and hoped that maybe she would like Steve once she got to know him. No such luck. At dinner, she was horrified by his lack of table manners. She was much too discreet to say anything in front of him, but I heard plenty.

Now she called me in California and was on the attack again. Her first words to me after "How are you?" were "Neile—how is that actor? That blond boy. Is he still in your apartment?"

"Yes, Ma. He's still there."

"When does he plan to move out?"

"He's not, Ma. That's his place, too."

"Don't tie yourself down, Neile. Why don't you wait till he does well first? And—will you be honest with me? Who's paying the rent?"

"Oh, come on, Ma. Relax, will you? Everything's fine. Worry about something else. Please?"

In fact I was paying the rent, but I would never admit that to her. She would just have to come to accept our relationship, no matter how long it took.

Hours later my phone rang again. It was the middle of the night and it was Steve.

"Hi, honey. What're you doing up this time of night?" I asked groggily.

"Well, I'll tell ya, baby. I've been bumping into walls lately. I miss you. It's no fun around here without you."

As a matter of fact, Julian had told me just the day before that Steve had become absentminded. She had been invited to lunch by her son. In the course of the afternoon she had seen him stick an ashtray in the refrigerator, which Julian had happily reported to me when the two of them had called me up. Even now I smiled as I envisioned the scene. Julian had happily wondered what I had done to her son. And I, on the other end of the phone, had briefly wondered why the two were together. This was highly unusual, but maybe Steve's attitude toward Julian was mellowing. At least enough so that she was allowed entry to our apartment.

What had actually transpired at that moment was

Steve's revelation to his mother that he planned to marry me. Julian was thrilled because, for the very first time in his life, Steve had confided in her. She was the very first—and only—person to know.

"You won't mind if I come out a week early, will you, baby? I'm going to make an honest woman out of you!"

"Oh, okay, fine. When?" (Did I know this was a marriage proposal? Of course not. I had always assumed that when a man proposed, he said, "Will you marry me?")

"I'll come in Monday and I'll catch up with you either on the set or at the motel. Sound good?"

I was still on the sound stage the afternoon he arrived from New York. Julie Wilson saw him first and I turned my head as I heard her say in that low, sexy voice, "Hello, lover boy. Welcome to California!"

"Lover boy" quickly swooped me off the floor and gave me a big kiss. Then he pulled me aside, and from his pocket he pulled out a ring and placed it on my finger. It was a wedding band he'd had designed for me in the Village. Because they were friends, the jeweler had accepted a $25 deposit with the promise that as soon as we got back into town the lady would be paid the balance. (As it turned out, for the next two years I'd be paying for the "balance" on several of his transactions, most of them having to do with his cars. For some reason this state of affairs never bothered me. It horrified some, though. Even my banker quietly told me to keep my bank account separate from Steve's. But our whole life was ahead of us and as sure as some people were that I was being taken advantage of, I was just as sure this arrangement was temporary. We had our whole life ahead of us and the future looked bright. If not for him, certainly for me.)

Anyway, sheer panic and confusion set in. I felt sick and yet I had to look happy. Steve was ecstatically informing anyone who cared to listen of our impending wedding. He said the following Friday would be the day. I didn't want to hurt him. I loved him. But marriage? Jesus Christ! I wasn't ready for marriage! I knew I had to talk to somebody—quick. That night I called Hilly Elkins and hysterically explained to him what was in store for me in just a few days. Hilly said, "First of all calm down, darling. Second, schmuck, say 'No.' Now, that shouldn't be too hard, should it?"

"Hilly, I wouldn't be calling you if it wasn't hard!"

"All right, what about this. He's marrying you for your money. You know that, don't you?"

"Oh, come on, Hilly, I want advice—like how do I get out of this gracefully without ending the relationship?"

Even if Hilly Elkins had known the answer, I doubt he would have given it to me. Really there was nobody I could ask who could get me out of this dilemma. This was my problem to solve, and I felt helpless. I knew Steve was not the type of man who could gallantly accept a "no" from the girl he loved. No matter how temporary. Rejection had dogged him all his life and not a hint could come from me.

On Friday I realized there was no way out. Marriage was in the cards for me on this day whether I wanted it or not. I wasn't ready for the kind of commitment marriage demands, but Steve was. That's all that mattered—at least to him. I suppose for somebody whose capsule review of his own life read, "I was looking for a little love and there wasn't much around," it had to be. In retrospect, I must have felt, deep down in my heart, no matter how frightened I was, that if we didn't marry right now, we would have eventually gone our separate ways. And that would have been difficult to take.

By six that evening, Steve was at the studio driving a rented Thunderbird. He had thrown together a few things in a bag for me. I ran to my dressing room on the lot, removed my makeup, showered, and was ready in half an hour. We said good-bye to everyone and drove out the front gate and headed in the direction of Mexico. I sat as far away from him as I possibly could. I was viewing him as an enemy. A non-hostile enemy, perhaps, but an enemy nonetheless. I smiled while my heart palpitated wildly. I kept telling myself to relax. After all, if worse came to worst, I could always get a divorce, couldn't I? So what's the big deal?

So as the sun settled somewhere in the Pacific, Neile Adams and Steve McQueen were embarked on a journey that would take fifteen and a half years to complete. Before that journey's end, there would be many glorious years, two adored children, and a staggering motion picture career that neither one of us could have envisioned in our wildest dreams.

And there would also be searing pain.

5

STEVE WANTED to be married in San Juan Capistrano. "Where the swallows are," he said. He wanted a nice romantic setting. He thought that after the ceremony we could either stay the night in town or go on to Ensenada for a two-day honeymoon. When we arrived at the Mission in San Juan Capistrano, however, the nice sister informed us that there was no possible way we could get married this night. Being the lapsed Catholics that we were, we had forgotten that the banns had to be published. That would make a three-day delay. The sister was most apologetic. Nevertheless, Steve took it as a personal affront.

"All right, then, we'll live in sin," he told her petulantly as he pushed me toward the car. It had been our first try at getting married and we had been unsuccessful. I was secretly pleased. Maybe my luck would hold out. I kept alternating between resignation and sheer panic. Steve was now hungry, so we found a restaurant where we could sit calmly and plan our next move. And before we knew it, more than an hour had gone by so that the other places that could have married us were already closed for the night. Finally, in frustration, Steve stepped on the gas. We had to get to the next town. Maybe there would be a justice of the peace who hadn't gone to bed yet. I don't know how fast we were going but it was "swift"—as he delighted in saying. As we approached San Clemente, two highway patrolmen saw us and tagged us. They were poised to give us a speeding ticket until Steve explained that "Really, all we want to do is get married." I suspect that they thought it was an invented story, but to be nice, they escorted us to the police station and introduced us to the police captain, who just happened to be friends with a Lutheran minister.

The captain growled, "Will he do?"

"Yes, sir," was all Steve said.

The Lutheran minister and his wife had been hosting a dinner party. But as soon as he heard the police captain's story about the plight of the two kids, the minister agreed, on the instant, to open up his church so he could marry us. And what a beautiful church it was.

And so on November 2, 1956, four months after we had been introduced, at approximately eleven thirty at night, Steve and I were married. For the ceremony, I wore a gray wool skirt and a gray shirt with a mandarin collar and Steve wore chino pants with a dark brown flannel shirt and his favorite brown tweed jacket. Our two witnesses were the highway patrolmen who had caught us speeding a little more than an hour before. As soon as the necessary papers were signed and as soon as we were congratulated by the people present, we thanked everyone profusely and hopped in the car. One of the policemen jokingly warned us about speeding. He said, "You're out of excuses now." We laughed and took off.

An extraordinary thing was happening. The panic I had felt earlier had left me as soon as we were pronounced husband and wife. I felt calm and completely relaxed. Steve, on the other hand, was looking at me as if I had suddenly materialized into Vampira—fangs and all. For all his self-assuredness before the actual vows, *he* was now nervous. So much so that he had to stop driving for a bit to collect himself. He was cold and clammy. I started to laugh. This was nuts, I said. Soon he saw the irony of the moment and in no time at all we were both laughing. After a while he started the car and we went to a drive-in to pick up some coffee and potato chips. Then we continued on to San Diego, where we spent the night.

My recollection of our honeymoon in Ensenada is one of furious activity. We had found a hotel on the beach, and as a jumping-off point for our various expeditions it couldn't have been more ideal. We had bought masses and masses of firecrackers, cherry bombs and rockets, and we'd fire away every time the opportunity presented itself. Steve would also drive the T-bird on the beach everytime he found it deserted, going as fast as the wind, with me hanging on for dear life. The car took a tremendous beating, but it survived till we got back to Hollywood. At one point Steve drove the car to an embankment that faced the beach, told me to stand behind the car while he set up a rocket, and then very carefully lit it. It should have gone straight up when it fired, except it didn't. What happened instead was worthy of a Charlie Chaplin comedy routine. The rocket, while bursting in flames, toppled over slowly and trajected itself toward Steve, who was standing nearby. Steve started running as fast as he could in big wide arcs to avoid a direct hit by a rocket gone mad. He was able to leap high enough for the rocket barely to go whizzing by between his legs, and the next thing we knew it had turned around just enough to come heading toward me. I dove under the car in time to hear it hit the side of the T-bird and fizzle out.

I went back to work the following Monday exhausted but happy over all the crazy adventures I had just been a part of. The only memento I have of that honeymoon weekend is a picture Steve insisted that I pose for so that I could show it to my mother.

It is the sort of picture that one has taken at a carnival or at a typical tourist trap. I sit atop a rented burro with a rented sombrero askew on my head. The photo was taken in Tijuana the morning after our wedding. But Steve himself refused to pose in this manner. He said it might come back to haunt him someday!

My mother, who had been so opposed to Steve, was now ecstatically happy to have him for a son-in-law. Suddenly gone were her reservations about his manners. She told me later that when she had learned of my living with Steve, she became fearful that the same fate that had befallen her might now befall me—that is, going through life as somebody's mistress, as opposed to being somebody's wife. It was important to her that I become a respectable woman. In those days a woman achieved respectability only through marriage.

Steve's mother was just as ecstatic over our union, although for a very different reason. For the first time in years, she and her son were able to speak to each other on a much nicer level than had ever been possible. She attributed this to Steve's new toned-down personality, which she felt was directly attributable to me.

So if we weren't all the best of friends, at least peace reigned over our mothers' corners of the world.

While I worked and he looked for work, Steve suddenly became obsessed with the idea of finding his father. His marriage to me and his plans for a family had resurrected the need to confront the older McQueen. (Curiously, it's a little-known fact that Steve also bore a hatred for his father. Not as well publicized as his feeling about his mother, but certainly it was just as strong. In an isolated interview in an unguarded moment, Steve described his dislike for his father as so deep that it threatened to adulterate Steve's life and relationships with others. He

admitted that this worried him.) His mother's last
contact with "Bill" McQueen had been in California,
and so on days when I was not toiling in front of the
cameras and on weekends, we would spend hours
trailing leads Steve had been given, no matter how
small or inconsequential they were. Sometimes directly after work, with my face still in heavy makeup,
Steve and I would grab a hamburger and milkshake,
then get in the VW that had replaced the Thunderbird as our rental car, and we would comb a neighborhood that he'd heard might have been a hangout
for his dad.

But Terrence William McQueen was a hard man
to track down. It had been made doubly hard because Julian, conveniently though understandably,
had forgotten to tell us of an episode that had transpired years and years before.

Julian had never liked the name Terry for a man.
She felt it was too weak. Since William was her husband's middle name, she saw no reason why she
shouldn't call him "Bill." Throughout her life, Steve
never heard his mother refer to his father as anything but Bill McQueen. Incredibly, through bits
and pieces that Steve had painstakingly assembled,
we would find him. But not this time around. For
the moment the trails were cold. It was time to re-
treat. Steve had a very low patience quotient. He
would throw himself in a project with an enormously
concentrated effort, but when that effort proved fruit-
less, he would lose interest and drop the project
abruptly—almost as if to recharge himself for the
time wasted or for the time to come when a sudden
renewed interest would again spark the flame. And
then he would resume with the same fury that had
consumed him in the first place. This was his way
until the day he died.

During those times when we were not looking for
his father, we would play. That could mean a variety
of things. He introduced me to rifle shooting. Then

he taught me about shotguns. Soon after that it was pistols. Westerns were now proliferating on the airwaves. He felt that sooner or later he'd be cast in one of those western shows and he wanted to be prepared. Actor Hugh O'Brien—television's Wyatt Earp—was reputed to be the "fastest draw" in town. Steve wanted to be able to challenge Wyatt Earp himself when the opportunity presented itself, so sure was he that he'd be cast in an episode. He wholeheartedly threw himself into this new exercise called the fast draw. He became quite good at it, but he never appeared in any of the "Wyatt Earp" shows. The opportunity to challenge O'Brien on his own turf never arose. And for that Steve never forgave Hugh O'Brien! Never mind that a whole crew of people, but not the star of the show, cast the actors. Steve never forgot this imagined slight. Thank goodness the need to get even with O'Brien never became a significant matter.

Another thing he taught me or tried to teach me was how to ride a bicycle. We would strap the bicycles in back of the little Volkswagen and then we'd drive to the deserted and dry Los Angeles riverbed and we would ride back and forth, back and forth. I never did get the hang of it. On one cold December day, we were pedaling furiously on the riverbed when a great big patch of green moss loomed up from one end of the riverbank to the other. As we approached the gooey mess, Steve yelled, "Careful, now! Keep your wheels good and straight!" I looked at him cheerfully and flashed him a "don't you worry" smile. Then I immediately found myself in the air, and before I could even gasp, found myself flat on my back! I was soaked through and through while Steve was beside himself with laughter. My teeth started chattering and I angrily tried to get up. I couldn't. Moss is not easy to negotiate when one's body is shaking! Steve came to my aid, and to get even with him, I gave a good yank and pulled him in with me. So much for bicycle riding.

Next came camping. While I enjoyed certain aspects of it, I decided this was one activity Steve could do with the boys. Most especially after I awoke one morning and saw a sign that said PLEASE DO NOT FEED THE BEARS.

All these things had been foreign to me. The world had so much more to offer than I ever imagined and it was a lovely surprise. I liked knowing that there were alternatives to our show business life-style. It made me feel superior, as if I were endowed with a knowledge that nobody else had.

Toward the end of December, while I was still filming *This Could Be the Night,* I was asked to guest on "The Walter Winchell Show." I had also just been asked to appear in the second Tropicana Hotel Revue, which was projected to open in September of the following year. Which meant August rehearsals. Which meant that the last half of the following year was already accounted for as far as my professional life was concerned. I was worried. I felt real concern about Steve's possible uneasiness and even possible resentment over the amount of work that kept coming my way while he still remained unemployed. I decided I had better tread lightly. Still, my salary had now tripled. It was a source of pride to me, and who else would I share that piece of information with? I was relieved to see that he was actually thrilled. The first thing he did was to return our rented VW and buy us a new car. To get us around New York, he said, when we returned. My means of transportation in New York was my feet and his was his motorcycle. Nonetheless, he bought us a cute little red MG. He delighted in making his daily rounds to agents' and producers' offices in this expensive new play toy.

The movie was winding down. All I had left to film was my big dance number. In the meantime, while I awaited a shooting schedule, I rehearsed for hours on end. I wanted it to be perfect. Robert Wise's next movie, also at MGM and also with Jean Simmons, was to start shooting immediately after ours ended. It was called *Until They Sail*, and Jean's co-star was Paul Newman. In between his preproduction meetings, and when he had nothing better to do, Paul would drop by the set and watch me rehearse the "Hustlin' Newsgal" number. Steve was always there, too, and sometimes I'd look up and see those two faces talking to each other. I'd think, My God, those are two young gods I'm seeing!

Paul was already a star. He had zeroed in on his screen personality, and was busy defining and sharpening it with each succeeding film. Steve, on the other hand, was still floundering. He had no idea how to transfer his personality onto the screen. I knew that there was only so much acting school could teach him. The answer for him was screen time. But how? When? Nobody was banging down his door. He had not turned in a good performance as Fidel in *Somebody Up There Likes Me*. Would he be given another chance?

I became determined to get him out of his Brando-Dean mold. Otherwise this man would never make it, and neither would our marriage. He was not the type of man who could tolerate being supported by his wife, although it appeared so at the time to others. But I knew he had that fierce midwestern pride about taking care of one's own woman. As it was, every now and then I'd detect traces of Norman Maine. For instance, sometimes after having had one too many, he'd come staggering back into our room just as I would be getting up to report for work. These were the times he would let off steam about his unhappiness over the work situation. I would reassure him that I didn't mind and that his time would surely come. He must be patient.

The fact was, however, there were many moments

of uncertainty on my part. I was not at all sure his time would come. But I would try and help him all I could until I could try no more. First I had to persuade the people who were behind me and mobilize them behind Steve. I knew I was going to meet some resistance, but I didn't care. I knew I wielded a little power because of my earning capacity. I was hot. Hilly's reaction to my proposal that he handle Steve was, "Darling, there are too many blond boys in Hollywood. Come on!" But eventually, I nagged at him enough so he agreed. The next step was my press agent. He had the ability to plant stories where stories didn't exist and to generate a feeling of excitement for a name nobody had ever heard of. Fortunately, he did not balk at the idea of handling Steve. The last step was a little tricky: I had to persuade my agents at the William Morris Agency— Stan Kamen, Lennie Hirshan, Sandy Glass, and Sy Marsh—to agree to handle Steve. These men were not too thrilled at the prospect of handling an actor who seemed headed for a mediocre career at best. But, if only to keep me happy, they agreed to take him on. In any case I was hoping we'd get back to New York before depression set in. I believe New York has a better atmosphere for unemployed actors. It has tremendous energy and seems to be constantly in motion, so that when one is not gainfully employed in one's chosen profession, time goes by unnoticed. Almost. There is an urgency in New York to get where you want to go, as opposed to the languid and laid-back ambience in California. If you get there, terrific, and if you don't, well—that's all right, too.

At long last I was through filming and we were on our way back home to New York. Steve wanted to drive back for two reasons. One was our new car, and the other was his desire to show me the country. I had never traveled from coast to coast by car. He said, "You can't be a foreigner all your life, you

know. You gotta know what this country looks like."
But I never did get to see much of the country so
long as McQueen was at the wheel. I learned quickly
that there was no such thing as leisurely drives with
my husband—only marathons where we had to finish in first place. I have this mental picture of us
overtaking one car after another while my eyes are
glued to the center dividers and the asphalt on the
road. Then in between, I catch glimpses of pine
trees here, a desert over there, and a city here.

Our trip to the East Coast took us less than five
days. He drove, we ate, and we hardly slept. He was
exhilarated when we arrived at 55th Street, while I
was so exhausted I went to bed and slept for two
days. As I crawled up the stairs to our apartment I
said, "Hey, honey, that was terrific. Now I know
what America looks like! A blur!"

Shortly after we had settled down again into our
familiar routines, Hilly Elkins called and said that a
Studio One production called "The Defender," starring Ralph Bellamy in the title role and William
Shatner as the assistant defender, was going to be
casting shortly. Stay put, he said to Steve. "I wanna
be able to reach you." We learned that the show was
a two-part episode to air the last week of February
and the first week in March. The part of the murderer, which was the catalytic part, was up for grabs,
and every actor in town was reading for it.

Steve's first reading had gone very well, and just
before he went in for the call-back he asked my
advice on an approach he was thinking of taking.
And that was to tell the director, Robert Mulligan,
that he wanted this part badly and he knew that he
could do a really good job with it. Because his first
reading had been excellent and there was no reason
why his second one wouldn't be, my reaction was
that he should tell the director *and* the producer *and*
the writer. Why not? I thought. What could he lose?
His enthusiasm, his earnestness, and his hunger for

the part might just do the trick. He agreed, and lo and behold the next day he had the part. Although his first big score was still a year away, the drought was about to end.

The show was a great critical hit and had an enthusiastic audience. (It eventually became a hugely successful television series starring E. G. Marshall.) Moreover, Steve's reviews had been excellent. Just as good, CBS received several calls from fans of Steven McQueen lauding his performance.

The show was also important to us on another level. This was the first time I had been with him through the very early stages of production and I was able to drop a gentle hint here and there about how he shouldn't play this role, based on the work I'd seen him do in *Somebody Up There Likes Me* and *A Hatful of Rain*. For instance, he had a wonderful smile and a delightful childlike sense of humor. I asked him if maybe when he did his scenes with his mother he could show the audience that smile. His role of the convicted murderer was heavy, but I felt that a motivation could be found to give the character another color and another shade. He saw what I was talking about, and indeed his scenes with Vivian Nathan, who played his mother, were poignant simply because he showed no self-pity. And for the very first time the viewing public was allowed a peek into his bad-boy personality. Score one for Neile!

6

THREE WEEKS AFTER the Studio One show, on Steve's twenty-seventh birthday, he showed up at the apartment with a huge baby German shepherd. He had seen the little doggie in the window of a pet shop and had promptly fallen in love with the animal. He named the dog Thor and promised to take care of him. I said you had better because I can't and I won't. I was aghast at this stupid purchase. We were very seldom at home during the day and I thought it unfair to the dog. Little did I know how unfair it was going to be to me. But after a while I had actually found it touching. Steve had wanted a dog ever since those early days at Uncle Claude's farm. Now he had a home to call his own and a wife to call his own. Now it was time to acquire a dog to call his own.

It was also his birthday, so I decided I'd best humor him. For the moment he was a child again. Through Steve's guidance and characteristic lack of patience, Thor quickly turned into the most ill-mannered dog it has ever been my misfortune to know. Over the years we would own more unruly dogs, but this one was in a class by himself. Steve simply was not temperamentally equipped to train man's best friend. In any case, I grew to hate the dog. He would relieve himself anywhere it pleased him. I knew the dog didn't know any better, but that didn't change the way I felt about him. The pity was that Thor could have been a fabulous animal.

When Steve moved in with me in the early part of summer, we had bought a cot for him to sleep on. My place, after all, was only a studio apartment. Besides chairs and coffee table, all I had in it was a twin-sized bed which doubled as a couch during the day. Moreover, everything between us had happened so fast that we never got around to figuring out just what sort of sleeping accommodations we should have. As soon as we came back to New York, however, the cot gave way to a thick, king-sized quilt Steve had picked up somewhere in the Village. He had always resented my sleeping on my bed while he slept on the cot. He had decided that since he was now a married man he was not going to sleep on a cot like a goddamn guest. Instead, *we* were going to sleep on the floor on the quilt that he had bought. With my money. Which we were now sharing with the beast, Thor.

Thor had decided that the best time for him to mess was in the middle of the night. There was never any mistaking that odor, especially in such close quarters. I had to force myself up to clean the mess—Steve was a heavy sleeper. I was a good sport for three nights running and then the party was over. If Steve wanted to keep Thor, then it would be up to him to clean up after the dog. I had warned Steve what I would do if he failed to watch the dog. And so the next time it happened I got up and dressed quickly, walked down to the next block, checked myself into the Warwick Hotel, and went to sleep. Steve got the picture, although he was mystified by my action.

Tax time was fast upon us, and the year 1957 was the first year we would be filing jointly. I found his receipts in his suitcase and to my delight I also found pictures from his days in the Marine Corps and pictures of his earlier acting jobs. I set aside the

receipts and started what was the first of many scrapbooks of our life together. Little did I know that I
was being the archivist for a future movie legend.

The visit with the accountant was not pleasant.
Steve was embarrassed to find that he had earned
$4,000 for the past year while my income was $50,000.
He also did not like the accountant's (or anyone's)
knowledge of the disparity in our earning power. I
kept telling him, "Look, honey, I just got there a
little sooner than you did, that's all. One day it will
be your turn." He really was not happy with the
situation and appreciated that I understood he
wanted to bring home the bacon.

We had six weeks free before either one of us had
to work. Steve was due in Philadelphia to repeat his
role in *A Hatful of Rain* at the Fairmont Park Theatre
during the latter part of June, then he would go on
to the Pocono Playhouse with the show for the first
week in July. In the meantime, I was contracted to
appear with John Raitt at the Pittsburgh Civic Light
Opera in *The Pajama Game* for the first two weeks in
July, and then ten days later, I was to do the show at
Kansas City's Starlite Theatre. After that, it was on
to Las Vegas and the Tropicana Hotel. That left me
exactly eight days in between, to go back to New
York and pack for a six-month stay. That meant that
I wouldn't be returning to New York until February
1958. How we would manage to see each other during my stay in Las Vegas never even came up for
discussion. Obviously Steve would have to come to
see me, since my schedule—two shows a night, seven
nights a week—would be inflexible.

We decided to take advantage of our remaining
time together and head south in our little red MG.
Steve wanted to show me the routes he and his
buddies had covered on their motorcycles on their
way to Cuba a little less than a year before. He and I
retraced his steps as far as Clearwater, Florida, where
a thumb infection knocked him for a loop. I had to

take him to the emergency room to have his thumb
lanced and stitched. All this arose from a cuticle he
had pulled with his teeth. On the way out of the
hospital he turned pale and I suddenly found myself
dragging his 168-pound frame with my 105 pounds
of dancing muscles. I was petrified at the possibility
of his fainting on me and then finding myself unable
to move and suffocating under his dead weight. But
he recovered. After a rest on the grass he was able to
pull himself together long enough to drive us to a
motel. The last words he uttered before he fell sound
asleep from the medication were, "Goddamn it, I
gotta teach you how to drive!"

En route home a few days later, we encountered
the edge of a hurricane. The rainstorm was something else. I recall sheets of water enveloping our
little car and the little thing involuntarily going from
one side of the road to the other. Steve decided it
would be folly to stop moving. He was afraid the car
would be swept off the road. By seizing the wheel
with a mighty grip Steve was able to keep us on a
straight and steady course as we inched along the
highway. My face was pressed against the windshield
and my eyes strained to guide us through the almost-
zero visibility. Eventually we found a motel and waited
for the torrential rains to abate.

Once the danger had passed I saw the same exhilaration he had exhibited after we had crossed the
country in record time. Later I came to recognize
that he needed these little adventures for his sense
of self. Like a gambler, he had a desire to conquer
the odds, and when that failed, he still reveled in
simply having been part of the excitement to begin
with. The element of danger was as necessary to his
survival as breathing was.

He had acquired a new maturity and a little more
understanding about himself in the last year, which
gave his latest portrayal of Johnny Pope in *A Hatful*

of Rain a new dimension. As I watched his first two performances at the Fairmont Park Theatre in Philadelphia, every now and then I could see the originality of his personality burst forth. But generally, I would observe this during those moments on stage when he was still. How interesting, I thought. As a musical comedy performer, I found that hard to understand, since I was always in constant motion on stage. And yet here he was, absolutely irresistible to watch in his most passive and unobtrusive moments. He would make an incredible Johnny Pope when he grew up, I said to myself. But despite the new awareness, something was still out of sync. It dawned on me that it was Kim Hunter. Like Vivian Blaine before her, Kim represented Woman as opposed to Girl, while Steve, on stage, was still a boy and not quite a man. And never the twain could meet.

It was during that summer Steve accepted my suggestion that he drop the *n* from Steven to make his name sound less formal. I thought Steven McQueen had a self-conscious ring to it, while Steve McQueen had the free-wheeling sound I could easily associate with the man. But for the next three jobs he would shift back and forth between the two names. It would take the combined efforts of Hilly Elkins and me to make him drop the *n* forever—just in time for the television westerns that would occupy his professional life for three seasons.

Our combined itinerary during that period would take us from New York to Philadelphia to Pittsburgh to Kansas City to Slater, Missouri, to meet Uncle Claude, back to Kansas City, back to New York, on to Las Vegas for me, on to Los Angeles for Steve, and finally on to Las Vegas for him and my Tropicana opening. In Los Angeles, Steve would read for the role of John Drew Barrymore's boyhood chum who grows up to become district attorney in the Harold Robbins movie *Never Love a Stranger*. Within a few days Steve was notified that the part was his. The movie's title was also prophetic: in the cast was a girl named Lita Milan. Steve told me after the picture he had had a fling with her. She would be the first in a long line of "flings" that would plague us—me— throughout our married life.

During quiet moments I sometimes try to understand the whys and what fors behind Steve's infidelities. It is difficult and confusing and taxing because contradictions come at me from many angles. On the one hand, I had a man whose philosophy in life was "God is my kids, my old lady, the green grass, trees, machines, and animals." For all his toughness, Steve was a little boy. He was also a man who found emotional safety in me and his children. He was tender, sentimental, sensitive, dominant, strong and steady as a rock. Our marriage was once described this way: "His control over his marriage is real, but it is also sometimes more apparent than real. He needs Neile more than she needs him. Her love is proof that he has managed to survive." I was McQueen's queen and there was no denying that. The man loved me, and I knew it. And yet, on the other hand, there was this quirk, this need in his personality to flex his muscles outside the marriage bed. At first he was not indiscreet, and I doubt I would have found out about his extracurricular activities were it not for his need to confess them to me to relieve him of his guilt. By doing so he transferred to me the responsibility of making it all all right. And I would make it all all right. It generally took a few days, but I was always able to rationalize his activities away. I knew that his bed hopping meant no more to him than a drive around the block. As he used to say, "You can only say 'no' so many times."

Obviously his indiscretions were not everyday occurrences, but they were enough to disrupt an otherwise spectacularly successful marriage. We had complemented each other well, together we equaled a whole. This particular bit of aberration I ascribed to his mother, who had treated him shabbily as a boy.

As for me, my combination Oriental and Latin upbringing had taught me that men separated love and marriage from their feckless romps in the hay. So, okay, I thought. I can handle it—I have to—as long as he doesn't flaunt it. This is what I told myself. I was so naive. And yet I was independent and daring and had interests of my own. I acted as a buffer between Steve and the world. Professionally, Steve never made a move without me—except toward the end. He trusted me and trusted my interests.

Later on, in an elsewhere time, his "meaningless fuck-flings," as he referred to them, would be the catalyst that made me tear asunder a seemingly indestructible marriage.

Las Vegas proved to be a triumph for me professionally. Everything kept coming up roses. My reviews were good, my salary rising, a new Broadway musical was on the horizon for me, and I was lined up to guest on all the major television variety shows. Thrillingly, my name started appearing on lists featuring stars of tomorrow. The October 1957 issue of *Redbook* magazine even placed the name Neile Adams ahead of Joanne Woodward, Natalie Wood, and Jean Seberg.

While my professional life was exciting, my personal life was chaotic, disastrous, and nightmarish.

While Steve was filming *Never Love a Stranger*, he commuted between Los Angeles and Las Vegas. With Thor. Darling dog. The animal and I had irreconcilable differences, and there was no way in the world he and I could become friends. When the film finally wrapped, it became the three of us unrelievedly together again under the same roof. Oh joy, oh rapture. It became impossible for me to get a good night's sleep, since Steve and I were on different timetables. And the dog, Thor, was an even bigger pain. Because of his enormous size, he required frequent exercising, which Steve was finding difficult because of the desert heat. In his restless state the dog would jump onto the bed to invite one of us to play with him. When he was rebuffed, which was often, he would then proceed to destroy the couch or the chair or the carpet. I became irritable most of the time when I was around Steve, and I couldn't wait to get to the club for some peace and quiet. Killing the dog was obviously out. I would have to divorce Steve in order to get rid of Thor.

Another irritant was the way Steve dispensed my money in the most cavalier way. He would generally wait for me in the casino while I removed my makeup and changed into street clothes. That, of course, was asking for trouble, since Steve seldom had any luck at the tables. On one such unlucky night, I had picked up my week's salary right after the first show and had given it to him to hold (I paid the bills). Steve and Dick Shawn (that darling, certifiably insane genius) had decided to have a bite to eat at a restaurant outside the Hotel Tropicana, and because the weather had cooled considerably, I had asked them to wait while I ran backstage to my dressing room to pick up a sweater. The entire process—the run from the casino to my dressing room and back—took no more than seven minutes. In that short time my week's salary vanished at the crap tables.

At the end of his second week's stay, he arrived at our motel driving a bright, shiny new Corvette. Another red car to replace the little red car. The MG had had a stick shift, which I had found impossible to negotiate. This Corvette, he said, has power steering. Just the thing *we* need to teach you how to drive.

I determined right then and there to get him out of town. I had a job to do and the man was driving me to distraction with his dog, his cars, and his gambling. He was bored. My hours were hard on him; he missed his pal. I slept until noon on good days and even later on bad days. Leisure time for me was almost nonexistent, since I left for the club at six thirty and did not finish working until one thirty in the morning. And so it went, day in and day out. I had come to the realization that here in Las Vegas there was no room for him in my life. But how does one say this to a husband? I hadn't any idea what marriage was when Steve and I got married. I had been caught unaware. We had jumped into it because we were in love and it was romantic and exciting, but what about now? I would look at him and the word "divorce" would come to mind. Then my mother's words would immediately take its place. "Better the devil you know than the devil you don't know." I saw the William Morris Agency and Hilly Elkins as my way out. I began hounding Stan Kamen and Sy Marsh about my husband's unemployment. I nagged Hilly. "Listen, fellas, you must get Steve something. Anything! He is driving me bananas! Do you guys understand that? Please, fellas!"

The "something and anything" materialized into another movie called *The Great St. Louis Bank Robbery*, to be shot in St. Louis. Like *Never Love a Stranger*, it was a low-budget "B" film. While the money was again negligible, this time Steve had the male lead.

On the day prior to his departure for St. Louis, I walked into our little motel apartment carrying a bag of groceries. Steve was practicing his quick draws with his Colt .22. He had just come in from the desert, where he had been practicing dropping a dime from the back of his hand and quickly pulling the gun out of his holster and firing at a target before the dime hit the ground. Incredibly, after his practice, he had neglected to check the gun's chambers thoroughly and had inadvertently left a lone bullet floating around in there. He said, "Look, honey!" and as I did a loud blast came from his direction and in the same instant I knew by the slight quiver of the grocery bag I was holding in my arms that I had had a narrow escape. The bullet had gone right through the paper bag and into the wall. After I had regained my composure I jokingly asked Steve whether the little incident had been an accident or a deliberate attempt on his part to keep me in line. He pulled me in his arms and gave me an innocent and enigmatic smile.

"I wanted you to have something to remember me by while I'm in St. Louis!"

I laughed but at the same time felt a slight uneasiness over his remark. After all, I thought, this is a man who goes around poking noses simply because an admiring glance or remark happens to come my way. Steve had once run after a carful of men during a walk in Central Park when a passenger in the convertible made the mistake of whistling at me. Steve pulled him out of the backseat and forcibly extracted an apology from the poor man. And Steve probably knew that Las Vegas was not the best place to leave an attractive woman unprotected. Already I had fended off the advances of one Johnny Rosselli. When his pursuit failed to elicit the desired response from me, Johnny appointed himself my guardian angel. I liked him enormously. I was not aware that in actual fact he was a high-ranking mafioso until years later when I read a book called *The Green Felt Jungle*. The book credited him with killing seventeen people. In August 1976, his dismembered body was found stuffed in an oil drum, floating in a bay near Miami, just two weeks before he was to testify before a Senate subcommittee investigating the assassination of President John F. Kennedy.

Howard Hughes touched my life ever so lightly. He was having me tailed by two men until Rosselli's men put a stop to it. Apparently, Mr. Hughes wanted to put me under contract and had instructed his people to find out how I conducted my life off the stage. Why he had taken an interest in me was never clear. I certainly did not follow the mold of Jane Russell or Terry Moore or Jean Peters.

I had very little time to socialize while I appeared in Las Vegas. One exception however was with Elvis Presley. He was then seeing a girl named Dottie Harmony, a chorus dancer who lived next door to me at the motel. They made a cute couple. He had made his sensational appearance on the "Ed Sullivan Show" just the year before, and the world was his for the asking. He would hang around with us in the lounge in between shows. He had an innocence about his sexuality that was most appealing. Open, vulnerable, and sensitive, he was also extraordinarily polite. He was the first person who ever addressed me as "ma'am." I was sorry I never saw him again on a social basis.

During the time that Steve was in St. Louis, we fought savagely every night over the phone. My weekly telephone bills at the hotel were astronomical. Steve only called collect. I dreaded his calls. As soon as I stepped into my dressing room the phone would ring and the inquisition would begin. Who did I see today? Who was I with at dinner? What man made a pass at me? How did I react? I resented his questions and I resented him. I was grateful he was far enough away so I could breathe. Incredibly, when he came to visit me on the weekends he would be so happy to see me that all our problems would fall by the wayside. His happiness at being together seemed to counterbalance his manicness. But then the cycle would begin again as soon as we were apart. As the years passed I recognized that his *need* for me transcended his love for me. I was all he had and when our children came, we were his whole world. Since he had no happy, sentimental memories of his childhood, he felt always at odds with the world unless we were within reach.

In the meantime, Steve at least had the good sense

to follow up our phone battles with love notes sent via Western Union that never failed to make things right between us. One of the first telegrams Steve sent me in Las Vegas bore this message:

I ADORE YOU I ADORE YOU I ADORE YOU I ADORE YOU
I ADORE YOU I ADORE YOU I ADORE YOU I ADORE YOU
I ADORE YOU I ADORE YOU WHEN WE START MAKING LITTLE ONES
WE WILL GET A LITTLE FAT ONE FOR YOU AND A LITTLE THIN ONE
FOR ME AND WE WILL MAKE THEM GO OUT AND SUPPORT US SO WE CAN BE TOGETHER MY LOVE IS WITH YOU DARLING NEXT TO ME YOU ARE THE MOST TALENTED PERSON IN THE WORLD AND NO MATTER WHAT THE BAND PLAYS WE WILL ALWAYS HEAR OUR OWN MUSIC I LOVE YOU AND I LOVE YOU

ESTEBAN

And the last telegram of that period read:

MY DARLING DEAREST THEY SAY THAT THINGS THAT COME EASY ARE NOT WORTH HAVING I ONCE VOWED AT AN ALTAR IN SICKNESS AND IN HEALTH FOR BETTER OR WORSE THIS PERIOD WE ARE GOING THROUGH IS VERY DIFFICULT PROBABLY THE MOST DIFFICULT PERIOD IN OUR LIFE YOU AND I TOGETHER WILL KEEP THAT VOW WE WILL SOON HAVE THOSE DAYS AGAIN TOGETHER OF HAPPINESS AND UNDERSTANDING COMPLETE LOVE AND COMMUNICATION ALL THE UNHAPPINESS WE FEEL THROUGH BEING SEPARATED WILL SOON PASS AND BE FORGOTTEN AND MAKE WAY FOR MORE BEAUTIFUL THINGS FOR A LIFE OUR CHILDREN AND OUR LOVE I LOVE YOU WITH ALL MY HEART REMEMBER THAT I AM ALWAYS WITH YOU

ESTEBAN

In deference to my Spanish background Steve almost always signed off with "Esteban." Rarely was it ever Steve or Steven.

Steve was anxious to start a family, while on the other hand, the idea left me panicked. My God, what would I do with children? While Steve talked, I smiled, said nothing, and had hot and cold flashes. It was hard to fathom what effect children would have on me, on our lives, and most of all, for the moment, my body—this body that was so generously supporting us. In the short run, I knew my moneymaking ability was the underlying motive that made him accept jobs indiscriminately, jobs that were probably doing more harm to his career than good. But it was also a situation that I was able to exploit to give me some peace during my Las Vegas run.

Then one beautiful golden morning Stan Kamen called to inform me that there was something in the very near future that Steve might be right for. "So just hold on, kid!" Stan was referring to a television pilot about a bounty hunter that was going to spin off from Robert Culp's very successful series "Trackdown." By coincidence, Hilly Elkins managed Bob Culp. By coincidence, Stan Kamen handled Four Star Productions, the company that produced "Trackdown." And true to his word, Stan saw to it that the kid from the Actors Studio got the part. A few days before Christmas, the segment of "Trackdown" entitled "The Bounty Hunter" went before the cameras. BINGO!!

On February 11, 1958, after a record-breaking run of six months at the Tropicana, the show finally closed. I was exhausted and in need of battery recharging. Two shows a night, every night, had been wearying. I looked forward to doing something different, other than dancing, for at least a brief while. Steve and I had rented a little house in North Hollywood on a street called Klump Avenue (Steve used to say, "It's embarrassing, you know, you give your name and your address and then people look at you kinda strange!") and become bicoastal people. Wisely, I had not given up the apartment on 55th Street.

After ten days of getting settled in L.A., I was summoned to New York to join Andy Williams on "The Pat Boone Show." While on the East Coast, Hilly had received an offer for Steve to star in a very low budget horror movie entitled *The Blob.* "Are you serious, Hilly?" We all fell on the floor laughing. *The Blob?* Hilly's response was "Why not? Better to be employed than not. Besides, CBS still hasn't made up its mind about going ahead with 'The Bounty Hunter.' So I suggest you take advantage of the time." Steve looked at me questioningly and I shrugged my shoulders and said, "Well, it'll keep you off the streets!"

"What if it's a hit?"

"Honey, it's a mom-and-pop operation from the sound of it. It'll disappear at the drive-ins."

And so it came to be that after my appearance on the "Boone Show," Steve and I hightailed it to a little community outside of Philadelphia where the horror flick was to be shot. The director was a minister named Irvin S. Yeaworth, Jr. I assumed he and the producer, Jack Harris, had joined hands because the producer had a very limited budget and the director had fashioned a very workable special effects operation in one of the rooms in the church building. It definitely looked like a Mickey Mouse operation, what with the miniatures and the special effects paraphernalia being housed in a room off the church. But Yeaworth's earnest belief in the project was so endearing it disarmed Steve. He agreed to do the movie if they "give me the $2,500 in my hot little hand" all at once instead of the small percentage that had been offered previously. Steve quietly wished that the movie would never see the light of day. But as the world knows, *The Blob,* upon its release, became not only a box office hit, but also a cult film—much to Steve's horror! For some reason audiences loved the blobby mess on the screen. Also, they found the ending amusing. The caption "The End?" was scrawled across the screen as the blob was dropped into the Arctic Ocean. Presumably to surface again according to the producer's whim.

More important, this film role showed us that he could no longer play high school kids. During the two years we had been married the transformation from boy to man had transpired. He was now twenty-eight years old and his performance was forced. Fortunately, by the time *The Blob* was released, the television series was on its way to catapulting Steve to national prominence.

As Steve was finishing up *The Blob,* I did two more variety shows before I was notified that I had been awarded the lead opposite Paul Muni in a new Broadway-bound musical called *At the Grand.* The show was expected to open in Los Angeles July 7 and in New York in December. A week later Stan called to tell us that CBS had bought Steve's pilot film! It was being renamed "Wanted—Dead or Alive" and the network had ordered twenty-eight episodes.

We were ecstatic for ourselves and for each other. After the Las Vegas experience, however, neither one wanted to broach the subject "what if." We each independently came to the conclusion that we would deal with problems as they arose. If they arose. One at a time.

On April 5, 1958, Steve McQueen began portraying a western character named Josh Randall who was unlike the run-of-the-mill bounty hunter of the Old West. He was soft-spoken and carried a sawed-off Winchester rifle known as a "mare's laig." This custom gun was worn in a holsterlike hook-and-clamp rig on Steve's right leg. By practicing with it day in and day out, he developed an amazing agility with the weapon as a handgun. (The "mare's laig" qualified as a machine gun and, because it was sawed off, was subject to federal law.) To render his trade as a mercenary more palatable to the American public, Steve insisted that his character generally bring in his quarry alive as opposed to dead. How quickly the new television star discovered how to use the power that is automatically bestowed on someone whose name is above the title!

Rehearsals for *At the Grand* commenced in the middle of May. The show was based on the movie classic *Grand Hotel,* which had starred Lionel Barrymore, Greta Garbo, John Barrymore, and Joan Crawford. Their roles were now being played, respectively, by Paul Muni (making his musical debut), Joan Diener, Cesare Danova, and Neile Adams. From the beginning the show was trouble-plagued. Muni and director Albert Marre became estranged (to put it mildly), and since all my big scenes were with Paul Muni, I was forbidden by the old man to take direction from the director. He said, "I will direct you." And so for our scenes together, Muni directed me, while Bella Muni, his wife, directed him.

On opening night Steve brought Shirley MacLaine, and after the show she gave me wonderfully constructive criticism. Unfortunately, I was the least of the show's problems. The audience reaction toward me that night and every night was enthusiastic. I had the closing song and the closing line of the show, and there was no doubt in anybody's mind that this show would make me a big star—provided, of course, that we reached Broadway.

In the meantime, there was an absence of order in my own household. Steve was now getting up every morning for a six-thirty call and going to bed at eleven. Four Star Productions wanted to have as many episodes in the can as possible before the show premiered in September. While *At the Grand* was in rehearsals, the only time we spent together was in bed. Otherwise we were living quite independently of each other. Steve was not happy about this, and I tried to compensate for it. We communicated by telephone several times a day and we left each other little notes. Soon he began signing off with "Love, your pen pal." As soon as my show opened, the situation eased up a bit. I made it a point to get up with him every morning before his day's shoot and make him his coffee (with three sugars) and sugar toast. We would have a bit of conversation before he left for work, and as soon as he closed the door behind him I would crawl back into bed and continue my sleep until it was my turn to go to work. Sundays were our "make up for lost time" days, and we would catch up with everything we had missed during the week.

Almost too soon, my departure for San Francisco was upon us. For the first time I felt stirrings of guilt and sadness at having to leave my husband, who now needed me and my support more than ever. There was no way I could resolve the problem unless I quit the show. And I couldn't do it. This is what I had worked so hard for the last few years. This was my moment. He knew it and I knew it.

Steve spent the next seven weekends with me in San Francisco. He almost always arrived in an agitated state brought on by his battles on the set with producers and writers. He was now beginning to define the character of Josh Randall in terms of his own personality and life experience.

The scripts being given him were too unrealistic. The "superman" sort of westerns were passé as far as Steve was concerned. When the script called for Josh to do battle with three giant gunmen or was told to "git" by a group of desperadoes, Steve's instinct told him the character should react the way

Steve himself would. That is, to "git" and then come back and shoot them in the back if necessary.

One story he relished recounting and which he always used as an example of what he meant was the time in the Marines when two toughs had given him a hard time. A fistfight was about to ensue when Steve bowed out, recognizing that he wouldn't be able to handle the two capably. Instead he waited in the latrine and when one of them came in he said, "Hey, you!" When the lone man turned, "I punched him and kicked the hell out of him. I made my point and was never bothered again."

It didn't always make him a very popular fella but as time and ratings proved, his instincts were right. And this was the name of the game as far as he was concerned.

The early reviews of "Wanted—Dead or Alive" were not promising. *Variety* said, "Steve McQueen, a new face in the electronic corral, is not a huge hunk of man to set a maiden's heart fluttering. He is lithe and lean and can handle up to six men at a time." (A little sarcasm there, as with other reviews.) From *TV Guide* came this: "There's this bounty hunter, Josh Randall (Steve McQueen), who ranges about the Old West, see? He studies posters of 'wanted' lawbreakers, then hunts them down, brings them in dead or alive, and collects the reward." The San Francisco papers (where I was then performing) were unanimous in their assessment of the show. They thought it too violent. The San Francisco *Examiner* chastised CBS for showing a most violent western. "The man-hunting hero, Steve McQueen, is a trigger-happy James Cagney type. In the first three minutes of the first show he shot a man in the back and broke another man's hand. Later there were two violent on-camera killings. Typical dialogue: 'You make a move and you're open from the scalp down.' For blood and thunder fans, great! For the squeamish, appalling!" And on and on it went.

These early reviews only made Steve more determined than ever to mold his character to his liking. He felt that Josh Randall had to display some human frailties in order to make the man more believable, more likable, and more vulnerable. He felt that John Wayne's sort of bravura was not compatible with this sort of hero. Actually, he was paving the way for the growth of Steve McQueen as an actor.

Simultaneously, there were rumors circulating around the Curran Theatre that *At the Grand* might close down after the six-week San Francisco run for rewrites. The possibility of reviving a show once it has closed shop seemed remote to me. It became even more remote when I discovered I was pregnant! I didn't breathe a word to a soul—not even to Steve. My plan was to wait to see what the decision on the show would be. If, by chance, they could pull it off and open on Broadway, I had every intention of being there opening night. Steve would have prevented me from going about my plans. Why make waves? I asked myself. But a funny thing happened to me on the way to the Big Time. Man and Mother Nature conspired to prevent me from fulfilling my destiny as a musical star. Instead they conspired to fulfill my destiny as wife and mother—but not before I snuck in an appearance on "The Eddie Fisher Show" on November 11 of that year.

Steve was ecstatic! At last he had his wife at home. Not only was I at home, but I was also pregnant and barefoot in the kitchen. For the quintessential male chauvinist pig—and I say that with much affection— that was the ideal! I had supported him for the last two and a half years, and now it was time to reverse our positions. He felt this was the right moment for me just to work intermittently and allow him to carry the workload. Actually fate had stepped in at the right moment. It's doubtful this young marriage could

have survived another long separation following on
the heels of the Vegas run.

As the popularity of his television show grew, so
did the number of personal appearance tours he
agreed to do. We traveled all over the country publi-
cizing the show. He delighted in introducing me to
his fans as "my Nellie with the belly." The audiences
at the fairs and theaters where he made his personal
appearances loved his brand of freshness. He had
developed a little patter that was designed mostly to
acquaint them with him and show off the "mare's
laig," while at the same time giving them a little dose
of homily laced with a dash of hip New York brash.
Example: "Yup, my ole lady and me, we got us one
in the oven!" Nobody in the public eye had ever
talked like that. Certainly no TV star. And the public's response was one of utter delight. The press
began to have a field day! They exaggerated his
colorful speech pattern and tried desperately to trans-
late the essence of the McQueen personality. What
generally came across, however, was a distorted
representation of the man. His original words and
phrases were baffling. His personality, in the beginning, was difficult to capture in print, especially when
he would pour it on so thick that he would become
unintelligible even to himself. He seemingly was able
to pick words out of the air before one heard them
on the streets and they became part of the national
vocabulary. Other actors tried imitating his speech
patterns, but what came naturally to Steve always
came out stilted and forced from somebody else.

In truth his unique conversation was part musician
talk, part jive talk, part street talk, and part Steve
talk. It took a little while before the media caught on
to the fact that here was a thinking man's kook.
When we first married and he started referring to
me as "my old lady," columnists like Hedda Hopper
and Louella Parsons thought him strange. Words
like "bread," "melon," "wheels," "juice," etc., had an

entirely different significance in Steve language. Yet to their credit, Hedda and Louella were able to detail him for their readers in very colorful and captivating ways. Significantly, since his way of talking was partly for show, at home he kept it to a minimum—just as he kept his "hearing impairment" segregated from home and family. Terry, Chad, and I were never subjected to the quizzical looks accompanied with "huh's?" and "what's?" and ear cupping.

Much newspaper and magazine space has been devoted to Steve's alleged hearing problems. True, he had had a double mastoidectomy as a very young boy. True, he had damaged part of the hearing in his left ear (about 30 percent) when he came up abruptly from the ocean floor while he and a friend were scuba diving in 1955. But it was also true that he could hear well enough to listen in on my phone conversations while he sat in the next room. The hand-to-ear gesture that he often displayed to reporters and strangers was nothing more than a ploy to give him time to think or just plain tune out when he became bored or annoyed. He delighted in using it to his advantage, and it was beneficial as a signal for me to join actively in an interview or a conversation when he wanted to bow out gracefully.

His salary for "Wanted—Dead or Alive" was $750 per episode, and not unnaturally, the first investment that he made for himself was a car—a 1958 black Porsche speedster that is still in the family. It now belongs to our son, Chad. (It was the start of a collection of vehicles that would total 135 antique motorcycles and 35 cars. The collection, sold at auction in Las Vegas in 1984, brought in over a million and a half dollars. It benefited the IRS more than it did the McQueen Children's Trust, as it has been presumed by some people.)

With the money I had accumulated over my working years, we also bought our first house, on Skyline

Drive in Laurel Canyon, and prepared for the arrival of the baby. Life had taken on a new meaning for me. My nesting instinct took over, and I found myself madly in love with my husband. Although I was sick most of the time, and decidedly fat, I looked forward to motherhood.

My newfound happiness suffered a setback one evening when Steve took a mysterious phone call and I overheard him say, "Look, I love my wife very much and we're gonna have a baby soon." I didn't have to hear the rest. Steve was full of remorse and said that he had been drunk one night and had met a girl, etc., etc., etc. For the next few days he brought me flowers and presents and cards. For a while I was so hurt that I refused to speak to him, but eventually we again became a happy couple.

One late afternoon Steve and I went out to shop for maternity clothes. He patiently sat through all my many clothing changes, and on the way out he decided to look at some sweaters. As he made his selection, I went around the counter opposite him and was in the process of looking at shirts when I started to feel clammy. I stood rooted to my place as I desperately tried to catch my husband's eye. I was now having hot and cold flashes—a signal from my body that I was about to pass out. I finally yelled out his name and as he looked I motioned for him to come to me. I knew that he absolutely detested being called to and gestured to in the way I had just done, but I hoped he could see I was in trouble. Unfortunately he didn't, and he gave me a cold, hard look instead—just as I started to slide down behind the counter. A salesman had apparently caught me, but when I recovered I was in Steve's arms. As was the pattern in both my pregnancies, these fainting spells were over in a matter of minutes, but Steve always found the experience unnerving. And it was inevitable that an unsuspecting fan would recognize him at such a moment and ask for his autograph with the classic line, "I know it's a bad time, but could I please have your autograph for my sister? She's a great fan and she'll never believe I saw you!"

"Get the fuck out of here, kid. Now!" came Steve's answer.

At about the time of this incident, a gift, like manna from heaven, fell in Steve's lap. He and I had agreed that he couldn't possibly afford to do another "B" movie or he would be consigned to them forever. His next film had to be at a major studio with a major star who could carry a film. Good, bad, or indifferent.

Enter John Sturges, who was preparing a movie called *Never So Few,* based on the book by Tom Chamales about 600 Burmese guerrillas led by a handful of Americans fighting off 40,000 Japanese during World War II. The film was to star Frank Sinatra and Gina Lollobrigida, and John gave the part of Bill Ringa, the resourceful, wisecracking, gum-chewing supply sergeant, to the young, fair-haired actor he had been admiring in a television series. It was inspired casting, and as it turned out, it was John Sturges, more than anybody in Steve's career, who would nurture that quiet and laid-back strength so necessary to the persona of this future film star.

By now "Wanted—Dead or Alive" was consistently among the top ten rated TV shows and CBS ordered thirty-nine segments for the 1959 season. To fulfill that order, off we went to Phoenix, Arizona, for location shots so he could still be free to do the Sinatra picture later that summer. CBS and Four Star were just as anxious as we were for Steve to break into movies. They felt anything their star did outside the series could only benefit them.

I was in my sixth month of pregnancy when we took off for the desert in the Porsche Speedster. I was already thirty-five pounds over my normal weight and looked as if I were ready to drop the baby at any time. It was one of those clear beautiful days when the horizon stretched forever. I was reclined on the passenger side dreaming about my baby while Steve maneuvered the car expertly—and quickly. He was happy. I was happy. Yet, as so often happens on these deserted stretches, a police car with red lights flashing suddenly appeared in Steve's rearview mirror.

"Oh, shit, baby. Cops!" We were already paying an enormous insurance rate and Steve could ill afford more moving violations, so I yelled, "Tell them I'm having a baby!"

In his best Stanislavsky acting method, Steve jumped out of the Porsche, ran toward the police car, and excitedly asked, "Where's the nearest hospital? I think my wife's in labor!"

"Follow us!" The police car took its place in front of our car and roared off. Steve was beside himself with joy. Not only were we riding well over the speed limit, we were being escorted by the law! However, when we arrived at the hospital the law men refused to budge until the good doctor had signed a clearance pronouncing me O.K. He said I was suffering from severe gas pains.

So much for the Phoenix adventure.

Frank Sinatra could not have been more generous with Steve in *Never So Few,* and John Sturges took advantage of this and worked with Steve to make his appearance a memorable one. John was a strong director and was able to guide Steve. Although on his series Steve had begun to give orders here and there, now he deferred to John's direction without question. He was impressed with John's credits and his reputation of being a man's man. Moreover, John respected and knew all about fast cars. It gave them another level of communication. Steve had just discovered auto racing and was gung-ho about the sport.

Because films are heavily insured, he was naturally forbidden to race during principal photography. Since he was the first of the actors to take up this hobby seriously, he was also the first to bear the brunt of its restrictions. Eventually, a compromise was reached on all his movies. No car or motorcycle racing would be tolerated during production, but he would be allowed to ride his motorcycle or any other vehicle of his choice to and from location. There was no way Steve could possibly leave his cars and motorcycles idle in the garage while he toiled for the establishment. He once said his machinery represented "his balls" and was a symbol of his rebelliousness—as if anyone could forget. So on he rode. It was important for him to provoke the establishment every once in a while, and he had a wonderful time doing so. And the cars became crucial in shaping his perception of the world around him.

7

BY THE TIME the second season of "Wanted—Dead or Alive" went on the air in the fall of 1959, the show was a bona fide hit.

We also had a new baby daughter, named Terry Leslie McQueen, born June 5, 1959. Shortly after her birth a huge fire erupted in Laurel Canyon, threatening to trap my infant daughter and me. Steve, in his haste to get to us, broke through a police line without informing them he had a wife and baby up the hill. A chase ensued, although the cop didn't catch up with Steve until the three of us had emerged from the house and then the patrolman understood. But that didn't prevent him from admonishing Steve. When the fire was contained I received an enormous bouquet of flowers with a note saying, "Welcome home, love from Dick, David, and Charles." After puzzling it over for a few hours I called the florist and discovered that the flowers were from Steve's bosses at Four Star—Dick Powell, David Niven, and Charles Boyer!

Frank Sinatra, who I think possesses the same rebellious and devil-may-care qualities as Steve, had become fond of him, so not long after Terry was born, Frank asked us to accompany him to New York and Atlantic City for a bit of fun and frolic. Along with us on this trip were Natalie Wood and Bob Wagner (during their first marriage). I gathered they were old friends of Frank's. We saw *Gypsy* and *West Side Story*, and we took Frank to Louie's in the Village, where Steve had scrounged for food in his early days. Louie was pleased to see "the bandido" back, especially pleased that Steve was no longer starving, and really, really pleased that we had brought Sinatra along.

We also went to Atlantic City for one of Sinatra's club openings, where he was billed simply as "Guess Who?" and for the very first time, we became privy to how a *big star* lives. Limos, room service at the snap of the fingers, the aura true stardom creates . . . it was a fascinating experience. Steve had said, "Yeah, I want a crack at that!" To which I had replied, "Yeah, me, too, honey."

We had also finally traced the whereabouts of Terrence William McQueen, Steve's elusive father. Steve's new burst of energy in the search for his father surged at about the time of our daughter's birth. Our child would know her father; Steve ached to know something about his.

Interestingly enough, the little information we had took us no farther than the Silverlake area, where Steve had spent a miserable time with Julian and her new husband. Steve left his agent's phone number at every bar and pool hall, imploring anybody to call in case his father or somebody who knew him materialized. Persistence and patience finally paid off. A woman called and after identifying herself as Bill McQueen's lady friend—only she referred to him as Terry McQueen—asked if we could meet with her after dinner? Of course, we said. We drove to an Echo Park apartment building. There we learned that time had run out for Steve's father just about three months before. The woman who had lived with him during his last months before he suffered a fatal heart attack told us that he watched the "Wanted" shows religiously and always wondered out loud whether the image on the TV screen belonged to his son. She was able to answer Steve's questions so fully that there was no doubt in Steve's mind that the man this woman spoke of had indeed been his father. Before we parted, the lady opened her purse and produced a well-used silver lighter with the initials TMcQ. It had belonged to Bill, and she wanted Steve to have it (it is today in our daughter Terry's possession and is the only legacy left to the children from their paternal grandfather). She also gave Steve a picture of the old man with some of his cronies at an earlier time. Sure enough, the man in the photograph was the mirror image of Steve, although she pointed out that Steve's dad was taller than he. (Much to my regret that picture vanished during the time of our divorce.)

Steve's father had been in the Marine Corps and had worked for the Flying Tigers Cargo Company in his later years. It is interesting to note that there is no mention of Bill in any interviews Steve gave until 1959. By that time Steve had created, with his unrestrained imagination, a role for his father that portrayed the old man in a romantic and virile light. Steve had him alternately flying with the navy or the marines, depending on which came to mind first, and finally had him die with General Chennault's raiders in China. There was no harm to this innocent manipulation of the facts, of course, because they gave Steve a more colorful background. But as the years rolled on, the accounts of his father's life became more and more heroic. Writers even began offering psychological interpretations of Steve's life as it related to his father's "flying career."

The series' reviews for the second season had improved. Steve was now being given credit for the success of the show. The unfortunate fallout that resulted from the industry's recognition of Steve's contribution to his series was the license he seemed to feel he now had to bully his producers. He began to demand more and more control of the scripts and had begun to question everything—the casting, the choice of directors—to a point of madness.

The first casualty on the show was the producer-writer. He had written many of the show's scripts and was the nicest and most mild-mannered man. His hobby was wood carving, and he had in fact made me a cradle for Terry. Off the set, he and his wife and Steve and I often went out to dinner together. On the set, however, Steve systematically undermined the man's role as head scriptwriter and line producer. It had the effect of belittling him in front of cast and crew, because Steve never handled these creative differences with finesse. Steve had only one thought in mind and that was to make the shows as good as they possibly could be. He very clearly stated, "I'm not here to win a popularity contest." This was an admirable trait but for the producer-writer the burden was heavy. Toward the end of the second season the man went on sick leave and never returned.

I went back to work as soon as I was able. I had been cast in a "Westinghouse Playhouse" and I was raring to go. And then I found myself in an "Alfred Hitchcock Presents," opposite Steve and Peter Lorre. Immediately after that, husband and wife signed on to go to Alaska with the "Bob Hope Christmas Show." Surprisingly, though, at least to me, I found that the new baby had altered my life irrevocably. The need to work was no longer a driving element in my personality. As much as I loved the interaction with the people on the set, playing house with my husband and baby was a hell of a lot more satisfying. I found myself turning down almost everything that was offered to me until the offers eventually dwindled to nothing.

For Steve though, life was just beginning. After

the first preview of *Never So Few,* Frank Sinatra had slapped Steve on the back and said, "It's all yours, kid!" It was a time for rejoicing! His screen personality was finally finding itself. All that hard work on "Wanted" was paying off. The western series had established a character that was heroic, courageous, and monosyllabic all at the same time, and the role of Bill Ringa launched a screen character who was both off-center and daring. With the passage of time, the two characters would be taken farther and farther along so that all the qualities came together in one person.

We ran out of the screening room hand in hand barely able to contain ourselves. In the parking lot I threw my arms around him and said, "Honey, I think we're gonna make it!"

"Hush, woman," he replied, looking skyward. "Not so loud. They might hear you and put the whammy on me before I even get started!"

"They wouldn't dare! Sinatra's just blessed you!"

We laughed, got in the car and went to Cyrano's, a coffee shop on the Sunset Strip, to celebrate our good fortune.

Sinatra's verdict on the night of that first preview had been accurate. The movie's reviews all spotlighted Steve. The *Hollywood Reporter* said that the film "provides a catapult to stardom for Steve McQueen, hitherto known principally as a television actor." In those days, and for a long time after, it was virtually unheard of for television actors to cross over to films successfully. Now Frank asked Steve to join him and his "Rat Pack" cronies in *Ocean's 11.* Unfortunately, as much as CBS liked to accommodate Steve in other ventures, the timing of the new Sinatra movie made it impossible to grant Steve his wish. CBS was adamant that Steve film twelve segments of "Wanted," back to back, right after our Bob Hope–Alaska jaunt. There were not enough shows in the can in case of any emergency. CBS was all too aware that their star was in demand for other projects and the network wanted to be prepared just in case an offer came in that Steve couldn't refuse.

As it happened, Steve did not go before the movie cameras again until his hiatus period began in March. Once again he would be working with John Sturges. Based on the Japanese classic *The Seven Samurai*, John's film was called *The Magnificent Seven*.

In the meantime, while he waited for filming to begin, Steve was getting impatient with his series—impatient with the small salary in comparison to the big bucks that movies paid; impatient with the slap-dash quality that is part and parcel of producing a weekly television series; and most of all, impatient with the daily grind that prevented him from blocking out chunks of time to devote to car racing. He had just traded in the Porsche speedster for a Lotus Mark 11, a machine designed strictly for racing. For street consumption, he bought us a prototype of the Jaguar XK-SS. (A fabulous-looking car that he paid about $4,000 for, this same car was later sold at auction for a staggering $147,500!) Steve had become so enamored with car racing that as soon as it was feasible he planned to star in a movie with the title *Le Mans,* which was to be produced by our newly formed production company with the impossible name of Scuderia Condor (as in Scuderia Ferrari and Scuderia Maserati, the Italian car stables). The plan was to get Brigitte Bardot to co-star with Steve in this extravaganza. At this time, the Bardot involvement was nothing more than a press agent's dream. She was a huge international star and Steve was still a home boy. But eleven years later, when *Le Mans* at long last went before the cameras, Bardot's star, sad to say, had already peaked while Steve's was still streaking across the skies like a giant meteor.

When he had first committed to the series, Steve had agreed to go for five seasons if there was a call for it. I did not think it right to renege on a contract because he was now in demand elsewhere. It was like biting the hand that fed you. Steve agreed, but for his efforts he did want a heftier raise than Four Star was willing to give him. To get his way, he embarked upon an elaborate scheme whereby we would be involved in a car crash in Hartford, Connecticut (he was there for a personal appearance), and he would then apparently become incapacitated because of a neck injury derived from the crash. This "injury" would prevent him from filming while Four Star and Hilly Elkins were in negotiations over his contract for the following season. "However," Hilly said, "if you go ahead with this crazy plan, the crash has to be real. I can't just make it up. That good an actor, I ain't! Then hopefully they'll realize that your body's ability to heal will depend on your raise. Then you can sit home for as long as you like and I have a clear conscience. Fair?"

"Fair!" He looked at me and said, "O.K. with you, baby?"

"O.K. by me!"—not knowing then that he had every intention of having me in the car with him while he crashed it! The day after his personal appearance in Hartford, we got into our rented Cadillac convertible, went for a drive around the town, then headed toward our hotel.

"Are you ready?" he asked as we approached the hotel.

"As ready as I'll ever be! My belt's buckled on tight. Is yours?"

"Don't worry about me. I'm fine." He leaned over, gave me a kiss, and off we went.

It was only a matter of seconds from the moment he stepped on the gas to going over an island and onto the wall. The hotel doorman was aghast. It was the last thing he had expected to see, right there in front of him! He ran to us to see if we were all right and the pandemonium that ensued was exactly what we had hoped for. The wire services carried the story about the "accident." They reported Steve had inadvertently stepped on the gas while coming to a stop. Luckily, "his wife, Neile, was unhurt although the actor suffered a minor neck injury."

When we got off the plane in Los Angeles Steve was wearing a neck brace. But Dick Powell was no dummy. He knew exactly what was going on. To humor Steve, however, Powell came to our house, even bringing along his wife, June Allyson, to see Steve's "injury" for himself and to commiserate.

Not long after that, the daily *Variety* reported, "After much hemming and hawing over his recent neck accident, Steve McQueen finally signed his Four Star termer."

John Sturges had selected Cuernavaca, Mexico, as the location for *The Magnificent Seven*. God, what a cast he had assembled. Steve, Charlie Bronson, Jim Coburn, and Bob Vaughn—they were all so young and virile and handsome. But this group of up-and-coming young stars was also equipped with a sense of humor that kept the company in good spirits. Yul Brynner, the only established and true star in the cast, and young German actor Horst Buchholz seemed to be odd men out—probably because they were out of their element. The other guys were all very macho, very American, and very playful. They *belonged* in the film's western setting and reveled in that hot and dusty desert.

I commuted to Cuernavaca from Los Angeles every ten days so as not to be away from Terry for very long. She was too little to bring to Mexico. I refused to chance it. Broadway was now far away from my thoughts, although I did episodic television when I could. All it required was a few days of concentrated working time. I was asked to do another "Alfred Hitchcock Presents." I was also asked to test for the

Anita role in the movie version of *West Side Story,*
which I was excited about. That would be shooting
here in Los Angeles, and I could have the best of
both worlds. If I got it.

In Mexico, things were hot between Yul Brynner
and Steve. A feud had erupted between the two and
Steve was leaking details about it to the press, although he wouldn't own up to it. John Sturges tried
to keep a lid on things, although he acknowledged
there were "some clashes. They're dissimilar characters. Yul is like a rock, Steve's volatile. Steve figures
Yul is being a Big Star, and he's not willing for
anyone else to catch flies" (meaning, to draw the
audience's attention by some piece of stage business),
"and Yul thinks Steve is being an undisciplined smart
aleck, always trying to catch a fly. He gets sore because Steve is always fiddling with his hat or something. I have to tell Steve not to busy it up all the
time . . . to just stand there."

Actually the reason behind all that fly-catching was
Steve's frustration at the lack of dialogue. He also
felt his character was not as well defined as Charlie
Bronson's or Jim Coburn's. He was right. It is a
tribute to Steve's tremendous screen presence that
he managed, given the company, to come off as *the*
star to watch.

We were in Cuernavaca for Steve's thirtieth birthday. I decided to surprise him with a party. Since we
were all holed up at the beautiful Hotel Jacaranda
(with the exception of Yul Brynner and Horst
Buchholz, who had rented houses), I rented the dining room and hired twelve Mexican musicians to do
their thing. I made sure there was plenty of food,
drink, and firecrackers. By the time the birthday
cake was rolled in Steve was sufficiently swacked to
invite cabdrivers and anyone else he happened to see
to come join the party.

"Come in, amigos. Join the party!" and he beckoned amiably.

At night's end, with firecrackers exploding all around Cuernavaca, we went cruising around the town. Steve spied a bus-stop sign and decided that it belonged in Bob Relyea's room. Relyea was Sturges' first assistant director and was as fearless a man as I have ever seen. The next day, having traced the sign to Señor Relyea's room, the Mexican police presented themselves and requested that "el señor Bob" please follow them to the police station for questioning. There was much consternation and it took producer Walter Mirisch's considerable clout for the Mexican police to forget the whole matter. It was nothing more than a bunch of good-natured gringos letting off steam, both sides laughingly agreed.

The following day as everybody staggered into the pool area, Bob Vaughn jauntily sauntered in wearing one of his colorful jumpsuits. Bob seemed to have one in every color.

"Come on in, Bob!" hollered Steve. "Water's great!" Actually what Steve was doing was egging him on. Bob didn't like the water and never went in the pool. What we didn't know was the man couldn't swim. As soon as Steve got out of the water he immediately headed for Bob and put his wet arms around him. Bob, obviously irked, said, "Goddamn it, Steve, you're getting me soaked!" Before he knew what hit him, Bob was in the water. In the deep end yet! Just as he went under he garbled, "I can't swim!" Of course nobody believed him. Not in this company. But the more I saw him flail about in the water the more concerned I became. The guys all thought it was a big joke. I finally pulled at Steve and said, "Shit, honey! I think he's in trouble. You'd better do something!" The guys hit the water at the same time and rescued Bob.

Thank goodness Bob Vaughn has a fabulous sense of humor. He laughed off the incident, which made him all the more endearing.

While we were in Mexico, Steve received word that

he had been named Rookie of the Year by the American Sports Car Association. It pleased him so. He used to say that if he hadn't become an actor he'd probably have become a motor racer. When a writer called him on that statement, reminding him that he'd once said that if he hadn't become an actor he'd probably have become a criminal, and asked him, which is it? Criminal or motor racer? Steve replied, "Let me put it this way. Motor racing is an elite, expensive sport. If I hadn't become an actor, I probably would not have been able to afford to go into it, so I would have been denied both outlets of my energy." Which was a terrific answer, I thought. For my part, I never, ever asked him to stop racing. Most of the time I could be seen holding the stopwatch. I simply respected his need too much. As somebody once said, his masculine nature resisted complete conformity.

He had to win. When the horse on the series broke Steve's foot he opted to get on the horse again. Most actors would have insisted on another horse. Not Steve. He figured one of them had to win and it was going to be him, by golly! The things that were difficult whetted his appetite. It was said that was the reason Steve did not become a criminal. I agreed with that perception. No matter how near he had come in his earlier years, it would have been too easy for him to jump the line and head in that direction.

The year was 1960 and Steve's third and final season as Josh Randall was upon us. The day before my test for *West Side Story* I learned that I was once again pregnant! That came as a big shock, since Terry was only nine months old! Gads, give me a break, I said to no one in particular. But Steve was delighted. He wanted a son and he was certain this next one was going to be a boy.

At Four Star, a new producer-writer was at the

helm. His name was Ed Adamson, and it wasn't long before production meetings reached a fevered pitch. Steve was treading on Ed Adamson's toes. Often. But Ed grudgingly conceded that nobody knew more about Josh Randall than Steve—what Randall would do and what he wouldn't do. It didn't mean that he liked Steve any better for his argumentativeness, but he did respect him for standing up for what he thought was right.

Steve did in fact have a quick and inventive mind and he wanted desperately—especially in his later years—to be known as a filmmaker, as Clint Eastwood and Warren Beatty are. But he really didn't have the temperament. He was a wonderful leader as long as there were administrators above him in the hierarchy. He was not able to handle the daily responsibilities or the minute details that the filmmaker must. Also he found it very difficult to delegate authority for any period of time. Eventually even the force of his enthusiasms could not take the sting out of his often abrasive personality. He also had the maddening habit of constantly reversing his decisions, which naturally made it impossible to run a company in a profitable and rational manner.

The full force of that abrasiveness was to be known by Richard Donner, later the director of such films as *Superman, Ladyhawke,* and *Goonies.* Dick was someone we had known briefly in New York. He was then a struggling actor and he and Steve had at times gone riding together. Dick had moved to the West Coast in 1960 and had started directing commercials. He ran into Ed Adamson at the Desilu Studios while he was directing Lucille Ball, Desi Arnaz, Bill Frawley, and Vivian Vance in a series of Westinghouse commercials. Ed watched the action for a while and decided to ask Donner to direct some "Wanted" episodes. He said to Dick, "If you can work with these guys, then you can work with McQueen!"

"Terrific," Dick said apprehensively, "but I think I should talk to Steve first, don't you think, Ed?"

"Hell, no. I'm the producer and you're hired. For twelve shows. What do you think of that?"

Well, it wasn't all that easy. Steve resented Adamson's hiring new directors without his knowledge, and standing on principle, Steve this time very plainly said "no." He said Dick was an actor, and not, for Christ's sake, a director! Dick's attitude was great. He said philosophically, "Well, nothing ventured, nothing gained!"

But Ed Adamson was a stubborn man. He was not going to give up that fast. He asked Donner to stay loose until the matter was definitely resolved. Surprisingly, Steve finally gave in to Adamson's wishes.

Suddenly Dick Donner found himself a director of episodic television. He drew a Friday for his first day on the job. He also drew a location shoot for that first time out, which even seasoned directors find extremely difficult. On top of that, he had a very hostile, very recalcitrant, and very uncooperative star.

Dick set up his first shot and Steve said, "Nope. That's not the way a gunfighter would do it."

"How, then?" Dick asked, nervously trying to please the star. Steve looked his director straight in the eye and said, "You're the director. You figure it out." Then he turned and disappeared into his trailer.

Needless to say Donner's first day on the job was disastrous. A full day's work had been wasted and all Dick could think of was he would never work in the industry again! He was beside himself as he walked toward the crew bus. Ed Adamson intercepted Dick and asked him to ride with him back to the studio. Ed was very supportive and very encouraging to the young director. He kept repeating to Dick that he'd be able to figure out how to handle McQueen. "Look, this is only the first day! I bet you by Monday you'll have him eating out of your hand!"

Dick went home that night and went on a drunken

binge. On Sunday he called Steve and said he wanted to talk. Steve ordered Donner to be at our house at 7:15.

Dick arrived at 7:04 and stayed out on the driveway for a full eleven minutes until it was time to ring the doorbell. I showed Dick into the living room, where Steve was relaxing with some of his buddies and he proceeded to ignore him—deliberately. Finally Dick blurted out, "I gotta talk to you, man. Look, no hard feelings, but I quit. I can't do it." Steve gave him a cold, hard look and said, "Nobody quits my show." Then he got up from the couch and commanded, "Come on. Let's you and me go for a ride in my new Jag." When they returned to the house Dick passed out on the couch. I remember covering him up with a blanket in the middle of the night. The next day Steve and Dick went off to work together and did two days' work in one. The episode came in on schedule and Dick's reputation was preserved.

Things went along famously on the series until Dick's sixth episode. He had mapped out a very tricky and artsy shot which had taken a while to set up. (I think it was the first time this shot had ever been attempted.) It required the camera to travel from feet to legs to hips to waist to chest and finally to face. The crew and Dick were hyped up. It's not often one is able to come up with an artistic touch like this in a western series, so this was exciting for them. Steve had been sitting in his chair, drinking coffee and talking with the crew and getting just a mite antsy as he watched the proceedings. Finally Donner gave the signal and the assistant director called a "Let's go, please!"

Steve very slowly got up from his chair and began to walk in the opposite direction. He turned toward Dick and said he was going to the bathroom. Dick was taken aback. After all, the man had been sitting there for a full half hour or more doing absolutely nothing! Donner controlled himself and carefully chose his words. "Come on, Steve, please. This'll only take us a few minutes! We're all ready!"

"Well, man, I'm not. This dude's goin' to the can."

Dick finally lost his temper and announced, in that big booming voice of his, "Everybody take five while Mr. McQueen takes a pee!"

Mr. McQueen went directly to Mr. Donner after he was done with his business in the bathroom and told him, "You will never work this show again." Then he took his place in front of the cameras and complied with Dick's direction for the shot.

Ed Adamson called Dick Donner that night and apologetically informed him that Four Star was paying him off for the remaining six shows he had been contracted to direct. The parting was amicable, as they say, and Richard Donner went on to bigger and better things.

Eventually, after time had dimmed the memory, Steve and Dick became good friends once again and evermore. But as writer Malachy McCoy observed of Steve's behavior at that time, "Surging ambition, drive and determination, a certain selfishness, a measure of arrogance and vanity—all qualities most of us possess but generally manage to keep under control— suddenly surfaced in Steve's personality. Viewed for themselves, such qualities are never likable, even if they are the instruments that normally make men successful. But nice guys don't win ball games. And Steve, visions of a bright future already opening before him, seemed determined to win the ball game."

In September of 1960, as I happily ate my way through my second pregnancy, Steve went to several cities in the east to help promote *The Magnificent Seven*. This was the very first "A" movie in which his name appeared above the title—directly below Eli Wallach's, whose name in turn was billed directly under that of the real star, Yul Brynner. It was important to get the message across to the public and the press that Steve McQueen was an emerging movie star. Consequently I had insisted Steve hire his own personal press agent at the start of "Wanted— Dead or Alive" instead of relying solely on the series' unit publicist. My instincts told me the publicist would work hard on selling Steve McQueen only as Josh Randall, whereas Steve McQueen had to be sold as a personality and actor who happened to be doing a role in a western series. And I was right. What had to be stressed again and again was his diversity. He was Josh Randall while filming the series, but he was also a different character when in another project.

We had been to the sneak preview of *The Magnificent Seven* and the audience reaction had been terrific. I thought that Jim Coburn and Charlie Bronson, by the nature of their better-written roles, came off better than Steve in the acting department. But undeniably the McQueen presence on the screen was there. As one reviewer put it, "If anybody's looking for a youthful successor to Gary Cooper, McQueen would seem to be the guy." But the *Hollywood Reporter*'s review was more to the point. "Steve McQueen, if he can get sprung from TV, where he is learning nothing and only getting older, is going to be a great big star."

This "getting older" aspect was concerning him. Paul Newman (who had become a friendly rival) and other actor friends had been encouraging him to get out of television before it was too late. I was adamant that he stay with the series until CBS canceled the show. I didn't think it wise to break a contract, especially since the network and Four Star had been so nice and accommodating. It also seemed to me that everybody was ignoring the fact that the reason Steve had walked away with these pictures was because he hadn't had the burden of carrying them. Luckily CBS itself inadvertently put the hex on the series by moving it from Saturday night to Wednesday night.

"Wanted—Dead or Alive" did not survive the time change and the ratings plummeted.

While Steve was relieved to be rid of the series, he was also terribly angry that CBS had killed a good show by moving it into a bad time spot. But he needed now to try and learn new things. He had gotten all he could out of the three seasons he had spent with the series, and it was time to move on to the big screen. On March 29, 1961, Josh Randall rode off into the sunset for the last time.

Before the demise of the show, a series of events added variety to our lives. We bought a bigger house on Solar Drive in Nichols Canyon, and I finally became an American citizen on November 18, 1960. Three days later Steve was in a big row with a neighbor. The neighbor, a man of fifty-eight, in contrast to Steve's thirty, had been complaining bitterly about the XK-SS and the sounds it made on its daily rounds in and out of the canyon. This man was something of an eccentric as well, and he was well-known for calling the police department to complain about anything and everything. Steve and I generally took Terry for walks up the dead-end street with our husky Mike-the-Dog in attendance. The dog was fabulous with the baby and always stayed close to her. (Hated dog Thor had been dognapped a year before. I will be eternally grateful to the woman in the Cadillac who absconded with him.)

On this particular Monday, I hadn't been feeling well. I was "heavy with child" and didn't feel much like walking. Steve decided he and his little sixteen-month-old daughter would nonetheless take their usual stroll. The holiday season was upon us and he was feeling neighborly. With Mike-the-Dog in tow and Terry in his arms, he knocked on the door of the neighbor's house with the intention of saying "Hi, let's be friends." He never got that far. As soon as Mrs. Neighbor opened the door and recognized him she started yelling something about the dog. The old man came rushing out and began screaming and pushing Steve off his property.

"Hey, man, watch my kid!" Steve warned.

"You're a coward! That's why you brought her!" the neighbor cried. "Get off my land, you coward!" and he shoved Steve one more time. Big mistake. Steve put Terry down by Mike-the-Dog and punched our neighbor square on the jaw. The neighbor was so stupefied that he held his jaw and said, "You hit me!"

"Right, motherfucker, and I'm gonna hit you again!" And with that Steve hit him again, then picked up Terry and began walking up the canyon toward our house. But not before he saw Mr. Neighbor get up and, out of his frustration, hit Mrs. Neighbor. It must have been a funny scene. We laughed for days over that. Naturally, there were suits and countersuits and a lot of newspaper coverage. But the judge threw the case out of court and the man behaved himself after that. At least, the police department didn't get calls from him again.

While in New York on the last leg of his promotional tour for *The Magnificent Seven,* Steve and Hilly took an interviewer to Greenwich Village to revisit his old hangouts. That was one of his favorite activities—retracing his old haunts and the places he had lived. (Once he and I went to a neighborhood in Silverlake and located the house he and Julian and his stepfather had lived in long ago. We knocked on the door and a man came out inquiring what it was we wanted. Steve said that he used to live there, to which the man replied "So?" and slammed the door in our faces!) After dinner, Steve called me at our new Solar Drive house. When he came out of the phone booth he was all smiles. "This was fun, a great contrast, looking at my old $19-a-month cold-water flat," he told Hilly and the interviewer, "then talking to Neile in the new house we bought for $65,000. God bless television," he added.

And on December 28, 1960, to add to our happiness, I gave birth to a boy and we named him Chadwick Steven McQueen. I was delighted because I knew I wouldn't be pressured to have another child—at least not anytime soon—since we now had what Steve wanted most. A son.

8

STEVE'S REALLY TIGHT friends over the years were Tom Gilson, Bud Ekins, Jay Sebring, and Elmer Valentine.

His best friend was Tom Gilson, an actor on the rise at the time I met him. He was under contract to Twentieth Century-Fox and he had just finished an Elvis Presley sort of role in *Rally Round the Flag, Boys*, starring Paul Newman, Joanne Woodward, and Joan Collins. Tom's temperament perfectly matched Steve's. He was rugged, rowdy when drunk, spontaneous, and very lovable. To both men life was basically a scam. Both had made the right turn—with one exception. While Steve could control the furies that raged within him, Tom, when under the influence, seemed always to want to show the world that he could go one step beyond. By doing so Tom met an untimely death at the early age of thirty. Steve served as pallbearer at the funeral.

I first became aware of Bud Ekins in 1961 when his name would crop up now and again whenever Steve mentioned that one of his motorcycles was being serviced in a San Fernando Valley shop. Bud was tall, ruggedly handsome, and a skilled motorcycle rider. Steve admired his ability and considered Bud a "man's man." He taught Steve the finer points of bike handling, and in the process, the two became great friends. Steve arranged to bring Ekins aboard

The Great Escape, the movie that proclaimed him a major star, as soon as the director and writer had agreed to using a motorcycle for his escape. Bud joined the Stuntmen's Union, doubled for Steve, and jumped over the wire fence to glory.

Jay Sebring entered our lives during the filming of *Love with the Proper Stranger*. He restyled Steve's hair and gave him a wonderful new look on the screen. Instead of the normal barbershop haircut, Jay used a blow dryer to shape Steve's hair. In fact, I think it was Jay who introduced the blow dryer to the world of men's hairstyling. He remained a close friend until his murder on August 9, 1969, by the Manson gang. Short, wiry, warm, and energetic, Jay was no ordinary barber. He was an astute businessman who was able to parlay a pair of scissors into big business. Sebring International, creators and producers of hair products for men, I feel, would have been as big as Vidal Sassoon had Jay survived. Jay was also the person who introduced cocaine into our household.

Elmer Valentine was the most gentle of Steve's cronies. An ex-cop from Chicago, he had been a bodyguard to, among others, Israeli Prime Minister David Ben-Gurion. Elmer was running a club called P.J.'s in 1963 when Steve and he became close. In 1964 Elmer opened a new club called the Whisky A GO-GO and when he wasn't busy running his club, Elmer could generally be found at our house. He and Steve made an odd couple. He had a calming effect on Steve and watched out for him like a mother hen. But in the fateful year of 1970, the year our marriage began to unravel, pressing business matters at home made Elmer *dare* to leave Steve alone in France on the set of *Le Mans* before my arrival. Steve's anger at Elmer's alleged breach of loyalty never found its right perspective. It took a year before Steve could call him again and the friendship of seven years never regained its proper footing.

I could often be found cooking breakfast for a

group of Steve's buddies. And always, on Thanksgiving, Christmas, and New Year's, the "strays," as we called the unmarried ones, were invited to join us for festive turkey dinners. I learned to live in a world inhabited by men and I enjoyed it. Probably because I was the head honcho's wife, anything I did or didn't do was greeted with approbation. As in *West Side Story,* I was Maria to their Jets and Sharks.

Twelve weeks after Chad was born, we bought our first house in Palm Springs. Tom Gilson visited us most every time we were down there. He and Steve would go to the high desert, pick up peyote from some Indians they knew, and then bring it home. Under Steve's direction I would put the stuff in boiling water, let it simmer for approximately thirty minutes, pour in salt and enough pepper to kill an elephant, and then I would watch as they gulped it down. Although the stuff was vile, the end result of being totally stoned was worth it to them.

It was a source of irritation throughout our marriage, this trying anything and everything new— whether it be peyote or LSD—but I learned to live with it to keep him happy. Having "grass" in the house was by this time a given. We had to be careful because the laws were just as harsh on the users as on the dealers. Steve had several hiding places built especially for his stash. To please him I became adept at drying and separating the seeds from the grass itself. We developed a complex system with the help with regard to their presence in certain parts of the house. For instance, whatever room Steve happened to be in was off-limits unless otherwise indicated. (And when the help were away, the house would become a beehive of activity; that's when we would dry and separate the seeds from grass.) Steve was adamant they not know about his drug use for fear they might sell this juicy bit of information to the press or pass it on to the police. And I was fearful for him. Steve indulged himself only after work and on the weekends. As far as the children were concerned, they grew up with the odor of grass in Steve's den, and we never made a point of differentiating to them the distinction between Mommy's cigarettes and Daddy's cigarettes. It wasn't until Chad was twelve years old that he recognized what Daddy had been smoking all these years. It was prevalent in school and there was no denying it.

When Tom Gilson died, Elmer Valentine became Steve's desert buddy. Many a time between 1963 and 1970 they traveled hundreds of miles together to bring clothing and medicine to the Navaho reservation near the Four Corners, that piece of land where Colorado, Arizona, New Mexico, and Utah meet. Steve delighted in that because it brought reality to his make-believe world. Although he loved being a movie star, he had nonetheless developed tremendous guilts about being paid so much money for doing what he felt was basically "woman's work." This became his way of paying penance. Still another was the pleasure of sleeping under the stars, miles away from the nearest town, miles away from his daily responsibilities, on the bed of his pickup truck.

Once when they came home from a trip, Steve immediately demanded I tell Elmer that he (Steve) did not snore. Apparently an argument had ensued during their last night in the desert when Steve had poked Elmer in the ribs repeatedly while complaining bitterly over Elmer's snoring. When Elmer had had enough he sat up and told Steve, "You do that one more time and I'm gonna punch you right out. You're a good one to complain. You snore louder than anyone I've ever heard!" It then became one of those "I do not"/"you do so" types of arguments, with both men finally agreeing that Neile would settle this. Well, Elmer won. Steve couldn't understand why I had never said anything about his snoring. To which I replied, "No need to, really. I do one of two things. Either jab your ribs or tweak your nose. *Voilà!*

Snoring all gone!" Steve became so incensed over this discovery that Elmer, in the act of placating him, said, "Yeah, not only do you snore, but you aren't different from any of us. You don't shit crushed pineapples like you like to think you do!" Steve, in spite of himself, sometimes balked when he was characterized as merely "one of the guys." So in order to separate himself from his "ordinary" friends in a humorous vein, he had coined a phrase that he quoted often: "We movie stars are different, you know. We shit crushed pineapples!" Soon all three of us, Elmer, Steve, and I, were doubled up in hysterics.

The Navahos had also taught Steve about their land. "Where there is room enough and time enough," they used to say. He dreamed of going back to the farm someday—not the Slater farm, but a place where he could stop running. A place that might afford him the peace that seemed to elude him. For various reasons it took him until 1978 to acquire this land of room enough. It was a beautiful fifteen-acre spread in Santa Paula. Sadly, when he did, there was not time enough to enjoy it.

Steve's next films, *The Honeymoon Machine, Hell Is for Heroes,* and *The War Lover,* served to establish him as a solid film actor as opposed to being just a TV star. Although neither of us particularly liked *The Honeymoon Machine* or the performance he gave in it as a navy lieutenant who uses a missile-tracking computer for gambling purposes—in fact, at the first preview, Steve became so distressed we had to walk out of the theater—his reviews were good ("Steve McQueen displays another facet of an increasingly impressive talent" and "McQueen apparently has a flair for farce, a welcome addition to the few actors who do") and the movie did respectable business. *Hell Is for Heroes* netted him even better personal reviews. As one critic said, "Steve McQueen, a young actor who has yet to give a mediocre performance, is arresting as a single-minded killing machine. His concentration and absorption are almost unique among young actors. His 'method' is his own. In the core of his armor of bloodlust is a flame of gentleness. It is a magnificent characterization."

The public, too, was beginning to see the McQueen personality. Comfortable now with his own form of naturalism, he detested the incessant comparisons with Marlon Brando. When accused by a writer of being another Brando, a method actor, and an exponent of the squint-mumble-scratch-and-think school of acting, he answered, "If you want to say Brando, say Brando. But what's Brando done in the last year and a half? You could call me a young Kirk Douglas or a Gary Cooper, but believe me, this boy's gonna be a star in his own right."

The War Lover made him an honest-to-goodness movie star. Filmed in London, it also gave us the opportunity to mingle with the British upper crust. We lived there from September 1961 to March of the following year. During that period we lived at #1 Chester Square, a town house that belonged to Lord and Lady Russell. For two young people who had been poor most of their lives, this whole trip, with its red-carpet treatment, was a kick!

London was also the home of Stirling Moss and other famous grand prix drivers. Stirling and Steve struck up a friendship, and Moss took him under his wing and taught him all he could about high-speed racing. Stirling was impressed with Steve's ability to listen carefully and learn quickly. Stirling Moss was the only man whose open flirting with me never incurred Steve's wrath, possibly because the legendary racing champion was Steve's only real live hero. In fact, it became a running gag. Stirling, when writing letters to Steve, would usually address his mail to me. And when he did write to Steve directly, there was always a glowing paragraph about me.

The idea of moving away from Hollywood first

came up at this time. We had put a deposit down on fifty acres of land near Carmel with the idea of possibly living there someday, commuting to Hollywood when necessary. Somehow the deal fell through and we never actively pursued property in that area, although we visited Big Sur and Carmel often. The idea was really more of a pipe dream. In truth, Steve would have gone mad in all that solitude. The press has often labeled Steve a "loner." And he perpetuated that because it suited his purpose. The truth is he needed and longed to be with people—his own kind of people. The Hollywood mainstream kept running hot and cold. It had no staying power for either of us.

His interviews in this period were sprinkled with "I'm thirty-one and I'm beginning to find peace" ("finding peace" was a recurring theme in his life). "I don't need any kind of happy-jack publicity. I want to be part of society. When I'm working I'm happy to go home at night, put a chair under me, and just sit. But I like privacy when I'm off." What he really meant was to indulge his growing passion for cars and racing.

As *The War Lover* wound down, Steve bought another car, a Formula Jr. Cooper designed especially for high-speed racing, and had it shipped home. During the course of the transaction, Steve, with Stirling Moss's help, convinced John Cooper of the British Motor Corporation to allow him to compete as a team member in the upcoming Sebring International Races. As soon as we arrived home Steve entered all available forms of racing competition to train for the Sebring. When the big day came, he failed to finish the race, but he had proven himself. This was no hobbyist's holiday. Being a member of the BMC team was tantamount to joining a big league football team in the USA. One simply cannot get on the track on a movie star's reputation. Stirling was proud of his pupil, and together the three of us celebrated Steve's thirty-second birthday, which happened to coincide with the international event.

In May, we were once again on a jet bound for Europe. This time it was Munich, Germany, for a reunion with the *Mag Seven* team of John Sturges, the Mirisch Company, Charlie Bronson, and Jim Coburn. The film was *The Great Escape,* and Steve had first billing over James Garner and Richard Attenborough.

It was the first important film in which he was top-billed, and he relished that. Also he and Jim were both products of television, and that one-upmanship was important to Steve. It irked him at this point that Jim seemed to have become interested in racing. Steve considered that *his* turf. He didn't like other actors butting in! And years later when Paul got into it, he was really irritated.

To house Steve, me, and our children, the company had found us a beautiful chalet in Deining, Bavaria. The forty-minute drive to the Geiselgasteig Studios was good for Steve, for it provided him his "creative thinking time," but not so good for the farmers who used the narrow roads: Steve made up his own rules as it suited him. John Sturges and company spent half their time keeping him out of jail. Every time Steve came on the set the German police would be right behind him. John would quickly reprimand him with, "You cannot drive through a flock of chickens and you cannot drive into the woods and then come back onto the road to pass somebody. You cannot drive faster than makes sense or you will hurt yourself." But when Steve was troubled, driving around was the answer. It helped to calm him.

And troubled he was during the first three weeks of the picture. Stirling Moss had recently been in a serious car accident, and we weren't sure if he would make it. The accident had reached Steve deeply in a way he couldn't explain and had left him depressed and edgy. He found it hard to believe that this great driver was in a coma and fighting for his life (happily, Stirling pulled through).

More immediately disturbing to Steve was his role in the film. Generally Steve was a nervous wreck for the week or two prior to principal photography. I learned to recognize the signs. He'd break out with a fever blister and generally act like a caged animal while he thought about and got a fix on his character. Those were the times when I'd let him "run free." I would make no demands on him nor make any inquiries as to his whereabouts. I gave him a lot of rope and this worked well for us.

But the part of Virgil Hilts was still ambiguous. Hilts had no real personality. He was bland and he was boring. Steve knew that, given this cast, unless he came up with something interesting for this role he would blend in with the scenery. He had absolutely no intention of letting that happen. He did, after all, have top billing and he didn't want to lose face. John Sturges, who was Steve's mentor, was trying to solve the problem. Together with writer Ivan Moffat, they labored until all hours of the night trying to do justice to Steve's presence in the film. Both John and United Artists felt that Steve was indispensable to their movie.

One day, to give the actors a morale boost, John Sturges and film editor Ferris Webster decided to show twenty minutes of hastily assembled footage. They thought it would be a nice thing to do for them. Steve, who had not shot yet, saw Jim Garner's wardrobe and became truly distressed. There was his main competition in the film wearing a white turtleneck, for God's sake! and looking very imposing. And here he was, with no film footage and an undefined wardrobe. Shit!!

As I recall Steve quit the film and rejoined it and was fired and rehired at least twice. I remember Stan Kamen leaving Munich for Hollywood on a Friday and returning by Sunday to negotiate—again! The poor man never even got a chance to go home from the Los Angeles International Airport before he had to turn around.

While all this transpired, Steve was driving around carelessly, getting rid of his nervous energy. He demolished two cars but came up with an idea he presented to John: What if Virgil Hilts used a motorcycle for his escape? *Now* they were cooking!

For good luck Steve wanted to wear the same sort of cutoff sweat shirt I had accidentally fashioned for him in *Never So Few*, only this would be a well-worn navy blue one. If anybody were to ask me what single moment in Steve's films could be pointed to as the jump-off point for his phenomenal career, my answer would have to be Steve's (in the person of friend and stuntman Bud Ekins) jump over that fence in *The Great Escape*.

Another piece of business that evolved spontaneously was Virgil Hilts' use of a baseball and mitt. Steve and John disappeared into that little prison cell used in the movie, and two hours later John emerged and asked "Beady-Eyes," the prop man, to get Steve the new props.

"Now let's roll!" boomed Sturges.

John was extremely patient with Steve as he struggled to find a way to make Hilts memorable. As Jim Coburn has said, "The thing was to get the film right. Steve obviously wasn't wrong because the film was a huge success. He had a special sense. He knew what was right for him and saw to it that everything was in that slot."

John Sturges taught him about reining in. Steve tended to overplay things, especially in comedic scenes, and John, ever the consummate director, would take him aside and quietly suggest to him, "Look, Steve, this is a minor thing but if you stay at this level throughout the film you will drive everybody out of the theater."

Another thing John had to work on with Steve was

his dislike of words. Here was an actor who was more comfortable with playing emotions than using words, and John handled him very carefully and told him that "you simply cannot stand there and just make faces. You have to speak or they won't know who you are and what you're thinking." While Steve always responded to John's direction, he remained forever partial to reacting.

By the end of October, with the exception of a month's break, we had spent a year in Europe for location filming. I had come to recognize that my career, for all its auspicious beginnings, was now in mothballs. Broadway was a dream of yore. There was no request from Steve to quit working. Rather, it was like the rounding off of a chapter. I had made an unconscious decision for love of children and husband. I did not want to split up the family unit. So wherever Steve went, we went. As far as Terry and Chad were concerned, home was where Mommy and Daddy were.

In February 1963 we bought a spectacular stone house on Oakmont Drive in Brentwood which we nicknamed "The Castle." The house stood on three acres and, despite its deceptively massive appearance and eighteen rooms, the house had been designed without children in mind. In fact, one had to go through Terry's room to reach Chad's, and if we'd had another child we would have had to add on. But we loved it and made it work for us. Terry's dream, as soon as she was old enough, was to have her father walk her down the curved stairway and give her away in marriage. Alas, this was not to be.

Overlooking the great crescent of the Pacific shore and the unending asphalt plain that is the city of Los Angeles, the house was sheltered by tall pines and citrus trees and adobe walls. It had massive remote-control arched oak gates that swung (sometimes noiselessly and sometimes not) from a thick abutment.

Then one went up a seemingly endless driveway to a huge courtyard which (as soon as we took possession) immediately became the parking arena of mud-caked motorcycles, since the three garages were taken over by automobiles and gym equipment. For the first time in his life Steve felt he was able to afford and house the proper barbells and assorted gear for his daily workouts. The New York bus-stop sign, which had served him so well but also reminded him of hard times, was unceremoniously dumped as soon as the new equipment arrived (a move he regretted many years later when he began collecting American memorabilia).

Steve was a fanatic about his workouts. When he missed one it was always for a good reason. Every movie contract stipulated that gym equipment be installed in his temporary quarters during location filming of over two weeks. (The only exception to this was the Hong Kong *Sand Pebbles* location, when we took up residence at the Peninsula Hotel.) Steve's assessment of himself for public consumption ("I sure don't get goose pimples when I look in the mirror") was definitely different from his assessment of himself in the privacy of our home. He was vain and he spent time in front of that mirror. I'd tease him about it, and we'd wind up having a contest on who was the best. His body was his religion. He worked out for two hours daily and made sure he was in top physical shape to make the action scenes believable.

The children were now two and three years old (their actual age difference is eighteen months) and busily and happily explored the new wonders of the world around them. We romped about that estate as joyfully as our little kids, with Mike-the-Dog and Kitty Kat, a new acquisition, right beside us. Ever the animal lover, Steve insisted that all forms of animal life (birds, bees, spiders) on the grounds were protected.

Just before we bought the new house, a silly misunderstanding in London had cost Hilly Elkins his position as Steve's manager. The break had been irreparable, and Stan Kamen subsequently assumed the guiding reins of Steve's career with William Morris Agency head Abe Lastfogel's helping hand and with me hovering in the background. Abe Lastfogel had just begun to realize the immensity of Steve's potential and was now taking a very active interest in the goings-on of his new star's career. A pattern had established itself early on. Stan would screen the masses of material being offered Steve and give him his recommendations, then send the most promising scripts over for me to read. The ones I thought best for Steve were then read and evaluated by him. It turned out to be a very good and efficient system since Steve didn't particularly care for reading—with the exception of car and motorcycle magazines. (He never knew what was going on in the world around him, but he certainly enjoyed life.)

There were only two films that we disagreed on. *Dirty Harry* was one of them. It had come on the heels of *Bullitt,* and he had no desire to make another cop movie. The other was *Two for the Road.* He found the script disjointed, but I admired Stanley Donen's talents and I begged him to do it. Also Audrey Hepburn was playing the female lead, and Steve had missed working with her in *Breakfast at Tiffany's* when he could not get sprung from the western series. But he disliked the script simply because he couldn't follow the sophisticated chronology.

The year 1963 was an exhausting one. He did *Love with the Proper Stranger* with Natalie Wood, *Soldier in the Rain* with Jackie Gleason, and *Baby, the Rain Must Fall* with Lee Remick. The name of Scuderia Condor was scratched—thank goodness—as the name of Steve's production company, and Solar Productions took its place. (We had toyed with the name Cherry Productions, which was a derivative of both children's

names, but had decided at the last moment to take
the name of the street where we had all come together.)
Having his own production company gave Steve
greater creative control and greater artistic leverage.
The name Solar Productions first appeared in *Soldier
in the Rain* and gave him a sense of tremendous
accomplishment. It made him a bona fide businessman.

When Steve and Natalie Wood starred together in
Love with the Proper Stranger, Natalie developed a
crush on Steve, perhaps because she and Warren
Beatty were already on very shaky grounds. Warren
was extraordinarily handsome and rather shy. Maybe
it was a pose to disarm unsuspecting females. I can't
presume. But I liked him. He had a way of talking to
a woman that made her feel desirable, as if she were
the only female around. His concentration is intense,
if brief, and it's a tough combination to ward off.

Natalie tried every which way to ensnare Steve
short of using a butterfly net, including resorting to
adolescent tricks like sticking her leg out of her trailer
steps, pretending she was talking to someone inside
just as Steve would pass by. It gave her an opportunity to "chat." Ugh. Steve was amused by the methods she employed and actually looked forward to the
next day's shoot to see what her next move would be.
But he resisted her advances for two reasons (at least
during this period; after he and I split up he succumbed to Natalie's charms, but that was years later).
She had been married to a man he was fond of, Bob
Wagner, and she was at present living with another
man he liked, Warren Beatty. I doubt the fact that
Steve was married to me even entered his mind.
Marriage had nothing to do with it. I was his old
lady and that was that.

I not only heard about Natalie's exploits from Steve,
but also from other persons I knew who were working on the picture. I found these stories annoying as
hell! Had Natalie Wood known me better, she might

have thought twice before going after my husband in such a blatant way. I do have this streak in me which requires me to settle a score given the opportunity. The chance came in Paris a little over a year later.

In September 1964 France's leading television magazine, *Tele 7 Jours,* honored Steve with its "Most Popular Television Actor" award. Steve was a big star in France. Most of the young people in Paris were wearing jeans in "le style Steve Mac-Queen" patterned after the Levi's he wore in "Wanted—Dead or Alive." A French company, in partnership with our Solar company, manufactured and distributed them. A department store in Paris had created a Steve McQueen Ranch on one of its floors to promote the sales of the western clothes. There was an unprecedented two-week-long celebration, which began with the magazine's award presentation at a huge luncheon and which culminated with the premiere of *Love with a Proper Stranger* on September 26, with the two stars in attendance. With Rupert Allan (one of the partners in the firm employed by Steve as his press representatives) expertly handling and monitoring the events, all the interviews and appearances with the press and public served to enhance Steve's disarming personality. Rupert's suggestion that Steve auction off his sawed-off shotgun from the series for a French children's charity was a clear demonstration of how valuable a really good press agent can be. The gesture was, not surprisingly, received enthusiastically by the French and made Steve an even bigger hero.

Natalie apparently arrived at our hotel the day before the premiere. Alone. Gone was Warren Beatty.

We had already enjoyed several days of celebration in Paris and we were riding high. Natalie called a few hours before we were to leave for the theater. She asked Steve if she could ride along with us. Steve didn't commit to an answer as he wanted to discuss it with me. I felt fate had dropped opportunity in my lap and I seized it. Sweetly, I reminded him that at the moment he was the most popular person in Paris. Neither press nor public could get enough of him and they watched his every move. "Naturally your co-star would want to come with us. Otherwise she would miss out on all that publicity," I said. "But it's up to you, honey. Let's do whatever you want. It makes no never-mind to me."

He thought a minute and then said, "Yep, you're right. I'll tell her we're going someplace beforehand and we'll meet her there."

Natalie was smart enough to detect what was going on and directed her driver to alert her the moment we appeared in the lobby. As I glanced back, I saw Natalie hurriedly get into her limousine. I nudged Steve. As soon as he saw what was happening he yelled to our driver, "*Vite,* let's go!" A wild chase scene ensued, but we managed to arrive at the theater a good three or four minutes ahead of Natalie. Those minutes were crucial. The press descended on us as soon as our car appeared and were making a great fuss over us while Natalie Wood's arrival went unnoticed.

Natalie was annoyed over the incident, as well she should have been, and complained to Stan Kamen. Being the gentleman that he is, Stan passed this information on to me so I could bring it up to Steve so he could make amends to Natalie. Over my dead body, I thought. I now felt vindicated and I could go on as if nothing had ever happened. Why rock the boat?

The year before in Wharton, Texas, in the fall of 1963, Steve and Lee Remick had been on location for *Baby, the Rain Must Fall.* Possibly feeling isolated from family and friends, Steve said he wound up in bed with Lee Remick. There was no reason for me to find out except for his compulsion to tell me. Not to hurt me—just to make it all right. For him. But I knew then that as long as I was around Lee Remick would never do another movie with Steve McQueen. In 1978, a few years after our divorce, when Steve was looking for somebody to play opposite him in *Tom Horn,* the name of Lee Remick briefly crossed his lips and I could easily have put in a good word. Instead I kept my silence. Possibly Lee would have passed on it anyway. But I felt a debt had been repaid.

9

IF THE EARLY SIXTIES had been a giant leap for us, both personally and professionally, then the middle sixties was a quantum vault.

Much has been written about Steve's being the reluctant movie star. The truth is that he *adored* being a movie star. This man was no recluse. At least not while he and I were married. He enjoyed the recognition, he found pleasure in the power he wielded ("Snap your fingers and your wish is granted") and the unconditional admiration given him by women. His momentary lapses notwithstanding, I wasn't at all disturbed over Steve's popularity with women. I wasn't surprised. I felt as totally secure in our marriage as he did. I was, after all, married to a man who genuinely relished having a wife and children. In one very revealing interview he said, "A man needs love or else he becomes a man with half a dream. Because when he gets it, then there's no one to bring it home to or laugh with at the whole fuckin' mess."

There was no denying, though, that his stormy nature sometimes made being married to him trying. But I was spunky, and my natural independence served both of us. As he once said, "It's this sort of thing—a woman can go along with a man because it's the simplest thing to do to avoid a row, or she can go along with him because she loves him. She loves me and that's why she goes along. But if she thinks something is wrong for me she'll give me a beef on it and I listen." It also fell on me to warn Stan Kamen and others who worked closely with Steve when he was feeling out of sorts or when he was in a good mood. It was no secret that Steve could be abusive and abrasive when he wanted to be. I would make light of those times by saying the full moon was out and "we all know how that affects Steve!"

We took 1964 off from moviemaking. Instead, we devoted ourselves exclusively to traveling, racing, furnishing our house, and other worldly pleasures. Since the middle of 1958, Steve had worked almost without a break, building a career that promised to reach the payoff. Now, as we awaited the release dates of *The Great Escape, Love with the Proper Stranger, Soldier in the Rain*, and *Baby, the Rain Must Fall*, he felt deservedly entitled to his own space.

Sure enough, as his movies started unfurling in theaters across the country, there was no doubt that the breakthrough had come. *Newsweek* had put it succinctly: "Steve McQueen's splendid amalgam of blinks, furrowed brows, smirks, quick smiles, pursed lips, shyness, catlike grace and occasional clumsiness is one more explosion of the four-part firecracker of his career for the year." Steve was suddenly in vogue. Together we were photographed for the covers of *Life* and *Look* and fashion photographer Richard Avedon shot Steve for the cover of *Harper's Bazaar*, the first time that magazine ever featured a male on its cover. Inside, Steve was photographed cavorting with Jean Shrimpton, then the world's most famous female model.

It was a heady feeling, this view from the top. Sometimes we'd be filled with the wonder of it all. *Wow*, we're here! We—are—actually—here! One of the things that made Steve so endearing to me was his enthusiasm for anything that I would buy for him. It didn't matter what it was. He would rhapsodize over a wrench as much as he would rave over an expensive script holder. And he eagerly gave me presents acquired in an unconventional fashion: jewelry bought from a man at a street corner; our pet Mike-the-Dog, whom Steve bought from a man peddling little pups in front of Schwab's Drugstore; and flowers bought at freeway entrances. We enjoyed indulging one another although once we had achieved a certain material level, it never occurred to me that one day the good Lord might take it all away. Steve, on the other hand, was always mindful of that possibility.

In April, with his wrist bandaged from a break recently suffered in a motorcycle accident, Steve appeared in his first Academy Awards show. At the Governors' Ball following the proceedings, Hedda Hopper remarked how handsome Steve looked in his tie and tails (which he was wearing for the first time). His reply was a heartfelt, "I was so proud to be on the show tonight. For the first time I felt I was a part of this great industry."

We gave our first big "Hollywood Party" at the Castle during a full moon in August of 1964. We invited everyone we knew—bikers and movie industry people alike. Through Elmer Valentine's Whisky A GO-GO, we had arranged for Johnny Rivers and his group to provide the music (John himself was just on the crest of rock stardom). Also, through Elmer, we had a girl named Joanie, who was billed as the first Go-Go girl at the Whisky, to come give lessons to anyone who desired to learn the Watusi. Among our guests were Lois and Jim Garner (they had bought an acre lot below us and had just broken ground), the Norman Jewisons, Tuesday Weld, Jim Coburn, George Hamilton, the Kirk Douglases, and Sharon Tate (still lovey-dovey with Jay Sebring). Carroll Baker was there, too, with her husband, Jack Garfein. So were Janet Leigh and Bob Brandt, George and Jolene Schlatter; Ben Gazzara and Janice Rule were there and so were Gena Rowlands and John Cassavetes. Eva Marie Saint was with her husband, director Jeff Hayden; there were Cloris Leachman and her other half, George Englund, and many, many others.

For some reason, I can vividly remember Natalie Wood's shoes although I cannot remember whom she came with. Probably her sister Lana. Natalie had clear plastic wedgy "spring-a-lators" with what looked like live guppies in her heels. I recall thinking, Well, what the hell. She was never one of our snappy dressers anyway.

Toward the end of the party, when I was ready to drop from exhaustion from dancing, I put my arms around Steve and leaned against him. As a joke, he lifted me up and ran me up the stairs into the bedroom à la Rhett Butler while everybody applauded. We came back down just moments later, of course, since we were, after all, hosting this soirée!

This party was the first true indication of our acceptance in the movie colony. There they all were. At our party. In our house. Steve and I marveled over that one for days.

Steve's career was now the dominant factor in our relationship. That was no problem for me. Since, for all intents and purposes, mine was over, I decided to help him in any way I could. I wanted my very own movie star! I had helped him overcome through those insecure early days of his acting career, and now I was determined to let nothing impair this happy marriage. And as far as he was concerned, he once told a reporter, "A woman should be busy making and keeping a home for the man she loves. At night she should be sleeping with him!" I faithfully adhered to his philosophy.

Racing continued to be one of the most important things in his life. I asked him only to be careful. Nothing more, nothing less. People interested in Steve's career tried to stop him and they never could.

One such time had been Steve's participation in the International Six-Day Motorcycle Trials in East Germany, which were scheduled just before the French premiere of *Proper Stranger*. He and Bud and Dave Ekins, Cliff Coleman, and John Steen had all been invited to represent the United States. Quite naturally Steve was thrilled. His first reaction to the invitation was "Man, I do like to live. Life is good and I mean to take a big slice!" Naturally, Steve's agents didn't want him to chance injury. And just as naturally, Steve prevailed.

The plan was for me to meet him afterwards in Paris for the festivities. In those days East Germany was a risky place to be, and Steve was concerned for my safety and comfort. So was I. Paris was plenty good enough for me. When I arrived in the City of Light, I learned that the U.S. team had performed magnificently. Cliff Coleman and Dave Ekins won gold medals and John Steen a silver one. Steve and Bud were on their way to the gold when both crashed on the third day. Bud broke his ankle and Steve, in an effort to avoid hitting a man crossing the race course, went over the handlebars. When I saw Steve, his face was a series of cuts and bruises, just as his business people had predicted. Yet somehow, rather than detract from his face, it added a new dimension to it. He was a fast healer and by the week's end there was hardly a trace of the injuries.

Steve and I enjoyed Paris enormously although we found it impossible to walk around the city without attracting the attention of hordes of autograph hounds.

One day he decided to outfox his fans. He asked Elmer Valentine, who was with us, to buy him a mustache and a Buster Brown cap. Not only did Elmer accommodate him, he found Steve a makeup man who applied the mustache as well as a little bit of makeup here and a little bit there and a goatee, so that by the time Steve walked out of our hotel he barely resembled the Steve McQueen everyone knew and loved. Elmer and he walked toward the Champs Elysées, sat at an outdoor café, and watched the world go by. No one paid him any attention. While he appreciated his anonymity for a short while, he became agitated when he felt the game had gone on for too long. "Hey, man, I'm a movie star. Fuck this shit. I don't like it." He couldn't wait to get back to the hotel, where he washed his face, grabbed me, took me to the Left Bank to shop, and let his public gaze at the adored movie star!

Actually, he was so unpredictable that he was predictable—at least to me. He would tell me he'd give anything not to be recognized in public, but the minute he wasn't, he'd go to great lengths to identify himself. Once for a Halloween party he decided to go as Bat Masterson. He wanted to be creative, so we colored his hair black, which made him unrecognizable, and when we walked into the party, the photographers snapped pictures only of me, which immediately put him on the defensive. "Hey, you guys, it's old Josh here! I don't let my old lady go to parties alone, you know!" And once in London, when he couldn't sleep after our long flight from Los Angeles, he decided to take a walk around Piccadilly Circus. I was too exhausted to tag along. Off he went wearing his yellow glasses and his cap to avoid detection. I had warned him before he left that the English were too cool to carry on over a movie star. He had said, "I don't wanna chance it." Surprise. Nobody paid him any attention, which stunned him. He did have a sense of humor about it all. He woke me up and laughingly told me that as panic set in, he removed his cap and then his glasses. Finally, when one person recognized him and asked for his autograph, he was so relieved and grateful he dashed back to the Dorchester totally spent and ready to sleep.

The Paris hoopla finally ended. Ekins and the

other teammates went home, Rupert was off to Monaco, Stan (who had also flown in for the premiere) to London, and we were off to Mallorca—"we" meaning Steve, myself, Elmer and Tom Donovan, and Sandy Kevin, two other buddies who had come along. Steve had been able to commandeer a French sports car plus a Volkswagen van for our trip. We left Paris just as the sun went down; we journeyed through southern France and over the Pyrenees on our way to Barcelona, where we were to catch the ferry for Mallorca. Tom, Sandy, and Elmer were in the van, and Steve and I were in the little sports car. Every hour we'd stop and trade places. At one point, while I was in the van with Tom and Sandy, and Elmer was in the sports car with Steve, we became separated. Two hours later, when we still hadn't connected, Steve turned to Elmer irritatedly and yelled, "Goddamn it, Elmer! I should be with my old lady right now. Instead I've got you!" As if Elmer had anything to do with our present predicament. We finally found each other at about four in the morning, when we were all dead tired but had no place to park our weary bodies. As luck would have it, the little godforsaken town we had accidentally discovered had a whorehouse. When Meestair Mac-Queen hopped out of the sports car, he was spotted by a prostitute watching us from her window. She was quickly joined by a few other ladies of the night, all of them chirping, "Meestair Mac-Queen! Meestair Mac-Queen!"

God bless those ladies. They took us in and turned over their bedrooms to us. In the morning, before we went our merry way, they fed us and then refused money for the use of their rooms. They were charming, every one of them.

After a year's sabbatical, Steve was back in front of the cameras, directed this time by Norman Jewison. Jewison was a fairly young director, extremely enthusiastic and very determined to give *The Cincinnati Kid* a look that was all its own. He and Steve made a good combination. Steve's role was that of a card-player who overshoots his luck. In the cast with him were veterans Edward G. Robinson, Karl Malden, and Joan Blondell. The female leads in the picture were Tuesday Weld and Ann-Margret.

After so much time away from acting, he found the first days of filming rather unnerving. He felt like an amateur in front of the cameras. He had sleepless nights and days of disorientation. We spent hours going over his lines. But with Norman's sure and steady guidance, it didn't take long for him once again to feel secure.

For the first time, Steve now had an honest-to-goodness office. MGM also assigned him a secretary, Betsy Cox, who was to remain with him faithfully until 1973. He came home one day fuming over Tuesday Weld's remark, "YOU!?! You mean *you've* got an office and a secretary?" She had apparently shrieked in disbelief, had laughed, then had left him standing there on the steps of the Thalberg Building, where his office was located. It had confused him momentarily and was one of the few times in his life he had been left speechless. He was furious at Tuesday, whom he otherwise liked. I told him, "Don't worry about it. You're making more money than she is and the bottom line is you do have an office and you do have a secretary and she doesn't." He saw the logic in what I said and decided to forgive her— which was rare, because, like me, he was not one to forget grudges. (Actually Steve and Tuesday had a special kinship. She was at that time still married to Dudley Moore, although their relationship was strained. I always said that Tuesday was Steve McQueen as a girl and Steve was Tuesday Weld as a boy. They had the same temperament and might have been twins in some other time.)

Under contract to producer Marty Ransohoff's

Filmways Productions was a remarkable-looking girl named Sharon Tate. Sharon and Jay Sebring met at Elmer's house one day and became a steady duo before Roman Polanski took her away. Sharon and Jay were frequent visitors to our house. I found Sharon to be nice and totally guileless. She seemed willing to do anything Jay asked her to. I don't think Marty Ransohoff approved of their relationship or of Jay's influence on Sharon, whom Marty seemed to be grooming into a Marilyn Monroe–like star. But I doubt he ever said anything to her.

The one and only time I tried LSD took place at our house one night with Jay and Sharon, and of course Steve. It was a Friday night and Steve had the weekend off. LSD was then the drug of the moment. Everyone seemed to be doing it and Steve was anxious for me to share this experience with him. The peyote days were over and this new sophisticated capsule had replaced it as his preferred form for altering his mind. I was apprehensive, unapproving, and very uptight about the whole idea. Drugs were not my cup of tea. Steve, however, was insistent, claiming that there was nothing to worry about. The four of us would be together and we'd have a wonderful time. "The nanny is in there with the children," he reasoned, "so there's nothing to worry about." To pacify me he said he'd only give me half a tab. "O.K., baby?" O.K.

It didn't take long for me to see an army of snails crawling through the gardens and up the walls of the house. I was aghast! I remember telling myself to tell the gardener that his work was growing careless. How dare he let those goddamn snails crawl all over the grounds! I don't care what Steve says about life being preserved on these grounds! I was obsessed about talking to the gardener. I don't remember sleeping that night. I waited until he came to work and told him to remove those snails as soon as possible. "I don't care what it costs!" After the gardener's gentle explanation that there were no snails, I realized that the drug had done its job on me. In fact, I don't even recall what happened to Steve and the other two. I didn't remember seeing them at all—only the snails! That experience was enough to validate my belief that drugs were no good.

Now if only I can get that across to Steve, I thought.

Steve emerged from his sabbatical year more eager than ever to do *Le Mans*, which had been retitled *Day of the Champion*. He was to star, John Sturges was to produce and direct, and Academy Award–winner Edward Anhalt was to write the screenplay for Warner Brothers. His dream movie had become a race against time since director John Frankenheimer was also planning to make a racing feature, *Grand Prix*. Steve had actually been asked to star in this one but hadn't felt good vibrations from either Frankenheimer or his producer, Ed Lewis, and had declined the offer. The big problem was how Steve was going to fit *Day of the Champion* into his 1965 schedule. He already had a July 1 starting date for *Nevada Smith* and a possible November start date for *The Sand Pebbles*. Lewis and Frankenheimer had nothing on their slates other than *Grand Prix*.

John Sturges thought he would expedite the schedule by beginning preproduction photography at road racing events, commencing at the Nürburgring in Germany while the script was being written and Steve was busy on his other movies. He guessed that Steve would be ready and principal photography could begin by May of 1966. To film the movie in two phases was chancy but not impossible. Stirling Moss and Sir John Whitmore had been retained respectively as production consultant and technical adviser, and they would prove invaluable to Sturges. The public was told that because motor racing was the crux of the film they knew only in broad terms what the screenplay would be about. Rather the film's atmosphere and racing scenes had to be accurate.

Consequently they could not hurry the shooting: too many cinemagoers were motor racing addicts for them to be fooled. The party line covered up the fact that the film was already sailing through muddy waters. The course had been charted and a collision was up ahead.

During that busy year Steve turned thirty-five and replaced Marlon Brando as the most popular star in Europe. He was also Japan's number one star and was one of the top five box-office attractions world-wide. Even the Soviet Union was mad about him. Two years earlier, he had become the first American to be awarded a prize in the Moscow International Film Festival for his performance in *The Great Escape*. He had been unable to attend the festival to pick up his Best Actor award; this year however he had again been invited to attend and to show *The Cincinnati Kid*. Although he had accepted, it became an impossible dream. The festival's date coincided with an earlier-than-expected start date for *Nevada Smith*. I couldn't have been more thrilled. I had no desire to go to Russia.

Steve did find time, however, for us to attend the Monaco Grand Prix that May. Princess Grace and Prince Rainier invited us to attend a dinner party at the palace. There were lots of royalty present, dozens of people wearing medals, a small orchestra, and uniformed guards with guns at the doors. Grace and I had been nodding acquaintances in New York. She had been beautiful in those days, and was beautiful still. If I had to trade places with anyone I would have traded places with Grace Kelly. Prince Rainier was a charming host, witty and gracious. He has a warmth about him that normally doesn't show in photos. With the exception of Freddy Heineken (of Heineken beer) and Rupert Allan, we were probably the only untitled guests there, although Freddy Heineken could have bought and sold most of them.

He must have been somewhere in his forties. I found him rather attractive—personable, seemingly in command of any situation, and very confident. At the party, he asked me to dance while Steve and Prince Bernhard of Holland were discussing cars. As Steve became engaged in conversation with other people around the room, Freddy kept me dancing. He seemed quite taken with me. Once in the course of the evening, as Steve and I twirled around the dance floor, Freddy Heineken tapped Steve on the shoulder and asked if he could again dance with me. Steve, annoyed at being interrupted, amiably said, "You can, pal. But she's very expensive!"

"That's all right," Freddy countered. "I am very rich!"

Steve, never very successful at controlling his temper, challenged Heineken to either a duel or a meeting outside. In a flash, Rupert was at our side and was able humorously to disperse the crowd that had suddenly gathered around us. Gads! The last thing I wanted was an altercation at the palace in front of Princess Grace and Prince Rainier. To make peace Steve threw a line at Freddy that was at once charming and conciliatory: "Listen, man, if I had your looks—I'd throw my money away." Knowing full well, of course, that he was better looking.

Nevada Smith turned out to be one of the most satisfying work experiences Steve would have. He and director Henry Hathaway took a deep and immediate liking to each other. Hathaway, the veteran western director, called Steve "son" and went to special pains to make this film the best thing Steve had done to date. For Steve, in turn, this crusty, lovable old man with the twinkling eyes and ruddy cheeks was the father he never had. It was not uncommon to find Steve on the set a full half hour before Henry, just sitting there in his chair and teasingly greeting him with a "Where've you been, sir?" Reporting to the set early was his way of showing the old man his respect.

The company moved about California for a great deal of their location shooting. Convict Lake, Mount Wilson, Mammoth. When the company was in Lone Pine I drove five hundred miles to the location to celebrate my thirty-first birthday with my husband. I wound up cooking dinner for Henry, Karl Malden, Arthur Kennedy, Marty Landau, and Elisha Cook, Jr., which was O.K. since we were out somewhere in the boondocks. I knew there would be no complaints about my lousy cooking; they were a captive audience. That night at the table, Steve had bragged about the seaweed pills and organic vegetables that we bought in a health food store. "Everybody in my household is strong because we eat real healthy. You can hardly hear the old ticker. If your heart's goin' fast, you're in trouble. Now watch me die of a coronary."

Suzie Pleshette, who was one of the two female leads, drew the swamps outside of Baton Rouge for her location scenes in this movie! It was a bummer for her. The first time I came to visit the set I looked so clean and pristine in my white pants and top that Suzie burst into tears as soon as she saw me. She didn't look too glamorous with the muddy, dirty, swampy outfit she had on. I felt bad for her but I laughingly yelled nonetheless, "Tough shit, Suzie!"

Because Steve was now a Big Movie Star he was able to refine a game he had been playing for a while. He continually went around without money in his pockets—secure in the knowledge that someone would surely bail him out if any problem arose. Cast and crew were generally willing to lend him money for cigarettes, lunches, gas, etc. Except that, naturally, they did expect to be reimbursed, which they never were—unless they balked. Soon they all became wise to Steve's scam. This little idiosyncrasy had ceased to seem charming, and Steve had to charge and send his bills to our accounting office.

It was also Steve's habit, at restaurants, to order double orders of everything. Double orders of mashed potatoes, double orders of yams and steaks. More often than not the food went to waste. One night during dinner, Suzie asked him why he didn't just order as normal people did, and then if he found himself still hungry, order another portion? His answer was a very revealing, "What if they run out?"

The hurricane that hit Louisiana in that late summer of 1965 brought *Nevada Smith* to a screeching halt. The rains had made it impossible to film for weeks, which in turn delayed our arrival home. The children were impatient for our return since we had promised them a few days in Palm Springs before we were due back in New Orleans for the premiere of *The Cincinnati Kid* on October 15. The premiere was to benefit the hurricane victims, and we had immediately accepted. Hurricane Betsy had messed up our plans with our kiddies, so we decided to go home anyway to spend at least a full day with them. I hadn't seen them in ten days and Steve hadn't seen them in a month and we missed them terribly.

On the second day home we received a phone call. Steve's mother, Julian, had suffered a cerebral hemorrhage and was at Mt. Zion Hospital in San Francisco. The fact that she had had the presence of mind to get into a cab and get herself to the hospital in spite of that blinding headache was a tribute to her indomitable spirit.

Julian had moved to San Francisco the year before in an effort to get closer to her son and his family. Steve, still unable to reconcile himself fully to her, had left it up to me to establish some sort of relationship with her and the children. I wrote and sent her the latest pictures of Terry and Chad and called her with the latest news in her son's professional life. I took the children to San Francisco to visit, and in fact, the only pictures we have of Julian are the pictures I took of her and her grandchildren at the zoo. She had settled in the North Beach area of the city because it reminded her of the Village. Her four-room apartment was furnished in "early flower child," and she tooled about in a Volkswagen bug that Steve had purchased for her. He had deliberately bought her a secondhand car instead of a new one "so she wouldn't get spoiled!" The years had been good to Julian. She was well liked and had numerous friends. She discovered she liked to sew as a creative outlet, and Terry and I found ourselves the recipients of many wonderful dresses. In fact, Steve and I found a dress on the sewing machine that Julian must have been sewing for Terry on the day she was stricken.

By the time we reached Mt. Zion Hospital Julian had lapsed into a coma. All we could do was stare at her supine figure and look at each other and hold hands. The doctors were not hopeful and on Friday, October 15, 1965, less than twenty-four hours after being admitted to the hospital, Julian Crawford McQueen Berri was pronounced dead.

It was the first time I had ever seen Steve unable to cope. It was left to me to handle the funeral arrangements. Julian's death produced heart-wrenching sobs and left him guilt-stricken and bereft. He had hoped she would recover if only to ask for her forgiveness for the unhappiness he had caused her. He was not able to unburden himself to her and he carried the pain around for a very long time.

On Sunday, November 7, 1965, Sharman Douglas, the daughter of our ambassador to England and a member of Princess Margaret's social set, threw a black tie party at the Bistro in Beverly Hills to welcome the princess and her husband, Lord Snowdon, to the small kingdom of Hollywood. Everyone was there, from Richard Burton and Elizabeth Taylor, to

Paul Newman and Joanne Woodward, to Frank Sinatra and Mia Farrow, to Jack Lemmon and Lawrence Harvey and Rock Hudson and Robert Mitchum, to Merle Oberon and Rosalind Russell and Shirley MacLaine and Warren Beatty and Judy Garland, and on and on and on it went. All the most glittering stars in the town. A genuine feeling of levity permeated the gathering. I remember Paul and Joanne Newman arriving in their Volkswagen with the Porsche engine amid the plethora of limousines. I also remember the outrageously funny Larry Harvey pulling his trousers down to show off his undershorts as soon as Margaret and Snowdon had passed by our group on their way to being introduced to everyone else who had come to honor them.

Sometime during the night I found myself in the ladies' room—alone—with Princess Margaret. She had walked in to find me doing a touch-up on my makeup. We exchanged pleasantries and soon found ourselves engaged in conversation over mundane subjects like Hollywood, children, Buckingham Palace, England, etc. As the conversation proceeded I found myself smugly congratulating me over the impression I obviously was making on the princess. Little did I know that the reason she kept talking was to get me the hell out of there so she could use the john in peace and quiet. Much later on I was told that when a princess walks into a bathroom, she is immediately accorded the privacy of the place. How was I supposed to have known that? We had two more dinners to attend that week for the Snowdons while they were in town. Two very small dinners. And while she animatedly conversed with Steve, she barely gave me an imperious nod of the head! The whole episode embarrassed me deeply. I hope she's forgiven and forgotten all about the incident and me.

Six days after our introduction to Princess Margaret and Lord Snowdon we were on our way to Taiwan for the filming of *The Sand Pebbles*. It was less than two years since I had read Richard McKenna's book and had brought it to Steve's attention. He had immediately identified with the character of seaman Jake Holman and was delighted when he was approached for the film version. We had been especially thrilled to learn that Robert Wise was directing and producing. The last time Steve had worked for Bob Wise, he had been a bit player. We had also eloped to Mexico while I had been in the middle of a Bob Wise production and Steve had been steadily unemployed. Now here he was, *starring* for this widely acclaimed director in a multimillion-dollar epic. What was also nice was that Solar was coproducing the film for Twentieth Century–Fox with Bob's production company, Argyle Productions. Co-starring with Steve were Richard Crenna, still a close friend, and Richard Attenborough, with whom Steve had worked on *The Great Escape*. Steve's love interest was the ever beautiful nineteen-year-old Candice Bergen.

My first impression of Candy was that of a Jewish American Princess stranded in a strange land with strange people.

I remarked to Steve how very pretty she was and that I found her to be very shy and so young underneath all her seeming bravado.

"And horny," Steve said. I wasn't sure I heard him right.

"Say that again?"

"She's horny, I said," my darling repeated.

I looked at him and shook my head in exasperation. "For you, I suppose?"

"No, in general, is what I'm sayin'," said my all-knowing master.

Poor Candy Bergen, I thought. Those guys who are here without their wives are going to be hitting on her. But Candy was smart. Much smarter and much more of an intellectual than I had initially given her credit for. From what I observed she wasn't particularly keen on socializing with the cast of ruffians. Instead she became friendly with the very gentle Sheila and Dickie Attenborough, who were more on her wavelength.

The film was to be shot in Taipei and Hong Kong and their outlying areas and was expected to take nine weeks. Because of our past experiences with foreign locations my instincts told me this movie would not come in on schedule, and I prepared us for the long haul, packing a trunk for each of us, leaving Mike-the-Dog with friends and closing the house down. And I was wise. The night before our departure Paul and Joanne Newman came to wish us well. The last words Paul said to us as they drove down the driveway were "See you in nine weeks!"

We came home seven months later.

Twenty years ago, Taiwan was the pits. There is no other way to describe it. It was dirty and malodorous, and because the country was technically at war with Red China, it was also, for all intents and purposes, a virtual military base. Army trucks continually rumbled through the crowded streets of Taipei and uniformed personnel were visible everywhere. The war in Vietnam had been escalating rapidly and Taiwan was being used by our troops for "R and R." Ten days prior to our production start a defecting Communist pilot crashlanded a Russian bomber outside of Taipei, and a week before filming began, Nationalist Chinese gunboats fought a furious battle in the Formosa Strait. We were all issued special identification cards and all of us underwent security checks. Bob Wise's production manager assigned an interpreter to each of the thirty-two key crew members.

For the filming of the best-selling novel a gunboat from another generation had been reconstructed down to the very last rusty bolt and had sailed the China Sea and the Strait of Formosa. Because the Taiwanese government had just begun a vigorous campaign promoting tourism and was mindful of the economic gain to be wrought from a major movie

production company, *The Sand Pebbles* had a far easier time of it than another Twentieth Century–Fox
film had had a few years back. *The Inn of the Sixth
Happiness,* starring Ingrid Bergman, had run into
script difficulties with the government. Rather than
allow Taiwan to dictate to them what their script
should say, Twentieth Century–Fox just packed up
and left. They instead went to Wales, where they
constructed their very own Chinese city. This time
the Taiwanese tried not to interfere (although,
unaccountably, we all noticed that our daily editions
of the *New York Times* would arrive with stories missing and pages ripped out). Even though I tried to
deny it, the place made me very uneasy. I was careful not to convey my feelings to Chad and Terry,
who were then five and six-and-a-half. As was our
custom, we had brought them with us, and they were
attending school. I wanted them to enjoy themselves
and the experience of living in a new land.

Steve insisted that we live in our own house rather
than stay with the rest of the crew at the comfortable
Grand Hotel, which was owned by Madame Chiang.
Our house was surrounded by farmland and came
with a Chinese cook and amah (nanny). Our situation wasn't all as pastoral as it sounds. Since Taiwan's
popular form of fertilizer consisted mainly of human
excrement, when the winds blew toward us all the
windows had to be shut. Steve used to say, "The
reason there's so much rice on this island is because
the rice can't wait to get out from under to get some
fresh air!" One day Steve took the children bike
riding about the surrounding countryside and for
some reason all three slipped and fell into a recently
fertilized rice paddy. When they returned home I
refused to let them in until I had stripped them and
hosed them down! Toward the end of our stay in
Taiwan the popular saying among cast and crew was
"You know you've been here too long if you can't
smell it anymore!"

Filming began in Taipei on November 22, 1965, a wet, dreary morning. The children had already left for the Dominican School and Steve was inside the house frantically trying to reach the production office. His jeep wouldn't start and we had a twenty-mile drive to Eight-Foot Gate at Keelung, where the USS *San Pablo* was berthed and where the day's shooting was to be. They located Clap-Clap Shapiro, a local who had been hired to perform odd jobs for the company, and dispatched him and a driver to our house. As we rushed out Steve said, "Never been late to a set in my life," and quickly commanded Clap-Clap's driver to move aside so *he* could drive. As the driver and Clap-Clap groaned, Steve assured them with, "Don't you worry, now. We'll either get there alive or we won't get there at all." I turned my head and saw the panic in their eyes. In the few days we'd been here these men had already heard of Steve's mania for speed. I suppressed my laughter. As he began racing the Buick on the MacArthur Freeway Steve yelled, "How are the brakes?"

"Fine. I hope you don't get us in a ditch, Steve," came the nervous reply.

"Hell, if we go, we go end over end!"

Steve slowed down for buses and big trucks. The rest were honked aside. When the Buick finally skidded into the Keelung toll station, Steve was relieved and said joyfully, "Hey, we got it made!" As Steve hit the brakes at *The Sand Pebbles* set he turned, grinned widely, and offered his hand to Clap-Clap. "Thanks, man."

Clap-Clap Shapiro and his driver were in a state of collapse and could barely mutter a sound! Steve had made the twenty-mile drive in thirteen minutes, and there was no production time lost.

The GIs stationed on Taiwan had welcomed the movie company with open arms and had given us PX and the Officers' Club privileges. I organized and taught exercise classes at the club for the military wives, and just before Christmas I went to Quemoy for the day to entertain the three thousand men on that island. At that time, the danger was very real and the military air transport bearing me and the other performers had to fly at low level in order to avoid radar detection.

As Christmas approached, the children, Steve, and I went shopping for a tree. We bought what we thought was the best Christmas tree and when we arrived home we discovered as we untied it that branches had been wired onto the trunk to make it look thick. It looked thick all right, except that the extra branches all drooped. After we recovered from the shock we laughed and decided to keep the droopy tree anyway and to celebrate Christmas in the best Taiwanese spirit. Perhaps as a reward for our good cheer, we learned that the Hollywood Women's Press Club had given Steve its "Golden Apple" for being the most cooperative actor of 1965 (this we looked at as a Christmas present)!

In Tam Sui, where the USS *San Pablo* was currently docked, a twelve-foot Christmas tree was hoisted to the foremast of the gunboat and was spotlighted at night as a tourist attraction. I believe the tree came from the black market, where one could purchase anything and everything for the right price. The day after New Year's the tree came down and filming resumed. Or at least the attempt was made. The weather had turned so unpredictable that four call sheets (which are actors' and crews' assignments) were issued daily. And even then, shooting around the weather caused long and frustrating delays. Boredom and restlessness inevitably set in. While the men couldn't go anywhere since they were usually on call or working, the wives could at least get off the island for a while when claustrophobia set in and go to Hong Kong or Singapore or other neighboring islands for a day or so.

I made two such trips, one to Hong Kong to enroll

the children in the Maryknoll School, which they would attend during that phase of the location (it was the same school I had been to as a child); and to Manila, which I was eager to see through my now grown-up eyes. It was an emotional journey for me— how far I had come in these seventeen years!

While we were on this location Steve became enamored of cinnamon toast for breakfast. He never liked to deviate from whatever was his fancy of the moment, so every morning I gave him his two pieces of cinnamon toast and coffee with three sugars and a lot of milk. One day he said, "I want two pieces of cinnamon toast to eat here and two for the road." I thought that was a reasonable request. The next day he wanted two at home and four for the road. I thought, well, why not? The man works a hard day. The day after that it was six for the road, then eight, then ten, then twelve. I became suspicious. I said, "You can't possibly be eating all that!"

"Why not? I like it," he said. So I went to the set, made a few inquiries, and found out he was selling the toast to the crew for ten cents apiece!

The cinnamon toast also became useful for bartering. Dick Crenna later told me that when he first came on location, he had found it difficult to establish a rapport with Steve. It wasn't that Steve was cold, but that he preferred to hang around the set with his kind of guys, mostly stunt men. Then one day Steve said to Dick, "Let's talk about our parts," and Dick thought, Oh, God, here's the superstar to tell me how to do it. They spent five hours in a hotel room discussing their roles, and it was a breakthrough. In that moment, Dick came to respect him. But Dick also explained that because of his role as the ship's captain in the film, he had been given the captain's cabin on the *San Pablo* for the duration of the shooting, thereby segregating himself from the rest of the company, including Steve. With a crew as large as *The Sand Pebbles'*, cramped day after day on a 150-foot

gunboat, that cabin was a real luxury. Dickie Attenborough had moved in with Dick, and then after six
weeks on the *San Pablo*, Steve walked in one day and
said, "If you let me in I'll give you my coffee and
cinnamon toast." That did it: Steve was in!

As is wont to happen during a long location, there
were two accidents. While I had been away Chad
had burned his tiny hand. Steve said he hadn't cried
or moaned and that had pleased Steve enormously.
Chad had just looked up at his father, who had said,
"Well, Chad, another burn, another scar. That's what
the world is all about, son." Then Steve had given
him a big hug. Steve believed with all his heart that
the true measure of a man is how much he can take
and not show it. The problem was that inside, though,
he churned like an angry sea in a typhoon.

In the second accident, several members of the
crew were dumped into the Keelung River when a
fifteen-foot camera boat sank. The boat was lashed
in tandem to two other boats bearing Steve and
Dickie Attenborough, but the actors escaped a dunking. The very expensive Panavision camera was saved,
but other equipment, including a sound control panel,
went to the bottom. The camera assistants had taken
a dunking, but all had swum safely ashore. Nonetheless, the incident set the film's schedule even further
back.

One morning Jim Garner called from L.A. with
some aggravating news. As soon as I was assured
that nothing had happened to our house (he was,
after all, our next-door neighbor) or to Mike-the-
Dog, whom we had had to leave home, I handed the
phone to Steve. I sensed something was very wrong
and when he bid Jim good-bye Steve stared straight
ahead, not saying anything. I waited patiently for
him to collect his thoughts. Then slowly and deliberately he said, "That fucker. He's just signed to do
Grand Prix! Wanted to tell me himself before I read
about it or heard it from somebody else. How about

that? You see, baby, you just cannot trust anybody in this business."

"Honey, come on now, be reasonable," I pleaded. "I hate to tell you this, but you're overreacting. Look. You were asked to do the picture, but you didn't want to. Jim is an actor. You cannot begrudge him for accepting a part that *somebody's* going to do. I mean, it could have been Paul Newman or Jim Coburn just as easily. Obviously the producers have to go for a big name. They're not dummies. They're not going to hand the picture to some unknown just because these stars are your friends! Honey, you do see what I mean, don't you?"

He did see, but he didn't like it. It was two years before Steve would speak to Jim, although even then he really never felt the same way about the man again. Steve pouted and felt he had been betrayed and that was that. I felt bad because we had shared so many good times with the Garners. For instance, just before we left for Taiwan, Paul Newman, Jim, and Steve and I went to the races at Riverside. On our way home, the man became annoyed because I had insisted on stopping at the next service station rest room. They had hoped to beat the traffic home. When they did stop I discovered to my dismay that there was a long line of women ahead of me. Unable to stand the delay any longer, I came up with a brilliant idea. I said to the girls standing there, "Hey, do you know there's a car full of movie stars around the bend?"

"Who?" they cried in unison.

"Why, there's Steve McQueen, there's Paul Newman, and there's James Garner!"

The girls looked at each other and ran like crazy, leaving me in sole possession of the facilities. I never did tell the fellas how a swarm of females suddenly discovered them!

Now, to make our scheduling problems worse, John Sturges arrived on March 2 in Taiwan to discuss *Day of the Champion* with Steve. *The Sand Pebbles* was way over schedule. No one knew when the company would be moving on to the next location (Hong Kong), nor could anyone assess how long we would be there. In the light of these realities, the planned May start date for *Day of the Champion* had to be pushed back. Even July was looking "iffy." So John zeroed in on August.

But there had been an unscheduled run-in over the validity of the Sturges-McQueen contract with the Nürburgring auto racing course. The producers of the competing *Grand Prix*, Ed Lewis–John Frankenheimer, had attempted to get an injunction against the Auto Club of Germany, with whom Sturges had a contract. However, the courts ruled the Sturges pact valid and twenty-seven reels of backgound film were released to John. To capture the track's atmosphere, Stirling Moss, now completely recovered from his near-fatal accident in 1962, drove a racing car with a camera mounted on top of it, traveling at speeds up to 175 miles per hour. The Nürburgring Grand Prix drew nearly 500,000 fans and was also covered by a helicopter.

Steve could hardly wait. Whenever he talked about *Day of the Champion* his eyes sparkled. He had found a kind of dignity in racing and the acceptance that had been given him by one of the toughest fraternities in the world was immensely satisfying. He was certain this epic would be the definitive film on motor racing. His hands were already itching for the wheels.

A few days after John's arrival in Taipei a large earthquake shook the area just before dawn. The damage to the island had been extensive and John, who was a philosophical man, decided he had had enough of the Orient and departed for the good old USA! He had concluded his business with Steve and there was no reason to delay his departure. How we envied him! For years after this Taiwan adventure

Steve and I believed that anything we had ever done wrong on this earth was paid for on that location! Oddly enough, the experience seemed to make our relationship closer and stronger, possibly because there weren't many female temptations and possibly because Steve was relatively drug-free.

March 24 was Steve's thirty-sixth birthday. After four months in Chiang country we were finally in Hong Kong. Home was only a few weeks away and we could now look forward to an easier time. We could see the light at the end of the tunnel. There had been a tense moment in Taiwan when the whole company had been allowed to leave—that is, with the exception of Bob and Pat Wise, Steve, the children and me, and one or two other key people. The government had held our passports claiming that the production company owed Taiwan more tax money. It was a lie, but we paid them anyway. There was no choice. It was a case of pay or stay. To celebrate our release from Taiwan we observed Steve's birthday twice in conformance with Chinese custom. According to the Chinese calendar each month has twenty-nine or thirty days, depending on the moon, and every fourth year has thirteen months; 1966 was a fourth-year cycle and March was the repeated month. Hence, two parties!

The few weeks we expected to spend in Hong Kong turned into three months, and at last we were headed for home. It had been a tough location, and the film still had a few weeks to go on the sound stages at Fox. Steve looked exhausted and was suffering from an abscessed molar. He had refused to see a doctor until we got home. When we got off the plane in Los Angeles, Steve literally threw himself on the ground and kissed the American soil he loved so much.

When Steve finally allowed the doctors to check him, they prescribed enforced rest. He had been close to a physical collapse. Not only had the over-scheduled *Sand Pebbles* taken its toll on his health, but location shooting for the previously completed *Nevada Smith* had been tough. And before that had been *The Cincinnati Kid*. It was time for a rest. The man was clearly out of gas. Production shut down temporarily on *Sand Pebbles*, and it became disappointingly clear that the racing movie had to be temporarily shelved as well.

In the meantime, while Steve rested, there were little surprises. For my birthday that year I came into the courtyard at our big stone house and was greeted with a Mexican mariachi band singing "Happy Birthday" while Steve and the children, standing beside a beautiful green Excalibur with a huge green bow tied to it, sang along. Steve was paying me the ultimate compliment by entrusting me with a "sporty" car. He had always kept me in big bulky cars like Cadillacs and Lincolns; now it was time for me to go around town in a car that befitted the McQueen image.

It was a generous gift and belied his reputation of being tight with money. John Sturges used to joke that in Hollywood, where the definition of infinity is waiting for Cary Grant or Jimmy Stewart to pick up a check, Steve's name should be added to that list. But when the expenses had to do with me and our kids, he was always generous. Sometimes amusingly so. I belong to a charity called SHARE, and one year during an auction I listened with amazement as the bidding went higher and higher for what I thought was the coat I was modeling. I heard one of the SHARE ladies yell out, "Steve McQueen bids $10,000!" I was aghast and exclaimed, "Shit, I can get this stupid coat for $600 and I don't even want it!" As it turned out, Steve, who had had one beer too many and some joints in the course of the evening, had unknowingly bought a square-cut emerald ring surrounded by baguette diamonds instead of the coat I had been wearing. When the ring was handed to him, he grumbled, "What happened to the coat? I don't want that!" It was left to Janet Leigh, who had brought me into SHARE, to explain to Steve quickly that he had in fact bid on the ring. He accepted his error like a good sport, and the ring found its way to me on stage with the message, "From your husband."

Steve also had a tender spot for needy children. Early on he had established an annual Steve McQueen scholarship at the Boys' Republic. When Nicaragua was hit by a mammoth earthquake in the early seventies he quietly bought $50,000 worth of food and medical supplies and hired a plane to bring it in to that beleaguered country. A few years before, he had rescued two boys who were about to be sent to a Florida jail for some minor infringement of the law. By taking full responsibility for them, he was able to have them transferred to the Boys' Republic instead. He also served as a board member on the Advisory Council of the Youth Studies Center at the University of Southern California. Steve took pride in the fact that he was the only actor so honored. When he attended his first board meeting it was also his first time on a college campus. And in Taiwan, Steve and Robert Wise gave Father Ed Wojniak, a priest who worked tirelessly for the betterment of that society, a check for $25,000 to start construction on a hostel for homeless and orphaned girls. Steve's association with the sophisticated and liberal Wise had had a stirring effect on him. He became interested in paying back his dues. He used to tell the children that you have to put back what you take out in this world.

But dealing with other people and dealing with the studios was another matter altogether. Steve could never resist "stealing" his movie wardrobe, no matter how tacky. He always came home with the clothes the day shooting wrapped. What he liked he stored in his closet and what he didn't like went to the Salvation Army. I once told him this compulsion of his made him look cheap. There was no reason to do it. He certainly could afford to buy anything he wanted. He thought about that for a bit, agreed with me, but was unable to discontinue the practice. He also scammed Columbia out of a Land Rover while promising to do promos for them for *Baby, the Rain Must Fall*. As soon as he received the four-wheel-drive vehicle he conveniently became unreachable when it was time for him to deliver his part of the deal. For a gag, he had the chemical formula for chicken shit painted on the vehicle door just as he had one day hung a sign on his motorcycle proclaiming him to be "The Mild One."

Steve was the first star to buy his own luxurious Condor motor home for the main purpose of having the studios rent the motor home from him—for his use—while he labored for them. We would occasionally use the motor home, equipped with bathtub, shower, stove, and stereo, for weekend trips. Mostly it stayed on a studio lot when he was not working. He delighted in saying, "Man, I'm so cheap, I throw my dimes around like manhole covers!"

Changes were taking place in the world in 1966. College students were protesting the United States' presence in Vietnam, and flower children in the Haight-Ashbury district of San Francisco were making their presence felt. Steve was apolitical and never voted in his life. Ironically, though, he was very definitely a mom-and-apple-pie patriotic type of guy. He empathized with our soldiers in Vietnam and was distressed by the situation there. Although he understood what the students were trying to do, he felt that they were wrong. He once told an interviewer, "There are a lot of people stepping up trying to find their own identity. But we have a responsibility to our country—our kids are getting killed over there—and this collegiate demonstration doesn't speak well for us over the world and it doesn't mirror what most of us feel." When asked what advice he had for our men overseas, Steve's reply was, "Tell them to keep their tails down."

In light of his own antisocial, sometimes rebellious behavior in the early fifties as a member of the Beat Generation, his personal conservatism might sound hypocritical. In truth, responsibility—to wife and children—had overtaken his youthful rebelliousness. "Today," he said with pride, "what I used to hate, used to rebel against, why, man, it's now part of my life! There's a funny feeling a guy gets when it's time to marry, and I felt this very strongly. I felt a terrible drive to succeed. I think my wife was responsible for that. It wasn't something I had basically. It was something that happened because I had somebody to take care of. She really shaped me up good. I was a taker and she a full giver."

That summer we agreed to take the Condor on a camping trip with our kids. The plan was to drive to Canada by way of Nevada, Utah, Colorado, on up to Wyoming, into Montana, then on to Vancouver, all the while stopping en route at the national forests. As a way of selling me on the idea, Steve had said there would be lots of time for picnics, walks in the woods, reading, and just lazing about by rivers and waterfalls while Terry, Chad, and Steve went trail-biking (I never did get the hang of motorized bikes). It all sounded so idyllic and wonderful. There would be no time schedule. We would take as much or as little as we wanted or needed to. So off we went.

We started out leisurely and slowly for a day or so as we had planned. Pretty soon we were picking up our speed, and I was having to cook while Steve drove this huge, cumbersome vehicle over winding roads at unheard-of speeds. I'd complain that I was nauseated and he'd say, "Just hang in there, baby, we'll be there soon."

"Where? Where's there?" I'd yell exasperatedly. The "there," of course, was a word that connoted many things—depending upon his mood—which he always kept secret from us. It could be a roadside motel where we would stop and take baths, it could be a creek, it could be a diner, it could be a little trail, it could be anything! The idea apparently was to keep moving. Then we'd stop to stretch our legs and off we'd go again. When he was tired of driving, I would take over the wheels while he slept or played with the children in the back. It was impossible for him to stop at any one place for a few hours at a time. It was mostly walk around, enjoy the scenery, and then on to the next scenic view. But for all the rush and tumble, we did have a good time. The children didn't seem to mind riding in the motor home while they watched those beautiful states whiz by. We played games, we sang, we jumped and exercised and did what most families do together on a camping trip.

With possibly one exception.

The head of this family pulled me aside when we arrived home three weeks later and said, "I've been thinking, baby. I'm gonna build us an empire." With that he patted me on the backside and said, "Let's go in!"

10

WE LAUNCHED our departure for New York and personal appearance tours for *The Sand Pebbles* with a sensational party in the courtyard of our house that lasted until the small hours of the morning. As soon as the tent went up, the set decorators from Twentieth Century–Fox immediately went to work to transform the Castle into the Red Candle Inn of Happiness, right out of the movie. There were colorful Chinese swinging lanterns, and scrolls, banners, and panels everywhere, lavish vases of flowers and greenery throughout the house, and a long buffet table of Chinese delicacies. The entertainment was provided by Johnny Rivers, now a big star, and a new rock group known as the Buffalo Springfield.

The invitations read "very informal," which in Hollywood can mean anything like tiaras for women and sneakers for men.

Joan Collins, as usual, was a party stopper in a red fishnet see-through dress (husband Anthony Newley was out-of-town); Jane Fonda, wearing a black vinyl miniskirt and jacket, was stopped at the bottom of the hill by a security guard because husband Roger Vadim's name had inadvertently been omitted from the guest list; Zsa Zsa Gabor was dressed in something that can only be described as a short, black sequinned tent, while her sister Eva wore a printed muumuu; Joanne Woodward was conservatively dressed in a white satin blouse and blazer and black pants; Stefanie Powers, ever the chic lady, arrived in a gray pinstriped trouser outfit; and as the hostess, I wore a colorful Pucci mini dress with matching tights *and* shoes, which caused Dick Crenna to joke, "Neile, it's a shame about your legs. I really do think that you should have had those varicose veins removed before you gave this party!" As for the men (Steve included), most of them wore turtlenecks, as befitted the times.

It seemed as if all of Hollywood was attending this party. At some point I heard Lee Marvin remark, surveying the crowd, "If the bomb hit tonight, the motion picture industry would be wiped out."

Because of the long driveway, we hired a tram for the evening to take our guests up and down the mountain. Terry and Chad had a wonderful time riding it up and down the road. Their main objective was waiting for the arrival of their idol, Adam West, then TV's Batman. Finally, at ten o'clock I had to put them to bed. When Adam at last arrived a half hour later, I took him by the hand and introduced him to the children. He was so sweet to them. When Adam retucked them in for the night they were the happiest kids I ever did see.

The very next day we were on our way to New York. Bob Wise was still editing the film down to the last hours before the first "official" screening. Still, we could feel the importance of this movie in Steve's career.

The rain and cold failed to dampen the crowd's spirits for the opening of *The Sand Pebbles* the night of December 20, 1966. The crowd started gathering outside the Rivoli at about seven o'clock, and by eight, the theater was jammed. There were Chinese ceremonial dragons bedecking the lobby and musicians playing. There were ladies in long dresses and furs and men in tuxedos. Penni Crenna looked sensational in a white ermine coat and I, still in my

Jackie Kennedy period, wore a long fur-trimmed magenta satin dress and coat. I remember spotting in the crowd Harry and Julie Belafonte and Pearl Buck and Hermione Gingold.

Directly after the screening, as Steve and I walked up the aisle, I looked at him and, barely able to contain myself, whispered, "What we have here, honey, is a real, honest-to-goodness, unadulterated, big-time moom pitcher star!"

He laughed, pulled me to him, and agreed. "This is it, baby. We Have Made It. I know it in mah bones." Then softly he yelled, "Oooowee!!!"

From the theater we went on to the New York Hilton for a dinner dance that was benefiting the Pearl Buck Foundation and the Korea Society. After dinner we excused ourselves and joined some new friends at the Moroccan consulate. The Moroccan ambassador had already extended us an invitation to visit his country ("Not bad for a farm boy," Steve had said). We had met the Princess Lalla Nezha and her lady-in-waiting, Kenza Alaoui, in Hollywood through Loretta Young and had liked them enormously. The after-hours party ended abruptly for me, however. I felt the flu bug hit me with a sudden vengeance. I fainted in the ladies' room of the consulate and when Steve led me out I could envision the other guests whispering among themselves, "How awful about Mrs. McQueen getting crocked and passing out. Tsk, tsk. Just imagine!"

While we were in the city promoting the film, the studio put a big black limousine and a little gray Volkswagen at our disposal. Steve didn't like to be driven around—in a limousine or otherwise—unless it was absolutely necessary. The Volkswagen gave us the freedom to move about New York undetected and the limo provided the necessary means of escape when that freedom was threatened. The two cars traveled in tandem during the day while we promoted the new film and went shopping. Over the

years Steve had adopted a way of walking down the
street like he was in a mad hurry in order to prevent
people from recognizing him until it was too late.
Sometimes it didn't work and he'd have to make a
dash for the limo. Still, he was grateful to his fans
and never minded signing autographs (the only time
he wouldn't was when the children were with him).
His feeling was "It's all right. I always wanted to be
someone, you know? And now that I am, all I've
blown is my obscurity, and that's not much to blow."
Because the crowds were sometimes huge and exhausting, he had had a rubber stamp made of his
signature in Taiwan, and he would sometimes carry
a stack of pictures with him which he would then
pass out to his fans.

During this New York visit we ran into Richard
Chamberlain. His musical *Breakfast at Tiffany's* had
recently closed after its first preview. Steve asked
Dick when he was coming back to California. "I
don't know," said Dick. "New York's kinda nice. You
have a big flop here and everybody still invites you
to lunch and dinner. In California you have a flop
and they cross you off the list."

Dick Chamberlain's remark touched a nerve in
Steve and troubled him momentarily. Like all actors,
I suppose, he lived in fear that he would wake up
one morning, and whatever it was that accounted for
his talent would be gone. Fortunately, those first
weeks of 1967 were wonderful. The critics loved his
performance in *The Sand Pebbles*. The film had been
rushed into a December release in order to qualify
Steve and the movie for the Academy Awards. The
studio's action had been justified. Steve's performance
showed his enormous emotional range ("with all the
simplicity and tenderness an actor can muster when
he trusts his own virility," one reviewer said). Indeed, *The Sand Pebbles* is one of my favorite Steve
films, although even then I found it excruciating to
watch him in a death scene. For sheer entertain-

Neile, 1936.

Life magazine, 1956.
(Burton Glinn, Magnum)

What Neile Wants, Neile Can't Get

A CONTRACT STALLS
A DANCER'S CAREER

When Neile Adams (*left*) belts out *A Girl Has Got To Do The Best She Can* while shaking off some clothes at the Versailles club in New York, she knows she is not really doing the best she can. Neile can purr her way through a love ballad, mourn convincingly through a blues and dance with the best girl hoofers in town. What she can't do is get out of the Versailles.

Twelve years ago Neile got out of a Japanese internment camp—she was born in Manila—and since then has been trying to make her way into a leading role in a big Broadway musical. A few weeks ago Broadway director George Abbott decided that she was just the girl to sing *Whatever Lola Wants, Lola Gets* in the road company of his hit musical *Damn Yankees*. But, the Versailles refused to let Neile out of her six-month contract, leaving her to brood over the thought that what Neile wants, Neile doesn't necessarily get.

The very first acting job, playing a
sailor in a 1952 Signal Corps film.

The car Steve won in a poker game and
demolished in a New York City pothole, 1954.
(John Waggaman)

My wedding picture.

The Bounty Hunter, which became
Wanted—Dead or Alive, 1957.

(left and below) With Charles Bronson
and John Sturges on the set of *Never So
Few.* (Courtesy of MGM/UA
Entertainment Co.)

Terry McQueen, the apple of her father's eye, 1959.

The car that would later be sold at auction for $147,500. (Curt Gunther)

With Mom and Steve at the Solar
house after Chad's birth.

Off to lunch (*The Great Escape*,
June 1962).

Bavaria, 1962.

A favorite picture of his. We had just moved into the Oakmont house.

The Castle.

Paris premiere of
*Love with the Proper
Stranger*, 1964.
(Michel Descamps)

Steve in his
French disguise, with
Elmer Valentine.
(Michel Descamps)

Hawaii, 1964.

The fashion plate. (Richard Avedon. Copyright © 1965. The Hearst Corporation. Courtesy of *Harper's Bazaar*.)

The only known photograph of Steve's mother, Julian, taken at the San Francisco Zoo shortly before her death.

Taipei, 1965. (Doris Nieh)

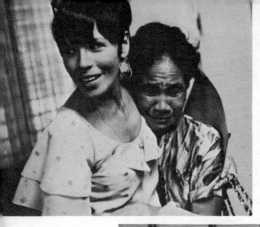

A tearful reunion with Binoy's wife, Manila, 1966. (Doris Nieh)

(below) After seven months overseas, home again.

Relaxing in the living room of The Castle, 1967. (Curt Gunther/Camera 5)

In San Francisco filming *Bullitt* on Steve's thirty-eighth birthday, before I found the hairbrush. (Mel Traxel)

Testing the new Indian motorcycle with Terry and Juliet Mills.

Partying in 1969. (Peter C. Borsari/Camera 5)

Steve referred to this as our "Andy Hardy" portrait. (Karl Gene)

The tycoon in his Solar office. (Mel Traxel)

Following the Sharon Tate murders, Steve never went anywhere without a gun. Notice his hip pocket.

With Peter Revson after Sebring race in 1970.

April 1971.

Christmas 1970 in Palm Springs. The bad times.

Just before Memorial Day.
(Peter C. Borsari/Camera 5)

Terry, Steve, and Chad at
Indian Dunes.

Steve and Ali,
1974. (Gary
Franklin)

The changed Steve, 1977.

(below) Chad's eighteenth birthday party, December 28, 1978. The last picture of the four of us together. (Eleanor Kaufman)

Steve and Barbara, 1979. (Peter C. Borsari)

The cabin he never saw finished, Ketchum, Idaho.

Chad, Neile, and Terry, 1984. (Marlene Callahan Wallace)

Al and Neile, today.

ment, *The Thomas Crown Affair* is my favorite of his films.

It was at this point that he began to relax and relish the idea of being a movie star. The Sunset Strip became his turf. At night we would drop by Elmer's Whisky A GO-GO to dance and mingle with the long-haired boys and miniskirted girls. The young people adored Steve, which was an achievement of sorts, considering the fact that Steve's hair was crewcut and his clothes were rather tailored sports models. "I'm off the streets," he used to say. "I'm people. I'm honest and I'm of the times. I don't give the idea I got ahead because of a letter of introduction from my father-in-law." It was fun, this business of being a movie star. "It's a good racket. And let's face it, you can't beat the bread!"

Steve was branching out. An official announcement came from Warner Brothers that Steve was moving into temporary quarters at the studio, while Jack Warner ordered the tennis courts to be replaced with a new two-story office building to house Steve's multimillion-dollar Solar Productions. Stan Kamen had negotiated a stunning six-picture deal with Warner whereby Solar would be responsible for its pictures without interference from the studio. Steve appointed Robert Relyea, formerly vice-president of John Sturges's Alpha Corporation, as his executive producer.

In retrospect, however, I think of this time as the turning point where Steve switched into that other gear that eventually clouded his judgment about what was most important in his life. The empire he had been dreaming about was now a viable and a very tangible thing. Solar meant power. Solar meant complete autonomy.

Back at the Morris office, Stan Kamen had just finished reading a script called *The Crown Caper,* which was to be Norman Jewison's next project. Norman had been thinking of Rock Hudson, among others, for the part of the urbane, sophisticated, and amoral Thomas Crown. Stan had other ideas. After all the genre and working-class roles Steve had played, Stan felt Steve needed a change of pace and that this vehicle would provide it. After reading the script, Steve became intrigued with the character but was unsure of his ability to pull it off. (He did have that disarming quality about him. He knew his strengths and weaknesses as an actor. "I have a certain range. I am aware of my limitations and that's probably half my talent.")

However, Stan and I were positive that Steve could do the part. Besides, we all knew that once the director and star were in accord, a writer could be brought in to tailor the script to the star. Steve was taking a maddeningly long time to make up his mind. Stan was afraid that the script might slip through his fingers, since Norman was talking to everyone else in Hollywood *except* Steve for this part. Unless Stan was told by Steve he was interested in the role, there would be no point in approaching Norman.

I decided it was time to galvanize him into action. Knowing that he subscribed to the "dog-in-the-manger" theory—that is, he didn't want it, but he didn't want anybody else to have it either—I knew it wasn't going to be hard to do.

At breakfast one morning I nonchalantly said, "You know, I really can't understand Norman's objection to you for *The Crown Caper*."

I thought he was going to choke on his French toast. "What do you mean?" Silence. "You're saying Norman doesn't want me?" he asked in disbelief.

"Honey, surely Stan must have told you that Norman is after Rock Hudson or Sean Connery. He sees Thomas Crown as this suave, sophisticated man. Now, you know there ain't nobody more dashing than those two!"

That did it. He put in a call to Stan and then Steve

launched a campaign to convince Norman Jewison that he was the right man for the role. Besides Stan's gentle persuasion, Steve called Norman every hour (for days, I think) trying to turn his thinking around. And the strategy worked. He exerted so much energy in the process that I think he just plain wore Norman down. Together, they created a slightly different Crown than had emerged in the first script, but it was surely a more exciting character than the original.

In the meantime, Solar Productions announced it had purchased the rights to the book *The Man on a Nylon String,* which was a fictionalized version of a true story. Production was scheduled to commence in late August of 1967 in the Swiss Alps. Negotiations were under way for George Roy Hill to direct the property, which Steve was also considering starring in. He wasn't sure if it would be wise for him to star in Solar's first solo effort. Since his deal at Warners gave him the option of not starring in the feature, I hoped he'd give the part to another actor. I disliked the story and thought the mountain climbing setting a boring background for a murder mystery. Moreover, the central character was an amateur spy. A simple, average guy. No ladies' man, no karate expert. No nothing. I felt it was all wrong for Steve. The thought of another foreign location didn't appeal to me either. I wanted to stick close to home. Boston, where *The Thomas Crown Affair* would be shot, was as far as I wanted to go this year. Solar had also acquired the rights to *The Cold War Swap,* which was another spy story and required another foreign location! I didn't like that one either. Too much of a downer, I thought. (Both *The Cold War Swap* and *The Man on the Nylon String* would fall by the wayside after Steve and Warners parted company.)

By February Steve was riding high. He and Julie Andrews had just been voted World Film Favorites by the Hollywood Foreign Press Association (the next day he woke Elmer Valentine out of a sound sleep with "Hello, Elmer. You are speaking to the world's most favorite actor!"), and he was nominated for an Academy Award for his role in *The Sand Pebbles*. (It was to be his first and only nomination.) We were in Palm Springs when we were notified. Steve was pouring concrete for the garage when I handed him the telephone. It was an exciting moment. He felt honored and overwhelmed. We roared down to Sambo's on his motorcycle, and we celebrated by ordering giant hamburgers and extra thick chocolate milkshakes with vanilla ice cream. And then on March 21, 1967, three days before his thirty-seventh birthday, Steve McQueen became the one-hundred-fifty-third star to put his handprints and footprints on the forecourt of Grauman's Chinese Theater. Over two thousand fans were there and God knows how many photographers. In true Hollywood fashion, we arrived in Steve's burgundy Ferrari as the crowd cheered. Amid the pandemonium we learned that Steve had set an attendance record, equaling that of Marilyn Monroe and Jane Russell, who had together immortalized their footprints in cement.

Steve, through our Solar Plastics and Engineering division, was in negotiation with Montgomery Ward to market a motorbike of his own design. This was big stuff because it eventually could involve a line of men's clothes. He most naturally had a few ideas for riding which would combine fashion and comfort. In the past few years, Steve had become quite the fashion plate. (Contrary to what the press alluded to as his "beatnik garb," Steve was a fashionable man. He had his own particular brand of stylishness. During the day it was jeans and chambray shirts or cutoff pants and no shirt, depending on the weather; for evening dress and for important meetings, Italian designer wear, particularly Brioni because their clothes were form fitting. It is true, however, that later, when Steve embraced the hippie movement, he also

adopted their mode of dressing. With a slight variation, Steve's hippie clothes were perfectly tailored to
his perfect physique.) He was featured in all the
fashion magazines—men's and women's—modeling
the latest sportswear and also the Cardin and Brioni
suits he favored at that time—along with the Mur-
ray's Space Shoes he insisted on wearing. Steve had
problems with his feet and knees and was almost
always in pain due to all the injuries he'd suffered in
motorcycle racing accidents. Then Danny Kaye suggested Steve try these shoes and they saved him a lot
of pain. He had several pairs made for him and very
rarely wore anything else. They looked a little odd
under those expensive clothes and also gave the mis-
taken impression that he wore lifts. Not true. At five
feet ten and a half there was no reason to. He was as
tall as Paul Newman and Bob Redford and Burt
Reynolds.

Steve desperately hoped to bring home the Academy Award. He felt that if the Academy "went American" that year, he just might. "But if the voting goes
English, then one of those cats will take the Oscar.
Probably Paul Scofield."

He was right. Paul Scofield won for *A Man for All
Seasons*. But Steve was a good loser. Although once
we were inside the Santa Monica Civic Auditorium
he kept holding my hand and telling his stomach to
settle down, he was riding high from the greeting
the fans had given him when we arrived. It seemed
they had reserved their biggest ovation for him, and
he was feeling loved by the whole world. To him,
being a movie star was better than being president
("Listen, in Taiwan most people don't know who
Lyndon Johnson is, but they sure as hell know who
John Wayne is"). As we were walking into the award
ceremonies, a reporter asked Steve what he attributed his success to. Without hesitating, he looked at
me and said, "Right there." It was one of life's magical moments for us.

*   *   *

A few days later, on one of those shimmering, cobalt-blue-sky days, I opened the front door to stare into a pair of smiling, slightly less blue eyes. They belonged to Paul Newman, who had come to spend the afternoon with us. As we sat around the pool having lunch, Paul casually mentioned something about a script that was being written by his friend William Goldman, a script he thought he and Steve could possibly do together. He said production was still a good year away, but it could be fun. It was a western film about two outlaws—*The Sundance Kid and Butch Cassidy* (as it was then being called). It would be a spoof on all those macho-men westerns and should be gently humorous. Paul was very enthused about the script and he went on to describe to us certain aspects about it that intrigued him, the unique relationship between the two men, the posse that glowed and shimmered in the distance as they tracked the two outlaws. As Paul spoke, I remember looking around me and realizing that I was surrounded by blue everywhere. The blue skies, the blue water, my blue bathing suit, Paul's blue eyes, Steve's blue eyes, blue towels, Steve's blue shorts, Paul's blue shirt! As the conversation moved on to other things, I was struck by something Paul said about his wife. "It's a great feeling for me to know that Joanne and I will grow old together. It makes me feel really good and secure." Down the years I have always felt great warmth for Paul, and it's probably because of those two sentences he uttered that sunny afternoon. Nice man.

By mid-June we were in Beverly Farms, Massachusetts, for the newly titled *The Thomas Crown Affair*. Our digs for the summer were located on the ocean, in a private compound of about a dozen gorgeous Cape Cod–style homes. Because these houses were all owned by families whose ancestors dated back to the *Mayflower,* and who had names like Crocker Snow,

Adam Winthrop, Forrester Smith, the neighbors christened Steve "the rebel among the blue bloods." There
were also a lot of children around, which made it a
terrific summer for my kiddies. Mike-the-Dog was
gone and a new puppy had joined the family, a
miniature schnauzer whom we named Annie (after
my best friend, Ann Smith). So Annie and Kitty Kat
came along to keep the little McQueens company.

Steve's leading lady was the terrific Faye Dunaway.
Having come off the very successful *Bonnie and Clyde*,
Faye was the hottest actress around. The teaming
was an electric one. Faye's clothes were sumptuous
and her hair and makeup were perfect. Steve, playing
the self-made Boston millionaire, was fabulously out-
fitted. And the creative Jay Sebring decided to lighten
Steve's blond hair, thereby accentuating that great
head for the camera. I don't think Steve or Faye had
ever looked as good as they did in *Thomas Crown*.

Over the years Steve had developed his own way
for preparing for a role. He read a script over and
over without memorizing any of the dialogue. He
discussed and dissected his character with his directors and co-stars for hours, and researched the role
as well, mostly by observing people.(Few people know
it, but Steve was a wonderful mimic, with a fabulous
sense of humor. He could do devastating imitations
of Marlon Brando, Walter Brennan, and Amos 'n'
Andy.) Once on the set, each scene was rehearsed
several times in order to allow him to explore his
character's emotions. Only then would he nail down
his dialogue.

On the first day of rehearsing *Thomas Crown* Steve
arrived on the set totally unprepared for Faye
Dunaway's brand of professionalism. She already had
her character and her dialogue nailed down. He
came home that evening awed by Faye, who had
come to work "so ready, so prepared that she threw
everything at me but the kitchen sink! I couldn't
believe it!" As soon as dinner was over he and I

spent the next few hours on the script memorizing
his lines. Norman Jewison was not going to see him
again lagging behind his less experienced co-star.

Beverly Farms proved to be the idyllic place to
spend the summer. On Sundays we'd have clam-
bakes on the beach and during the week, while Steve
worked, Terry, Chad, and I would explore the quaint
local villages. And when action shots were filmed, I
took the children to the set to watch their dad "make
like Errol Flynn," as I used to say. Steve had pushed
himself hard to meet the athletic demands made of
him by this film. But because he was in excellent
shape, he had little difficulty. For the film's polo
sequence, for instance, it took Steve only three weeks
of working out with the Myopia Hunt Club before "I
was right up their rearview mirror." Then there was
the gliding sequence, which was later put so brilliantly to music. Even his golf game looked terrific,
which was astonishing for someone who'd played
only miniature golf with his wife and kids. The first
time he swung the club in rehearsal he almost made
a hole-in-one! Norman stared in disbelief. And then,
of course, there was that dune buggy sequence filmed
on the sand dunes of Cape Cod. My admiration for
Faye Dunaway tripled the day she gamely lowered
herself into that buggy and took off with Steve at the
wheel. It took a whole day to film this rampage but
Faye managed to keep on smiling despite the skids
and the spins into the surf. Take after take.

That summer of 1967 was carefree and delicious,
and as I innocently went about my business of savor-
ing life with my family, forces were already conspir-
ing to undermine my happiness.

That summer, movie personality Jayne Mansfield
died of injuries suffered in a car accident; Billy Joe
jumped off the Tallahatchee Bridge; Muhammad
Ali refused induction into the army; Martin Luther
King, Jr., spoke against the war in Vietnam; and the
flower children heralded communal living, free love,

spiritualism, and LSD. It was their "Summer of Love," and in our own way, it was one of Steve's and my last.

When *The Thomas Crown Affair* wound down and as soon as Terry and Chad were settled in school, we went to Europe for a holiday. (My mother always came out from New York to keep an eye on the children if we were to be gone for any length of time.) While in London Steve startled me by glee-fully confessing that a few years back, he and some friends had been the first people to bring LSD into London. True or not, there was no way for me to verify the statement. However, I did give him a rather condescending, "I'm sure all of England thanks you, my darling."

At the end of the year a writer named Mike Tomkies remarked that I appeared to be an excep-tionally happy woman. More so than any star's wife he had interviewed in the last ten years. I smiled and answered, "I am. This is our happiest period. Right now. These last two years. Not only because of the security Steve's success has brought us, but because our personalities seem to be maturing together.

"It's hard to explain," I continued. "I know I'm beginning to feel more complete. C-o-m-p-l-e-a-t—that kind of complete! We're more aware of things—I understand him more now than I ever did. In a way, I think you don't really love anyone until you settle for yourself as a human being."

I spoke too soon.

Steve was beginning to alarm me. His use of grass was escalating steadily. What used to be indulged in after work or after dinner and before bedtime was now being used freely at all hours of the day. Coke was also becoming part of his daily consumption. He seemed to find a drug connection everywhere—in and out of the country. We'd have words and his response to me was always the same: "Look, honey,

I'm not working right now and I deserve time out for good behavior. Right? Right. I've been working my buns off, you know?" And then, in his Amos 'n' Andy imitation, would add, "I needs mah time to howl, woman!" All delivered in a way that made me feel guilty for even questioning him.

I couldn't disagree with his reasoning, and I wasn't smart enough to come up with the quick comeback. But his drug use bothered me. I sensed it distorted his view of the world. I began to resent Jay Sebring's presence in the house. Jay and his damned briefcase! Jay's briefcase with his combs and scissors . . . and the little packets of coke. And yet it was Jay who helped me convince Steve he should do a movie called *Bullitt*. The script had been waiting for Steve when we arrived home from Europe. As usual, I did the first reading. But when I told him that *Bullitt* was a cop, Steve immediately said, "No way am I playing a cop. Those kids call 'em pigs, man! What are you trying to do to me? Why, those kids would turn me off so fast it'd make your head spin!"

After several days of trying to persuade him otherwise, it was still no sale. And then one afternoon, as Jay was giving Steve a haircut, Steve brought the new script into the conversation. Both men were as high as kites, and I took advantage of the situation by getting Jay to agree with my reasoning that playing a cop might actually enhance Steve's image with his young fans rather than compromise it. Everybody was of the opinion the script wasn't particularly good, but I felt very strongly about the salability of the title. I knew Steve could play *Bullitt* in his own oblique and unconventional way. The way he was. And along the way he, and the moviegoing public, would maybe get an education—that cops aren't all bad. That they're only doing their job. Actually, Steve's feelings about police authority had thawed out considerably since those early days. (Good-naturedly, at the suggestion of his p.r. firm, Steve had taken out an ad in *Siren*, the California Highway Patrol's official publication, which read, "Merry Christmas, fellas. PLEASE! Steve McQueen.") But the drug culture was upon us, and he was again leery of authority.

Not only was Steve's screen personality representative of a new generation of dropouts and gentle misfits who suddenly seemed to be all over the place, but the man himself began to feel a special kinship with these kids, as though he represented them personally. A few years back, these young people would have been part of his world. They would have been members of the Beat Generation. They were rootless and antisocial and, like Steve, some of them were products of broken homes. Theirs was a world of instant gratification. They found their kicks in fast cars and motorcycles and drugs.

The tone of Steve's interviews was changing. Gone was patriotic Mr. America: "Whether you dig the long-haired boys and mini-skirted girls or not—whether the unwashed look of the beards appals and shocks you or not—just remember this: ten years from now, maybe less—they'll be running the country." When asked if maybe this generation seemed more con things than pro, Steve countered with "This could be a reflex action in self-defense. After all, everybody is more con than pro *them*." And in yet another interview, he said he liked to think of himself as "an interpreter. I represent a whole lotta guys my age who finally looked around and said, 'Hey, somebody's been lyin' to us': guys who suddenly found out they're a lot smarter than some of the head honchos sitting up there, pushing buttons in the front office."

His age was gnawing at him. But the young people he wanted to be identified with had warned, "Don't trust anybody over thirty." Suddenly, even I, his beloved wife, at thirty-three years of age, was looking old to him. He fervently longed to be a member of this *now* generation. If he couldn't be a part of it because of his chronological age, then he would join them in spirit and in deed. These young kids were mobilizing the country! It was astounding to him. They were antiestablishment, just as he had been in his youth. But then the country had been in a different frame of mind. Then there had only been "good wars." Now we had a "bad war," and Steve wanted to relive his youth through these kids.

Suddenly, I had a husband with two personalities: a self-destructive juvenile delinquent and a responsible, loving husband and father.

11

IF I WERE to pick a specific event that signaled the point of no return, it would have to be that morning in early January 1968 when an anonymous phone call disrupted our breakfast. A man's voice said cryptically that an underground book had just been released containing a list of all the known and unknown homosexuals who were in the public eye. "I thought you'd like to know that your name is on the list," said the voice on the other end. Click. The phone went dead and the blood drained from Steve's face. He was thunderstruck. There was a long pause as he looked at me unseeing. Thinking hard. Then finally he recounted the mysterious telephone call. We both fell silent trying to grasp the situation, trying to grasp what it all meant. In the end we both agreed that, one, this book was a sleazy publication and consequently no one would see it; and that, two, no one in his right mind would ever think of Steve as gay. I mean, *Steve*!! We decided just to think of the publication as a nuisance and to forget it.

But Steve became possessed. His ego couldn't handle the innuendo. It seemed to violate everything he stood for—most notably his macho image. We had our lawyers try to track down the publisher, but it was an impossibility. The name of the publishing house was phony and the trail led nowhere. Fortunately for their own reasons the FBI became inter-

ested in the case, and within two weeks the books
had disappeared from the underground market, just
as *Bullitt* started to roll in San Francisco. But the
incident had shaken him. That, plus the drug culture and the sexual revolution, conspired to draw
him into a mid-life crisis.

The metamorphosis was incremental. Subtle changes
taking place in our personal life. Some were imagined, but most were certainly real. While we had
agreed years before to bring the children with us
anytime Steve was involved in an overseas shoot,
location filming in the United States was a different
matter. There was no need to pull the children out
of their familiar surroundings—unless it was sum-
mertime and school was out—when I could easily
commute back and forth, from him to them and
from them to him. Besides, when we were gone
Terry and Chad always had their grandmother with
them at the Castle, which gave us a good, secure
feeling, knowing that the children were being properly looked after. I would join Steve on location as
soon as I felt the children could do without Mommy
for a while. But now my husband was insisting I join
him only on weekends during this San Francisco
shoot "because this was gonna be a tough location,
baby." My presence was suddenly being constrained.
Naively, I chalked Steve's attitude up to nerves. This
was Solar Production's first independent film and
Steve, as head of the company, had a right to be
nervous.

For one thing, Warner Brothers had just been
taken over by Seven Arts (something that Jack Warner had neglected to mention). An ex-marine named
Kenneth Hyman now headed the studio. Hyman was
a different breed of studio chief. He was not used to
coddling movie stars. He was from the East Coast,
was a businessman, and was determined to be involved in all the different phases of production of
films that were to come out of his studio. Solar, on

the other hand, wanted the autonomy that had been the basis of the original Warner-Solar contract. Steve's feeling was, "There are so many fingers involved in the pie when it comes to making movies that by the time the compromises are all made, sometimes you don't have much left of value. I understand the reasons, even sympathize with them, but I still want to do the things that seem right."

One of those things had been the now classic car chase, brilliantly directed by Peter Yates, who was making his first American film. The sequence would go on to spawn a legion of other car chases in films and telefilms for years afterwards. But none has ever achieved the originality or the excitement of *Bullitt*'s. I remember when Peter screened the first assembled footage of the car chase to the production crew. Bob Relyea came over to the house bursting with excitement and announced, "The public will forget the motorcycle chase in *The Great Escape*! Wait till they see this car chase. They'll go bananas! It is *great!*"

After *Bullitt* had been a week into its San Francisco location, Warner-Seven Arts demanded the company come home. Ken Hyman saw no reason why the rest of the film couldn't be shot on the lot, car chase included. Naturally the Solar group saw differently. Steve was incensed and refused the order. Filming continued as planned. He felt there were enough problems with the script, which was literally being rewritten on the set, without the studio's interfering.

Stan Kamen, after several meetings with Warner-Seven Arts, came to San Francisco and met with the Solar contingent in the Presidential Suite of the Fairmont Hotel. After the initial greetings, Stan came right to the point. "Fellas, our six-picture deal is now a one-picture deal!"

The group's reaction was not one of angry disbelief; rather, it was one of relief. Now they could proceed undisturbed and in peace. Steve was a lot less distressed about the situation with Warner-Seven

Arts than I thought he should have been. He felt no particular bitterness toward Ken Hyman; his first thought had been, Fuck 'em! He was a superstar and he was certain that Stan and Bob Relyea would find a home for Solar.

Two weeks after the meeting at the Fairmont Hotel, while Stan was busily seeking a new home for Solar, Steve in a rare forgiving gesture asked Bob to call Ken Hyman to smooth things out a little bit. "Ask him to come and look at the film. Tell him he'll like it!" Hyman was not inclined to be conciliatory. Relyea said that Hyman's curt reply was, "Well, I guess I'll catch it at the theater, folks."

End of conversation. End of contract.

A new pattern and a new Steve emerged in San Francisco. Steve began acting like a spoiled brat. As a movie star–tycoon on his way to building his empire, he began flexing his muscles. He demanded, for instance, that a pool table be installed in his rented apartment. The apartment was on the twelfth floor and the elevators were small—certainly not big enough to contain a pool table. "There's no way we can get a pool table up there, Steve. It's just plain impossible."

"Well, you guys think about that for a little bit more and tell me what you can come up with. Just remember, I want that pool table!" said the star.

The answer was a crane. They had to fly the pool table into the building with a crane. Not only that, but the rented apartment's huge front window had to be broken and repaired in order to swing the pool table into the living room. Peter Yates had been impressed and remarked, "You only get your way if you have power, and McQueen has power."

This remark of Peter's was applicable also to the welcome that was given Steve by the city of San Francisco. A sergeant and two patrolmen were permanently assigned by the police department to control traffic and provide security for Steve. The trio

was also used as an advance team to get things ready
before the company arrived for location shooting.
And Steve and Don Gordon (a close friend and
fellow actor) were allowed to ride in squad cars at
night to observe police business so they could better
understand the life of the homocide detective. And
because he was in San Francisco, right in the midst
of the youth movement, he felt moved to tell a reporter that young people "need leaders—constructive
leaders able to deal with them academically and po-
litically. And on the stage and screen they need to
see it as it is. That's the bag I'm in right now. . . .
The problem today is very basic—just a plain lack of
understanding. There is no rapport between today's
youth and their parents and cops. If all young people grow up hating cops, it is going to be a pretty
scary world."

He had finally come to realize that policemen were,
after all, only human, with the same hopes and dreams
he had. There's no question he believed what he was
saying; and to my practiced eye, there was also no
question Steve McQueen was now very impressed
with himself and with the impression he was giving
the world.

That Steve was growing full of himself there was
no doubt. Once in his dressing room, in the presence
of screenwriter Harry Kleiner and Peter Yates, I
witnessed a furious tirade over the word "obsequious." It had outraged Steve that he didn't know what
the word meant and he bellowed, "Obsequious . . . obsequious! What kind of a word is that? I don't know
what the hell it means and if I don't know you can
bet your sweet ass that those people in the theater
ain't gonna know either!" The word was part of a
sentence Kleiner had given the intellectual Bob
Vaughn character to say to Steve. To keep peace the
sentence was changed.

Steve was also registered as T. Crown downstairs
on the switchboard, and the name Thomas Crown

was printed on his mailbox. He also had his private
number (which presumably only I and one or two
other people had) listed under the name. He was still
giving out very positive and upbeat interviews regarding our life together, like, "I don't want to let
the money I'm making run away with me. Solid
values and beliefs I won't give up. The most important things in the world are my old lady and my
kids." To another reporter he philosophized, "There
are lots of divorces in this business for one reason.
You take guys, put them in the limelight—and trouble. Until then they're O.K.; but before long they
realize that all during the day they're surrounded by
all these people giving them love, love, love. So they
think, 'Why am I not happy all the time?' At home
you've got to work for the love you get. Earn it. The
hero suddenly thinks why should he work for this
love and respect when he can get it outside for free?
And the next thing you know he's off with a chorus
girl from the Sands."

He had, in fact, articulated for public consumption the feelings I had discussed with him at length—
which was all right with me. I think unconsciously I
already felt threatened and hoped my feeling of
uneasiness would pass. Since Steve enjoyed reading
his interviews and devoured everything that was written about him, I felt that maybe by reading his own
quotes the wisdom of his words might sink in. Steve
had the uncanny ability to believe what he was saying
at the moment. He preached against the evils of sin
like drugs and adultery and yet had a hard time
living it. (For instance, publicly, the Cheech and Chong
movies espousing drugs enraged him. Privately he
did what they did on the screen. When Ringo Starr
came to our house, he talked of the dangers of drugs
and belief in one's own publicity.) I think he wished
he could have been that person. He wanted to be
looked up to, and yet he couldn't bear to be left out
by the young people. He was so transparent to me,

and yet I was helpless. I knew firsthand that being a movie star made dealing with the outside world difficult, and I tried to be tolerant. After all, I was the woman "who shared the storms and sunbursts of life with this complex man" (as a reporter once wrote). I knew only too well about the predatory females who lurked at every corner.

What I didn't know was that he was already "entertaining" women in his apartment. I was not to learn about this "entertaining" until much, much later. But instinct told me the direction his life was taking, and I was being gently pushed away. I didn't understand why, and neither did he. Years later he would explain, "I felt compelled to do it and I couldn't stop. That fuckin' list [in the underground book] had twisted my head so bad, baby, that I felt I had to prove to the whole goddamn world I was Steve McQueen, super stud." Still, there was nothing overtly different in his behavior, which made it easy for me to disregard the warning signs. I kept repeating to myself, "It's all in your head, kid. Forget it."

To close observers, Steve was also becoming paranoid. Rick Ingersoll of the press relations firm that had been taking care of Steve for years had asked his secretary to get Steve on the phone. When Rick picked up the phone Steve chewed him out about the secretary's knowing his private number. "Now I'm gonna have to change my number!" he yelled. "Next time you dial yourself. I don't want strangers having my number. You got that?"

In a way it was reminiscent of another over-the-phone incident that had occurred when Rick, in an effort to help Steve on one of his earlier films, had told him to lighten up his behavior on the set. Rick had heard that Steve was causing a lot of problems. "Who told you?" he had asked menacingly.

"I don't remember," said Rick, not wanting to implicate anyone.

"Goddamn it, Rick, I've got enemies on that set and I wanna know!"

"Steve, I don't remember!"

"I don't believe you," Steve insisted.

Finally, exasperated with the line of questioning, Rick defiantly asked, "Are you calling me a liar?" Which in turn elicited the only response possible from Steve, convinced as he was that Rick had challenged him. "Maybe you'd like to step outside and settle this!"

The whole conversation was ludicrous, but in frustration, Steve fired Rick instead, which had made Rick's partner, David Foster, turn pale. Happily, in time, the matter was straightened out and all was forgotten.

This latest incident, though, was a bit more vicious and not quite so easy to ignore. Steve apologized to Rick a few days later, but unfortunately something had already been lost in the translation.

One Sunday, while still in the middle of filming *Bullitt,* we decided to catch a new movie that was breaking box office records. It was called *The Graduate* and overnight it made Dustin Hoffman a star.

As we left the movie house I could see Steve was bewildered. I kept looking at his face to see if I could detect in it what was bothering him. It was clear he wasn't ready to talk over just yet what it was he felt. I knew he had enjoyed the movie. His eyes had been riveted to the screen during the entire two hours. For a minute there I thought he might have been offended by the sacrilegious way the cross had been handled.

He remained thoughtful for a bit and then he blurted out, "What's gonna happen to us, do you suppose?"

"Us? What do you mean? Why should anything happen to us?"

"No, no. I mean 'us'—like Newman and me—you know?"

The man could be baffling sometimes. "No, I don't know. Tell me."

"God, baby, I can't believe this guy's going to be a movie star, can you? I mean, he is one ugly cat. Good actor, yeah, but he sure is homely!"

Dustin Hoffman's emergence in the cinema as a leading man dumbfounded him. Steve couldn't understand the public's fascination with this unconventional-looking actor. Time and again after that, Steve would stare at his image in the mirror and say to me, "Look at that, baby, take a look at that face and that body and tell me the truth. Who would you pick, him or me?" We would then both laugh, although I knew that he was serious.

Dustin Hoffman seemed to arouse my husband's insecurity over his durability, his ability to stay at the top. He called it the "brass ring" and spoke of "his lock on it." The good roles would continue to be offered to him, I knew; but as Steve aged I also knew they would not *always* be offered to him. And that would kill him, I thought, to relinquish those parts to someone who he felt didn't even look like a movie star. It was a strange way to feel, since Steve himself hadn't fit the Hollywood mold when he was making his way. Through the years he had challenged that leading-man mold, bending and twisting it until it conformed to his own persona. Now it seemed to him that a new generation of actors was emerging, intent upon fashioning *their* own mold— and he didn't like it.

On his thirty-eighth birthday I flew to San Francisco and went directly to the location. During the lunch break a cake was brought in, and the cast and crew sang "Happy Birthday!" I hadn't brought the children with me because it was midweek and we had decided school was more important. My plan had been to stay the week and then go home.

Although most of the action sequence had already been filmed, still on the agenda was the airport sequence, which included an encounter between Steve and a Boeing 707. That didn't thrill me a lot. I tried to talk him into using a double. I didn't care for stunts, and I shudder even today remembering *The Cincinnati Kid,* where Steve ran across those railroad tracks as a train whizzed by. I hadn't known about that one until after the fact because he hadn't shown me the call sheet. Rather, he had come home that night and matter-of-factly announced, "I did a stunt today." Anyway, this upcoming scene at the airport promised to be equally as dangerous. The plan was to have Steve run across the runway in pursuit of his quarry, just as a big jet fires its engines ready to begin its take-off run. Then Steve would either have to throw himself on the rough tarmac or else have a head-on collision with the steel monster.

Steve almost always performed his own stunts. The hairier the better for him. He thrilled at "living on the edge of infinity." And he was good at it. I was concerned about the other person—the pilot—on whom he had to depend. Would the pilot's instincts and reflexes be as keen as Steve's? Curiously, I had fewer qualms about stunts involving cars because Steve was always in command of his own vehicle. I knew he could maneuver himself out of any dangerous situation, as I had seen him do time and again.

As it turned out my worrying had been for naught; the stunt was successful and the risk taking had been worth it to him—especially since he had loved every minute of it! On film the sequence looked stupendous and dangerous, and the look of realism had been achieved.

When they resumed shooting on the streets of San Francisco that afternoon of the birthday celebration, I stayed on to watch and exchanged pleasantries with Steve's co-star, Jacqueline Bisset, who I thought was the most beautiful of Steve's co-stars, and then went on ahead to the apartment to shower, change, and cook a birthday dinner for Steve. When I got out of the shower, I spotted on the dressing table an unfamiliar-looking brush—a woman's—with long blond hair.

I stood there transfixed, staring at it for a long time hoping that maybe, just maybe, if I stared at it long enough it would disappear. Steve's words kept rushing at me vividly. *It's gonna be a heavy location, baby. I don't want to have to worry about you, too.* Indeed! That son-of-a-bitch! I picked up his radio and threw it against the mirror!

The mirror cracked and shattered from top to bottom.

"Good! I hope the whole thing falls on your goddamn head!"

There were flights back to L.A. leaving every hour on the hour, so all I would have to do was get myself to the airport. I was on my way home. There was no doubt about that. But first I wanted to give the creep his birthday present. I dressed and waited. The more I waited the more furious I became. By the time he walked through the door I was a raving maniac and he had been reduced from a creep to an asshole.

"Happy birthday, asshole!" I screeched as I flung the brush at him.

His mouth dropped. My greeting had momentarily confused him.

It took him a few seconds to recover and realize what I had discovered.

"Wait, baby, wait! Where're you goin'? You know it doesn't mean anything!" he said, trying to grab my arm as I went past him to the door.

"Don't touch me!" I turned and faced him squarely. "I am going home right now and I want you to do me a favor. Don't try to stop me and don't call me when I get home. I'll talk to you when I'm not too angry!" But really, I wasn't angry, I was in pain.

I didn't wait for the elevator. I ran all the way down the stairwell and into a cab.

For days after that scene in San Francisco, there was a frenzy of clichéd excuses—"I was drunk"—and a flurry of clichéd offerings—flowers and phone calls on the hour—before Steve made his way back into my good graces, if not my heart.

Always there were the children to think of. And then there were my mother's admonitions—"You make your own bed and you lie in it." As well as her all-time favorite, "Better the devil you know than the devil you don't know."

That year—1968—proved to be a long, long one. The mirror had cracked and the damage was already irreparable, but neither one of us "was hip to it yet."

By the time Steve returned from San Francisco the script that Paul had told him about the previous summer was ready. Only it came to Steve in the persons of David Foster (another partner in the public relations firm that represented Steve) and Bob Sherman, a talent agent. Both men at that time were starting to branch out as producers and had been entrusted with the script by William Goldman's agent. As soon as the studios became aware that McQueen and Newman were seriously interested in the property (still called *The Sundance Kid and Butch Cassidy*), a bidding war erupted among the studios that immediately blew Foster and Sherman out of the box as prices for the script skyrocketed into the hundreds of thousands of dollars. When the smoke had cleared, it was learned that Twentieth Century–Fox had paid William Goldman $400,000 for the script, thereby making him the highest paid screenwriter in motion picture history.

But a little problem arose.

Steve wanted billing over Paul—which was ridiculous, considering that Steve had made his film debut

in 1955 in a minor part (which was basically the
problem) in *Somebody Up There Likes Me,* starring Paul
Newman. Paul Newman had also gathered a few
Oscar nominations along the way, compared to Steve's
one, and Paul was as much a major star as Steve.

I thought Steve was being shortsighted, but he was
adamant. Then one night he woke me up and asked,
"What if I ask him to flip a coin for the top spot?"

"Come on, honey. Paul will never go for that. Put
yourself in his place." I turned around and looked at
him. "Would you?"

"Yeah, I would. You know I would," he replied as
he propped himself up on his elbow.

I had to smile. "Bullshit, honey. We both know
you wouldn't." He truly wanted to do this movie with
Paul, but he had boxed himself in by stubbornly
insisting on top billing. He thought flipping a coin
would be the way to save face and it would give him
a fifty-fifty chance of coming out on top.

Newman was no fool. He said no.

Then Freddie Fields, Paul Newman's agent, came
up with an idea that was wholeheartedly approved
by Paul. And that was to give Steve billing on the left
(which is the first position), while Paul's name would
be on the right, but raised higher than Steve's.

Or vice versa. Take your pick, Paul said. (Obviously, Paul didn't care about power trips. He was
secure enough not to need to. He simply wanted to
protect his rightful place.)

It was an innovative idea, but Steve couldn't decide. He asked Freddie's advice. "Which one would
you pick? The lower first or the higher second?"

Freddie said he thought Steve should choose the
lower.

Steve was thoughtful for a while and then agreed
with Freddie.

But by the time Freddie got to the door, relieved
that the billing problem had been surmounted, Steve
had changed his mind. He called to Freddie and

said, "No, no, man. I don't like it. Tell Paul I wanna flip coins."

Well—so much for *Butch Cassidy and the Sundance Kid.*

Meanwhile, Solar Plastics and Engineering patented a seat designed for dune buggies and four-wheel-drive vehicles and called it the Solar seat. Steve himself had designed this seat and was proud of the fact that the patent bore his name. In addition to the Solar seats, we were also manufacturing gas tanks, motorcycle fenders, and other parts for these recreational vehicles.

The Solar factory had a labor force of about thirty.

On the other end of town, Solar Productions was in preproduction for Steve's next movie, which was scheduled to start toward the end of summer. It was called *The Reivers,* and old friend Mark Rydell had been signed to direct. Solar Productions had found a new home base at Cinema Center Films, which was the new film division of the Columbia Broadcasting System.

This Solar employed several first-rate production people, their secretaries, Steve's Betsy, a public relations firm. Steve was having the offices decorated like an Italian villa, with lots of antiques, expensive wallpaper, plants, and key lighting.

Steve watched his empire grow with enthusiasm but with little or no regard to what was being spent. "You gotta spend money to make money," he exulted. "Besides, baby, money's rolling in. We ain't poor no more, you know!"

In reality both Solars were a couple of engines consuming gasoline at an alarming rate. I suspected it, but Steve was much too busy playing Howard Hughes to concern himself with such trivialities. And I assumed if and when the time came, our business manager would warn us about dwindling funds.

We went about our business as usual, and more

and more I saw changes in his attitude toward me and toward life in general. The one thing that never wavered was his attitude toward the children. He loved them and they knew it—no matter how strange Daddy acted sometimes.

We bought a new vacation house in Palm Springs, a much bigger and grander one than I cared to own in the desert. The house was in a new development called Southridge, which was located on a private road with a guardhouse at the entrance to the development. Since Steve had become a giant star it had become necessary to isolate our homes from the general public. Otherwise we often found ourselves at the mercy of crazies who thought it was their right to come to our house and demand to meet Steve because "I'm a big fan and I came all the way from Michigan to meet him!"—which happened many a time.

To prevent anyone from building right next to us, we also bought the lot next door. The house had two bedrooms upstairs, one for us and one for the children, and another bedroom downstairs for guests plus a separate guest house. Our bedroom had a porch, which looked onto the courtyard and swimming pool below. The whole house had floor-to-ceiling glass windows and sliding glass doors. It also had several structural steel beams outside which I had painted in different colors, making it unique. As soon as we closed on the house, I immediately went to work with decorator Peter Shore, whom I had known since our Solar Drive days and to whom I had entrusted the Oakmont Drive house. When the renovations got under way, Steve gave me a directive.

"Just think of this as my pad, baby, O.K.?" he said. "Decorate it as if it belonged to a man, a bachelor. No feminine stuff. You know what I mean?"

The man is serious, I thought. He's not kidding.

"Ah . . . just what are we proposing to do here?" I thought I'd best get the ground rules straight.

"Look, honey, this has nothing to do with you and me. I just want to feel like I have a house of my own. That's not too much to ask. The Oakmont house is more you than me [which was untrue], so I want Palm Springs to look like me." He said those words with such sincerity that I just stood there like a dummy, nodding my head!

My life was being thrown into disorder. I was feeling disconnected from the man I had married. At times it felt as though I were living with a stranger. Something was going on with him, and I couldn't get a bead on it. It was frustrating. It was the sort of thing one feels but can't put into words. Neither he nor I could communicate it to the other. But then it was becoming impossible to talk to him sensibly, since he was stoned most of his waking moments. His way of dressing was becoming very "mod" and very "hip." It was a self-conscious Steve who walked around in extra-wide bell bottom pants and a tank shirt and a self-conscious Steve who walked around with a mustache and love beads and gold chains. I noticed the gold St. Christopher medal I had given him in Las Vegas many years before had now vanished from around his neck. I had given it to him with the inscription, "To part is to die a little." He was a sentimental man, and he had never been without the medal and chain since that day I had given it to him. The medal is visible in all his movies up to and including *Bullitt*, with the exception of *The Cincinnati Kid*, when the chain had been in the jeweler's shop for soldering.

There was no point in inquiring about the medal. Steve had obviously removed it to make way for the love beads. (It did resurface in *Le Mans* briefly and then disappeared, never to be seen again.)

We were preparing to leave for Boston for the world premier of *The Thomas Crown Affair*, which he had happily consented to attend. Quite naturally everything was geared to Steve's presence during the premiere and the few days preceding it. Everything had been coordinated by Rick Ingersoll, who was also going to be traveling with us. Plans had been finalized and Boston awaited our arrival.

At half past midnight—just eight hours prior to our departure—Steve had a change of heart. He didn't want to go and asked me to call Rick to inform him. In a rather strained way, I opened the conversation. "Hi, Rick. Steve's sick and won't be able to go tomorrow."

Rick, aware of my husband's inability to follow through with plans without creating a rumble, immediately picked up my tone over the phone. In a very controlled manner he asked to speak to Steve.

"Rick. Man, I can't go. My ears are giving me trouble and the doctor says I shouldn't fly."

"Who's your doctor, Steve?" Rick asked as quietly as possible so as not to give the impression he was getting upset.

"Dr. Tarr," Steve said. "Dr. Lester Tarr."

Rick went on the offensive. "Oh, great! He lives just down the street from me. You don't mind if I talk to him, do you?"

"No, no, no! I don't want you to talk to him, goddamn it! I don't wanna go. That's it. Period!"

"Steve, it is now three in the morning in Boston. There is nobody I can get hold of. Preparations and scheduling have been arranged with your knowledge and cooperation. The entire plan cannot be changed. You must go."

Steve was pensive for a moment and then he asked, "What do you suppose Jeff Livingston will do if I cancel?" (Jeff Livingston was vice-president of advertising and publicity for United Artists—the studio responsible for the movie.)

Rick's response was "He will probably cut his throat."

Steve laughed softly and reluctantly said, "O.K. I guess we're going. See you in the morning, sport."

Steve did not speak to Rick for the entire plane trip.

However, once Steve ascertained it was going to be "first class" all the way, Rick was forgiven and the Boston trip proved to be a memorable experience. Steve was given a citizen's award by the state legislature and he in turn delivered a short speech to the esteemed group. "Steve McQueen Day" was then declared. Private parties were given everywhere in our honor and we even handed out prizes at a charity horse-racing event. But the premiere was the highlight of the trip. It was absolute bedlam, but it was exciting. When we got to the theater Rick and two deputies ushered me in as quickly as possible, while Steve had to be hoisted by policemen above the crowd when it looked like he might be trampled. As he was being carried into the theater, he looked the epitome of a movie star in his black tie and a white jacket with those baby blue eyes laughing all the way.

Steve and I were elated as once more we shared a special moment.

12

THROUGHOUT THE SUMMER of 1968, Steve was still giving out interviews that proclaimed our happiness to the whole world. "I like being married. I like my wife. Love is one thing, but I like her also—very, very much. She's part lover, part friend, part mother, part sister, but above all, we're pals. She's game as hell. If I get up off the couch at twelve o'clock at night, which I have done, and say 'Let's go,' we take off. Before we had the kids we could go on a moment's notice. Now I sometimes have to wait and get them out of school." "My wife is the very heart of my home," he said on another occasion. "Everything revolves around her. We're a close family."

These interviews gave me hope. Whatever it is that he is going through right now will pass, I said. He loves me. I just have to give him time and room to sort himself out.

That strategy was easier said than done. The renovations on our new desert house on Southridge were completed in six weeks' time. But the words "my pad" kept whirling around in my head, and with that in mind, in two days I spent somewhere in the neighborhood of $100,000 for the furnishings alone (a considerable sum today, but much more in 1968). I bought coldly and with a vengeance. I was feeling completely detached and alienated from the place and increasingly from him. I swept through the stores

203

with a "that, that, and that!" This was a big departure for me, since I don't buy anything unless I have a feeling for a particular piece. Everything in the Castle represented a part of our lives.

Then suddenly Steve decided we would go to Europe before he began his next picture, *The Reivers*. Claudia Cardinale and her husband, Franco Cristaldi (whom we had met when she and Steve were co-presenters at the 1964 Academy Awards), had invited us to visit them in Rome. The Cristaldis had two separate houses—one for her and one for him. They lived a mile away from each other just outside Rome. Her house was a renovated farm house designed for informal living while his was a bit more on the formal side, although his was equally as warm and charming as Claudia's. Franco's house contained the most elegant screening room I had ever seen. It was a salon, really, with red drapes and red and beige wallpaper and little shaded lamps lining the walls. I believe it accommodated twenty people.

I was fascinated by the way Claudia and Franco lived. She was a reigning movie queen and he a powerful and respected producer. To all appearances, their marriage was of the modern variety. And yet she was permitted very little latitude as far as her personal movements were concerned. When she visited California without Franco she would be escorted everywhere by one or two bodyguards. Steve and I, for instance, could not take her out alone. Whether the function be public or private, the bodyguards went, too.

Rome with Claudia and Franco was a real treat. They were gracious and enthusiastic hosts, showing us everything there was to see. We dined, we danced, we walked, we shopped, we sang, we sightsaw and gaped at the wonders of Rome. Steve was back to the Steve I knew and loved—funny, warm, and tender. The only thing that marred our trip to Rome was a brief episode with the notorious Italian paparazzi,

who had spotted us late one afternoon while we were
shopping. Probably because they were taken by surprise by Steve's presence on the Via Veneto, they
converged on us in a frightening way, and Steve and
I were forced to take refuge in a furrier's apartment
above his store. Furious negotiations ensued. In the
end we agreed to come out and pose for pictures if
they would leave us alone afterwards. Actually they
were very nice, though a little hysterical, and they
did keep their word.

For our last night in Rome, we decided to try a
lovely restaurant we had been told about. Steve and
I dressed in matching black leather outfits (and black
leather boots for me) we had purchased that afternoon. And of course we stood out like sore thumbs
in a sea of elegantly dressed people. But Steve's
philosophy was, I'm a movie star, darling. We can
wear anything we want. Nobody's gonna throw us
out! Dining in the restaurant, to our surprise, were
Cloris Leachman and three of her children, friends
from sunny California who had proudly ordered
their entire meal in Italian. We sat down to join
them and Steve immediately ordered two steaks and
two Coca-Colas—in English. Steve didn't believe in
ever making the effort to speak anyone's language.
"They hate you anyway!"

Our next stop was London, where we visited with
Sheila and Richard Attenborough and Mary and John
Mills. The Millses' daughter, Juliet, is a good friend.
The Attenboroughs took us to our very first soccer
game, which we found rough, tough, and exciting.
John Whitmore, one of Steve's racing buddies, was
there, but Stirling Moss was in Bermuda, so we missed
seeing him. Besides the socializing, we attended the
theater as often as we could. Steve had new suits and
jackets made by Doug Hayward, and I did my rounds
of the shops in London.

For this trip Steve had forsaken his new "hip" look
and dressed like a normal person. However, London

was bustling with its version of the flower children, and it was like a call from the wilds. The Playboy Club, an unlikely port of call for a married man, especially if said married man is on vacation with his wife, became a pit stop for Steve. Not for the nymphets that abounded there, but rather for his grass and "a-little-bit-of-coke" connection—or so he said.

Carrollton, Mississippi, was a time warp. It was America still in the early 1900s and it was perfect scenic locale for *The Reivers*, the film based on the William Faulkner book about a young boy's initiation into the world by two fun-loving rascals.

For Steve, however, it was another matter. We were billeted in a two-story motel along with the other cast members and the production crew in the tiny town of Greenwood. Our rooms on the second floor had to be boarded up at the railings due to the curious eyes of the onlookers. The presence of a superstar in their midst had electrified the townspeople, and they came to the motel religiously, day after day and night after night, hoping to catch a glimpse of Steve.

I arrived in Greenwood with Bruce Lee two weeks after the company set up shop. Bruce was a sight. (This was about two years before he became a household word by way of his Hong Kong–made karate–kung fu movies.) He went everywhere in his karate outfit and people thought he was my bodyguard. Before Steve left for location, Bruce had come over to visit and give him a refresher course in kung fu. I liked Bruce; he was a really good influence on Steve because he believed in clean living. No cigarettes, no drugs, no caffeine, and plenty of good health food and vitamins. Taking care of his body was a top priority for Bruce, while Steve seemed intent on abusing his. Oh, he did take vitamins and he did work out, but he smoked like a fiend, drank his coffee–with–three sugars, and, most serious, he was now heavily indulging in drugs.

Until now, Steve had never been late for filming, had always known his lines. This movie was different.

He was king at the box office, head of his own production company, and intoxicated by the sweet smell of success (and God knows what else). He now viewed himself as a filmmaker. His demeanor changed. He became contradictory and ornery and made life hell for director Mark Rydell. Mark called this "Steve's looney-bin period." He continually questioned Mark's directorial judgment (adding insult to injury, Steve did this in front of cast and crew). Mark was reluctant to have a confrontation, since he had gotten this job through Steve's "good graces." In desperation, Mark would call Norman Jewison for advice on how to handle Steve. Norman must have been at a loss himself, because this was a new Steve.

The unit photographer also came under attack. He made the mistake one day of marking the envelopes containing the pictures he had taken on the set "For Mrs. McQueen's approval." This practice was more or less routine, since I generally did mark the pictures that were suitable for release—that is, pictures that looked good—when I was on the set. In the past we had found it more convenient to deal with the on-the-set pictures in this manner. Not anymore. Steve felt it was demeaning to his stature in the industry.

When we arrived home, *The Reivers* had to shut down for four weeks due to an accident. Mitch Vogel, the young boy in the movie, had been practicing riding his horse during a lunch break when unexpectedly the sprinklers went on. The horse had become spooked and Mitch was thrown off and his arm broken.

During this enforced shutdown, Steve and I threw ourselves a twelfth anniversary party at the Candy Store, and Steve gave me a big canary-yellow heart-shaped diamond ring. It was, he said, for "being with me and earning your bread" on all those locations. And then he added, "If it weren't for you, baby, I'd still be snarling and clawing my way out of the jungle. Thank you."

I was touched and once again I felt all that other stuff was not worth worrying about. All would be well.

While Mitch Vogel recuperated, Steve demanded that Mark put together a rough assemblage of what had been shot so he could view it. Mark knew it would be disastrous to show Steve anything but the daily rushes. A director has an overall view of his movie and can visualize missing scenes because he knows how they fit into the scheme of things. Not an actor. Especially not this actor, who was making no secret of his antagonism toward his director. Steve would sometimes wake up in the middle of the night angrily denouncing himself for having hired Mark.

And now the stage was set for a showdown.

Mark tried to stave it off by going to Bob Relyea.

"Bob, this is no good. I just know this is suicidal. We only have six weeks' worth out of a fourteen-week shooting schedule. How the hell is he gonna make sense out of that? Give me a break! He's gonna hate it!"

Bob had about as much power to say "no" to Steve as Mark did. Steve wanted the rough footage and he wanted to see it real quick!

As Mark predicted, Steve went berserk when he saw the rough assemblage. He demanded Mark's immediate dismissal. Fortunately, Gordon Stulberg, the head of Cinema Center Films, put his foot down. He was behind Mark Rydell a hundred percent and there was to be no firing. Mark stayed.

Mark was now Steve's enemy for having survived his wrath. He made life really wretched for Mark. After two or three takes Steve would refuse to perform, most especially in scenes with Rupert Crosse, who played the other reiver and whose acting juices didn't cook until the eighth or ninth take. Mark developed a system. When the scenes involved Rupert and Steve, Mark would stand in for Steve until the eighth take. Then he would ask an assistant to get Steve out of his trailer. It was the one job the assistants hated. They were petrified of going to his trailer because he would hurl epithets at them. The crew had become very sympathetic toward Mark and kept out of Steve's way. He was the boss and he was the star and they were frankly terrified of him.

Then came the day of filming the movie's climax, a horse race that had to be won by the young boy in order for the reivers to retrieve the car they had lost on a bet. Mark had pointedly informed Steve the setup was going to take a little while. "We'll give you enough warning so you'll have enough time to get ready, all right?"

Steve glowered at his director and turned away and grunted.

Mark had everything all set and ready to go before he made a move to call Steve to the set. He was prepared to have Steve keep him hanging for up to fifteen, twenty minutes. That was better than calling Steve out when Mark wasn't quite ready. Although it wasn't likely, Steve could conceivably come out right then and there and, God knows, all kinds of problems could arise. There's no point to it, Mark thought. Better me than him right now.

Mark had nine cameras positioned ready to roll, the racehorses were in place, the principals stood patiently, the whole place was properly lit, and hundreds of extras only awaited the director's command for "Action!" to do their stuff.

And Steve refused to come out of his trailer.

He refused to come out until he was good and ready. He wanted to show them just who was the rightful boss. And when he did come out, a few hours later, he was wasted. He went directly to center stage, smiled his charming smile, and innocently asked Mark, "Hi! You been waitin' for me?"

Bullitt had been released at year's end and quickly became a top grosser. Never mind that the script was muddled and convoluted; what mattered was McQueen and all that action. The car chase alone was worth the price of admission, thanks to Bill Fraker's camerawork and Peter Yates's direction. The film was listed by the *New York Times* as one of the year's best, one of only three American films to make it that year. Peter Yates became an important international director and Steve won the NATO (National Association of Theatre Owners) Male Star of the Year Award for the year 1969.

Solar Productions, now a very successful production company, basked in *Bullitt*'s glory; and during interviews, Steve talked a lot about one's dignity as an actor, the dignity of the filmmaker, and his dignity as a human being. "I've got a feeling I'm leaving stardom behind, you know. I'm gradually becoming more of a filmmaker, acquiring a different kind of dignity from that which you achieve in acting."

God help me, I recall thinking, he has become so full of himself. He is actually boring to listen to. What happened to his sense of humor? What happened to that looseness? But how could I get that through to him? He was in no mood to listen. He was reveling in all that power—not to mention all the adulation coming to him from every corner of the earth. How the hell was I to deal with that?

And now it really did start. He was getting all that free love from the outside. Coming home and having to work for love seemed unfair to him.

He seemed to have suddenly placed unrealistic expectations on happiness. He had to be happy every day at every moment of the day, and when he wasn't, he blamed me. After all, if he weren't married, he reasoned, he wouldn't have the feelings that made him feel guilty and, therefore, made him unhappy.

On top of all this, plans were being made for Solar to go public. It all sounded so-o-o grand, although I wasn't quite sure what it meant—only that we were to retain 60 percent of the company and the remaining 40 percent would be sold to the public at $9 a share. I simplistically thought this probably was the way to recoup all that money that was running through our fingers like water.

Early one evening John DeLorean, then the big chief at Chevrolet, and his then wife, the beautiful and young Kelly Harmon, came to the Castle to toast Chevrolet's new affiliation with Solar and Steve McQueen. Chevrolet had just agreed to supply a fleet of cars to Solar for the production company. It was also to deliver some Chevy Blazers to Solar Plastics for racing the Baja 500; Solar would equip the trucks with Solar seats. On top of that it was agreed that a new Chevy pickup truck would be made especially for Steve. In return all Steve had to do was drive the cars. (Steve rejected Chevrolet's offer to become the company's spokesman, and DeLorean was satisfied that the public simply see Steve driving his Chevies.)

When the call came from Detroit announcing that Steve's brown pickup truck was ready, Steve called the company go-fer, Mario Iscovich, only eighteen years old, into his office and gave him an hour's worth of instructions on how to get the truck from Michigan to the Castle as fast as possible, safely and unscathed. Candidly Steve had told Mario he didn't trust anyone with the truck and was relying on him to follow his driving instructions to the nth degree. "Don't fuck up, kid," were Steve's parting words to Mario.

Mario had just met Steve recently and was in awe of him. A gentle, overweight Jewish-Argentinian who was raised in the San Fernando Valley, he also liked his job (in his position as jack-of-all-trades at Solar Plastics, Mario had become an invaluable asset) and had no intention of "fucking up" as his boss had warned him. The kid drove sixteen hours a day for three days to get the truck to Steve, and all Steve did was scowl at Mario for not having done it in two days!

Steve was developing a grudging admiration for Mario. He was eager as hell, which Steve liked. But Steve was also a very suspicious man, his attitudes exacerbated, I now feel, by his heavy use of grass and coke and beer. He kept trying to figure out "where this kid was at"—then a favorite phrase of Steve's.

One day Mario received some bizarre instructions from Willow Springs, where Steve was supposedly racing. He hadn't been in the office when the call came, and the message indicated that Steve wanted Mario to see him race. "Take the charter out," the message had read. Mario called Willow Springs and found out that Steve had already raced, but since he couldn't communicate directly with Steve he found himself in a quandary. "Do I go or do I not go?" Mario decided he should go. He was, after all, an employee, and the instructions had been to go.

The charter plane landed Mario right by the raceway and he saw a red-faced Steve running toward him yelling, "What the fuck are you doing here?"

Mario, in shock, could only say, "Steve, you told me to come!"

"Goddamn it, you little shit! This is a secret operation! Do you see any race cars around?" And as an afterthought, Steve added, "You think I'm Mr. Moneybags taking that charter? Huh?"

Mario was beside himself. He didn't know what to do. "Do you want me to go home?"

"I'll take you home," the pilot interjected, feeling sorry for Mario.

"*No*, goddamn it! He's staying!" Steve shouted.

After several uneasy moments, Steve meandered back to his 908 Porsche Spyder and his mechanics and Mario went to Steve's trailer, where Jimmy Jimenez, Steve's driver, gave Mario a taco to steady his nerves. Unfortunately Steve walked in just as Mario started to eat. He went right up to Mario and yanked the taco away from him, saying, "What the fuck are you doing eating? You haven't worked hard enough!"

By this time Mario was totally confused. He said to himself, My God, I've got a major prick on my hands! Not only that, he's paranoid, too!

Despite the untidy beginnings, Steve grew to love and trust Mario, and the kid came to understand and forgive Steve his wild personality swings.

Mario and I also became close friends. He was the younger brother I would have liked to have had and I was the older sister he had imagined for himself. We had the added bond of being Latin and speaking Spanish fluently.

In February of 1969 our friend Rupert Allan asked me to join him on his yearly trip to Monaco. I immediately said yes since I desperately needed to get away from the craziness that was beginning to engulf my life. Maybe I could come up with an answer while I was away and on my own. I had toyed with the idea of seeing a psychiatrist but I knew Steve would be vehemently opposed to it, sure as he was they were nothing more than a passing fad. (I had seen one in 1963 without telling Steve. I had consulted with the doctor on how to handle my husband, who was driving me up the wall because I had let my hair grow out during the German location for *The Great Escape*. Steve preferred my hair short and said something derogatory about letting my hair grow almost every day. And because he did I became more tenacious. At first I was able to laugh it off, but by the following year it had gotten to me. When I saw the psychiatrist and explained to him what my predicament was, he said, "Well, you ought to be grateful he's not unhappy with your legs. Those you can't do anything about. Your hair you can. So why don't you cut your hair and get it over with?" I laughed as I saw the logic of his advice and immediately went and got my hair cut short.)

I determined to leave all my worries behind and have a wonderful time in Monaco. It was the time for Monaco's yearly television festival, and the place was bustling with actors. Princess Grace, as usual, was wonderful to me, making sure I was seated at her table. I had been asked to present the Best Director award, and on a whim I brought along the same dress I had worn at the Golden Globe Awards dinner the year before. The dress had caused a sensation because the full lavender jersey skirt seemed to cascade down from the center of my lavender sequin-studded bra. The dress came with a lavender jersey Grecian-style coat. It was all in very good taste, but a bit risqué then.

At dinner Grace kept encouraging me to take off my coat, but I was a bit reluctant. Finally, after much urging from Her Serene Highness, I acquiesced. And she jubilantly said, "Ah, that's better!" She was a super lady. She liked to refer to herself as the "bourgeoise" princess, but to me she was the *only* real princess in the world because she was so breathtakingly beautiful.

Rupert and I went on to Spain from Monaco, then to Paris, and then to London and then home.

Steve picked me up at the airport and my homecoming was a little strained, although he said he was happy I was back. And then he announced he had just rented Vincent Price's beach house at Leo Carrillo Beach for the duration of the year. I laughed and said, "We're the only people I know with three houses in Southern California. One in town, one in the desert, and now one at the beach."

"Aha. But with a difference," was his wry reply.

"This one is my crash pad. That means I want your word you're to tell me before you use it."

I no longer doubted that the profound personality change Steve had undergone was here to stay. I felt totally helpless but did and said nothing because frankly I had no idea how to tackle the problem. Nothing in my life had ever prepared me for what faced me now. Here was my husband going through life as if he were a kid turned loose in a candy store. This living legend was fast approaching middle age and he felt life passing him by. His mid-life crisis, it appears, was exacerbated by the new sexual permissiveness that was sweeping the world. Once discreet about his affairs, he now felt compelled to flaunt them. As he was to say later, "I went through this town like Grant took Richmond." And so I went about my life as normally as I could. We still interacted as man and wife and still interacted as a family. But there was no harmony. It was heartbreaking and hollow at the same time.

It was Easter vacation, and Terry and Chad and I had driven to Palm Springs in one of the station wagons supplied by Chevrolet. Steve was already down there, having driven the night before with Mario Iscovich, whom Steve had begun to confide in. I hadn't expected Mario, but I was grateful when I saw his smiling face welcoming us to sunny Palm Springs.

It was "pretend time" for everyone. Steve and I had become so estranged from each other it was difficult to carry on a conversation. The children could feel the tension in the air although we all tried our best to distract them. Mario, who was obviously aware of the situation, inadvertently became the babysitter for a few days as he entertained them and took them into town. He was a considerate and sensitive young man who I know fervently hoped our problems could be resolved.

Years later Mario told me, "Steve was stoned all the time. That house on Southridge was a veritable whorehouse. He picked these girls up from any-where. He even picked up hitchhikers! I used to ask him, 'Why do you do this? You're gonna blow it all, Steve. You've got a great wife and you've got great kids!' His answer was, 'Hey, look at me. I'm the leading sex symbol in the whole world, man. I want it all.' I didn't know what to tell him. I just knew he was crazy!"

I was outside by the pool one afternoon, thinking what a nice job I had done decorating this house on Southridge despite the lack of feeling I had for it. Mario was riding bicycles with Chad and Terry, and Steve was upstairs in a euphoric state. I was dis-tracted from my thoughts by a young, open-faced man who called to me from across the pool.

"Hi," he said. "I'm the electrician. Is Mrs. McQueen around?"

I had called the electrician because of a faulty wall socket in the children's bathroom.

"Oh, hi," I answered. "Thanks for coming so fast. I'm Mrs. McQueen. Come. I'll show you where the problem is."

I noticed a slight hesitation and then he said, "I didn't recognize you with your hair dark like that. Sorry."

I caught my breath and as steadily as I could I asked, "Do you like it better this way or the other way?" To which this not-too-bright man shyly re-plied, "Well, I like blondes most of the time, but on you dark hair looks better."

I left the man in the children's bathroom with instructions to let himself out as soon as he was through. Then I went into our bedroom, where I found Steve, spread out on the bed, looking up at the ceiling and puffing away on a roach as the music blasted through the walls.

I walked past him, showered, dressed, and informed him I was going home. By myself. "You take care of the children for the next few days. I've got to get away from you for right now or I'll go mad. I'll tell the children something that'll make sense to them."

Having Mario there at the time was a godsend. The children were safe in his hands, I knew—as they were in Steve's, for that matter. Steve did have limits. He was always capable of pulling back and functioning well within the boundaries of saneness when he had to.

When Easter vacation was over we decided he should stay in Palm Springs or at the beach. Nobody had to know we were separated. We were not ready for the world to know that. Steve's absence from the Oakmont house appeared normal to the average eye. He was the peripatetic type anyway—what with his bikes and cars—and the children were able to accept that.

For Terry's tenth birthday, we all reunited at Disneyland. Terry's friends, Chad, Mom and Dad. Steve came from Palm Springs and the rest of us came from Brentwood. I had been apprehensive and had decided to go through with the outing for Terry's sake. It turned out to be a wonderful day. Steve was great with the children. He brought them all Mickey Mouse watches. And his attitude toward me was warm and complimentary. By the end of the week we were together again. He had missed me, he said. "What I go through once in a while has nothing to do with my love for you, you know. That's here and that other thing is there," he explained. It wasn't easy to accept the bullshit, but I kept telling myself I had to make the marriage work if only for the children's sake.

What I didn't realize until much later was my need to make it work for my sake. I was afraid to face the world without this man by my side because so much of my life was wrapped up in his.

For my thirty-fifth birthday Steve surprised me

with a party at Upstairs at the Bistro. I was caught totally unaware. With Betsy Cox's help, Steve was able to get my group of friends together. Jim and Lois Garner, Henry and Ginny Mancini, the George Schlatters, Don and Bek Gordon, Ann Smith, Stan Kamen, Sue Mengers, and a few others I can't remember. I do remember Jay Sebring had arrived with a trampy-looking girl and Steve threw them both out angrily with a "Not around my old lady, man!" We had a terrific night and everything seemed to be back on track again.

Solar was in the process of producing its first film without Steve, *Adam at 6 A.M.*, starring a young Michael Douglas and Joe Don Baker. Steve had also agreed to finance Bruce Brown's motorcycle-racing documentary, *On Any Sunday*, which turned out to be a real winner. When it was released in 1971 the *New York Times* called it "a clearly envisioned, simply told, beautifully made documentary."

Then Charles Champlin, the Los Angeles *Times* film critic, called to ask if we might be willing to open our house to a delegation of Russian editors touring the United States under State Department auspices. The Russians, Chuck said, had wanted to meet Hollywood. With that in mind, Steve recruited everyone from Ringo Starr to Peter Sellers and Jennifer Jones. Steve had returned from his *Reivers* location with a supply of moonshine whiskey in mason jars. He now pressed it on the Russians, who coughed appreciatively and pronounced it a superior beverage. To a local journalist attending the party he said, "You can't have any; you didn't like my last picture enough." Then he grinned and extended the jar.

After this Russian party we decided to spend the weekend in Palm Springs. Steve wanted to put some time in with his motorbike. The Baja 500 was coming up, Sebring looked like a real possibility, and *Le Mans* would at last begin filming in June of the following year; he wanted his reflexes as sharp as

possible. I was uneasy about the Palm Springs house.
The house seemed to have a hex on me. I prayed all
would go well.

It didn't.

I found a strange dress in my closet and I said,
"Oh God, here we go again." To add insult to injury,
Steve tried to convince me it was Elmer Valentine's
girl friend's dress.

I went to New York for a few days—again to get
away—and on the flight home, still despondent and
angry, I found myself sitting next to a highly respected actor of the brooding European variety. He
was dark, wildly handsome, and romantic. This charming Casanova was also the proud possessor of an
Academy Award for Best Actor, having won the
gold statuette for a riveting performance a few years
back, in a film laden with other heavyweight stars.

During the flight, he lavished all his attention on
me. I suddenly felt wanted, pretty and feminine.
Quite the opposite of what I had been feeling at
home. And as our conversation progressed I found
my mind wandering ever so often, thinking of home
and Steve and the last few blatant trysts he'd had.
How dare he soil the nest, the son-of-a-bitch! The
more I thought about it, the angrier I became, although I must have kept it well under control. Casanova explained he was going to California to discuss
his next film project. He would like to see me, he
said. He would be staying at the Beverly Hills Hotel
and he would be there for a few days and it would
please him enormously if I could meet him during
his stay in town.

My first reaction had been to say, "No, I'm a
married woman. I don't believe in cheating on my
husband." It is a fact of life in Hollywood that when
a fairly attractive woman is married to a superstar,
she becomes even more attractive to other men in a
perverse way. Ever since I had committed to settling
down and being a wife and mother, the thought of

having an extramarital relationship of any kind had never crossed my mind.

And yet, on this day, feeling put upon and taken for granted by my husband, I found myself smiling at the handsome Casanova and having no doubt at all that soon I would be in his arms.

My vengeful idyll with the handsome and foreign Academy Award–winning star proved to be a Pyrrhic victory, a fact I wouldn't be aware of for another year. Presently it amazed me how clever I was in covering my tracks. I would drive to the Beverly Hills Hotel in my Excalibur rather than a nondescript car, having come to the conclusion that the more visible I was the less suspicion I was likely to arouse. I was terrified Steve might find out. It will be instant death, I kept repeating to myself. And yet I couldn't make myself stop. "At least I'll have gotten him where he lives, the son-a-bitch!" At the moment it was what mattered to me. And yet when the brief affair was over, I was surprised to find myself guilt-stricken and feeling even emptier than before.

Steve continued to stay on at the beach or in Palm Springs, depending on where the action was for him. He would come by every two or three days to spend time with the children and then make his excuses about having to be alone so he could work on his scripts. I continued to live life as best I could. I went to parties and other social events with friends and more often than not Steve would surprise me by showing up unannounced. And when it was imperative we show up together, we did. One such occasion was a small dinner party at Danny Kaye's. Danny was cooking one of his famous Chinese meals. Sharon Tate was there, looking beautiful in a chic black maternity outfit. She was then four and a half months pregnant and positively glowed with impending motherhood. Roman Polanski, her husband, was in Europe and she had come alone. As fate would have it,

it was the last time I would ever see her. Steve would
see her a few more times because of her relationship
with Jay Sebring. Jay remained a close friend to
Sharon after her marriage to Roman, and occasionally Jay and Steve would visit Sharon at her Cielo
Drive house.

In public Steve and I would act just as any other
married couple did, so that very few people were
wise to the truth. But the loving manner that had
once characterized our relationship in public and in
private had long since vanished.

Shortly after my liaison with the Academy Award
winner ended, I awoke to find my husband standing
on the porch outside my bedroom door. It was 3:00
A.M. Steve didn't have his keys so he couldn't get in
unnoticed. I said, "What do you want, Steve?" For
one brief moment I thought he had found out about
my affair and it was showdown time—until I realized
the man was barely holding on to himself. He was
flying high.

"Let me in, baby. I feel sick," he whispered.

"Go find yourself a doctor, Steve. I'm tired and
I'm going back to bed."

"Please, honey. I really am sick. I need you you
take care of me." He was sounding desperate, but I
didn't want to give in.

"Good night, Steve. Go find yourself one of your
girl friends to take care of you."

"Please, baby. I really am strung out. I need to
come in." By now he was begging and I hadn't the
heart to send him away.

I opened the door and let him in. He put his arms
around me and I could feel his body shaking and he
felt clammy. "Hi, Nellie," he said. "God, I'm so tired."
There was no doubt about that. He looked as if he
was ready to drop from exhaustion. He had been on
a coke binge for days and needed to dry out. I
wondered silently as I looked at him who he was

hanging out with these days. I wasn't sure I really wanted to know.

I spent the rest of the night and the first hours of the morning tending to Steve's needs. Taking off his clothes, washing him down with warm water and alcohol, making him tea, letting him talk. Fortunately, going down to the kitchen was unnecessary since we had an efficiency unit upstairs.

What had started out as fun and games many years ago had gone far beyond that. But was this what is known as an addiction? I certainly didn't know. Steve was self-indulgent and he was self-destructive, but he also had great willpower. He had the ability to stop and recognize the danger signs of going over the edge. He would get scared and then he'd pull back. There'd be a lull for a while when he would espouse the evils of drugs and talk about how it screws up one's head. Periodically he would also go through his game of cleaning everything out that was in the house. He'd either give his stash away or throw it down the toilet. All of it. And then in a matter of hours panic would set in and he'd have somebody bring him the less "harmful" grass. Days would go by where he would have nothing stronger than grass, but pretty soon it would escalate to coke and the cycle would start over again.

On Thursday, August 7, 1969, Jay Sebring came by the house to give Steve a little trim. When I said good-bye to Jay that afternoon little did I dream it was the last good-bye. Steve and Jay had agreed to meet up with each other the following evening after dinner at Sharon Tate's house. Jay wanted to visit with Sharon before going to San Francisco for the weekend and to remind and reassure her that while husband Roman Polanski was away, Uncle Jay was there if he were needed.

Steve had looked at me inquiringly and asked, "You don't mind, do you, baby?" The question was meaningless. I was beyond minding. And anyway

Steve did what he wanted to do. All I did was go through the motions.

As it turned out, luck was with Steve that following Friday night. He had run into a little chickie whom he fancied and decided to forgo Jay.

By late morning of the following day came the news of the gruesome murders on Cielo Drive. Both Sharon Tate and Jay Sebring had been murdered in a bizarre fashion. Also murdered were two of Sharon's friends, Abigail Folger and her boyfriend, Voytek Frykowski.

There was fear in the air. Nobody talked of anything else for days. Steve was in shock. His narrow escape had been too close for comfort. Steve told me he had run into Elmer Valentine the night before and had decide to go slumming with him instead. (The truth was revealed to me several months later.)

Sharon Tate was buried the following Wednesday. We did not attend her funeral. Not knowing what madness was still out there, Steve felt one funeral for the day would have to suffice. We elected not to attend Sharon's and to go instead to Jay's funeral, since he had been a much closer friend than Sharon.

Those of us who came together in one car sat in the front and second rows of the church. The group included Steve, me, Elmer Valentine, Henry Fonda, Warren Beatty, and Jim Garner. Steve carried a gun in his breast pocket. Just in case. At the church at Forest Lawn I was shocked to find Jay in an open casket. But considering his violent death, the morticians had done a masterful job.

As we sat waiting for the service to start, a strange man climbed up to the altar where Jay's body lay and began a bizarre chant. Nobody knew who he was and it galvanized everyone present to attention. Warren Beatty, who was sitting next to me, was ready to throw me onto the floor, fearful that some sort of altercation was about to occur. He was aware Steve had a gun and was concerned what might happen if anybody opened fire. But somebody removed the man who was chanting in front of Jay's body and order resumed.

For the next few weeks the whole town, it seemed, was under investigation. Certainly the police went through Jay's phone book and contacted everyone in it. Steve never went anywhere without a gun now. Even I had to sleep with a gun under my pillow—as per Steve's direction. Paranoia ran rampant everywhere and several weeks later, when it was learned Steve McQueen's name had been on that murder list, Steve called on his friends from the CIA to help secure our house.

Then finally, after many, many weeks, Charles Manson and his Family were apprehended, and though no one could comprehend the reason for the wanton murders, Hollywood, once more, breathed a little easier.

In the fall of 1969 we did two Baja races. And in between we went to Phoenix to test the Baja Boot, Solar's very own dune buggy. Present all three times were Steve, me, Mario, Haig Altounian, Steve's head mechanic, and Jim Garner. Being the unforgiving man that he sometimes was, it had taken Steve two years to force himself to speak to Jim after the *Grand Prix* incident. But now the two men were friends again, though on a rather tenuous footing because Steve was not particularly keen on sharing the limelight.

Steve was back to smoking and snorting, and in Phoenix one night we drove to the Playboy Club for dinner. We had a new trailer home with us, a Cortez, and as the parking attendant directed us to a parking area a bit away from the building, Steve decided to drive the trailer home right onto the front steps of the club. He stepped on the gas, drove over the curb, and in the process ruined the undercarriage of the Cortez. Steve was laughing hysterically. He thought it was very funny, although nobody else did.

I believe that one of the side effects of drug abuse is paranoia. Steve had illusions that people were coming after him. For instance, we'd be driving from somebody's home to ours when he'd look in his rearview mirror and immediately suspect the car behind was following us. "Somebody is out to get me!" And so we'd go zigzagging from one road to another, and instead of being home in fifteen minutes, it would take an hour.

There were other changes. Where he had once sneered at the Hell's Angels, he now saw them as folk heroes. Also, the Woodstock Festival of that summer impacted itself in Steve's imagination in a serious way. The kids had shown the world that "one should do what makes one happy." Steve dug it because "it was meaningful, man!"

For Christmas vacation and for Chad's ninth birthday, we decided to take the children to Sun Valley. Steve and I were once more together—if one could call it that. This was not my Steve. It was somebody else's Steve. Spurning his London wardrobe and his "businessman" image, he was back to sporting his hippie mustache and his bell bottoms. His outrageous flirting with young—really young—girls infuriated and embarrassed me. I removed myself from his side as often as I could. There was no point in ranting and raving. Face it, Neile, I kept telling myself, the man is simply out of control. His demons had been steadily eating away at our relationship. We had a good time together only when we were surrounded by other people. And even then I kept my distance. For the children's sake, when they were around, I pretended all was hunky-dory.

Toward the end of that year, just before our Christmas vacation, a man named William Maher became an important part of our lives. Solar Plastics and Engineering's manager, concerned with the amount

of money the company was losing, called his friend
Bill Maher in Chicago and asked him to come out
and do a little troubleshooting. Bill agreed, but only
for a little while, since he had other businesses to
attend to. Steve had given the manager his blessing
in the matter of consulting with Bill Maher. Then
after Steve's first meeting with Bill, he thought it
might be a good idea for the new man also to take a
look at the inner workings of Solar Productions, to
see what could be done to keep costs down. It was
finally dawning on Steve that the *Bullitt* profits were
being depleted by the two Solars. He liked being "big
man," but the overheads were high.

Weeks went by as Bill Maher continued his investi-
gations into the inner workings of these two compa-
nies. Bill was amazed that after the initial meeting
with Steve, he had almost no further contact with
him. Steve didn't seem to be interested in the first
stages of his findings and it irked Bill. He didn't like
being taken for granted even though he was being
paid for his work.

Three months later, Bill, at last, heard from Steve.
He invited Bill to come to the house for a meeting,
then informed him our business manager had also
been invited.

When everybody was seated in Steve's den at the
Castle, Bill very tersely said, "Steve, I hereby give
you my notice to quit. I've been offered another job,
and before you say anything, you're broke." Before
Steve could respond, Maher continued, "You are
bankrupt. And don't let anybody tell you otherwise."

With that, our business manager said, "Well, I
wouldn't say he's bankrupt exactly. Steve is just not
solvent."

So there it was. We actually had no cash! It had
taken only two years. How can that be? Thank God,
Steve was still a huge star. If we were lucky we could
get ourselves out of this mess before it was too late!

Steve made some fast decisions that day. He offered Bill Maher a job to put our finances in order, and our association with our business manager came to an end.

I've heard it said that men who lose businesses they've created become emotionally incapacitated because so much of their ego is involved in the creation of those entities. If so, maybe the events that were soon to follow engendered so much rage in Steve because his dream empire had collapsed. Coupled with this would be his betrayal by the one person in the world he trusted.

II

The End: 1970–1980

13

IN THE LIFE OF Mr. and Mrs. Steve McQueen, 1970 was a cataclysmic year. The upheaval was such that neither one would be the same again.

For better or for worse came to pass, and the loss of innocence was complete. And as two people are always different from each other, so too, is the healing process different.

A stranger looking in would have laid odds on the male half of the partnership's surviving the emotional upheaval much better than the female half—who, after all, had become so immersed in her spouse's life that to think of herself after fourteen years together as someone other than his wife seemed impossible.

In fact, the reverse would prove to be true.

Most probably, the events that were to lead to the final disintegration of my marriage to Steve might have been averted had I not come to Le Mans that summer. But fate has a way of egging on the gods that control us so that what happens to us seems almost predestined.

Plans for Steve to participate in the twelve-hour Endurance Race at Sebring in March had long been set in motion. The timing couldn't be more perfect. The filming of *Le Mans* was to commence in the summer, and all Steve would have to do was make a passable showing at Sebring and a flurry of publicity was assured. A new 908 Porsche Spyder was supplied by the Porsche people for Steve's use, aware as they were of the windfall that was sure to come, win or lose. Not only that, but the soft-spoken Peter Revson, a respected driver in his own right, consented to be Steve's co-driver. They made quite a duo, the violently colorful movie star and the handsome millionaire sportsman.

Aside from the twelve-hour Endurance Race in Sebring, Florida, Steve very much wanted to drive in the real twenty-four-hour race of Le Mans, with Jackie Stewart as his racing partner, no less. Jackie Stewart was too sensible a man. He didn't need McQueen. Stewart was being touted as the next racing champion of the world. (Graham Hill held the title at the time.) Steve was good, very good. But Steve was still an amateur who couldn't compare with the world-class grand prix drivers who did this sort of thing for a living. As a matter of fact, Jackie Stewart was heard to remark that he disliked racing at Le Mans because there generally were too many amateur drivers behind those powerful cars.

The weekend before we were to leave for Sebring, Steve decided to enter the annual motorcycle grand prix race at Lake Elsinore, California. Bruce Brown had his cameras trained there for *On Any Sunday*, and both men thought it would be a good opportunity to capture Steve-the-competitor for Bruce's documentary. Despite our personal problems Steve insisted I accompany him to all these events. And I kept going in the hope that my presence would somehow obliterate the continuing estrangement we felt toward each other.

Steve took a spill during the fourth or fifth lap and hurt his foot. Despite the pain, he was unaware that he had broken it until after the race.

Now he felt the world was watching to see what this movie star would do. Breathe a sigh of relief and forgo Sebring? He certainly had the perfect excuse.

But Steve wanted to prove something to himself. He stubbornly refused to bow out of the race. He craved the other drivers' approval too desperately. He wanted to show he had the right stuff.

Even I was not prepared for the incredible fortitude his mind and body were equipped with. With a specially constructed cast for his left foot, Steve and Peter Revson went on to capture second place overall—second only to Mario Andretti, who announced after the race, "This was the toughest race I've run and I'm lucky to have taken it!" After which Andretti bent down and gave Steve a big bear hug. Steve emerged an honest-to-goodness hero that day. He deserved every bit of the accolades that came his way, as well as the Hayden Williams Sportsmanship Cup awarded him that night.

For the race at Sebring, Mario Iscovich had been given the responsibility of arranging all the accommodations for the Solar group and coordinating everything, including Steve's arrival and the mechanics' presence in the pits. It was not an easy assignment, for Steve's movements around the race area had to be curtailed somewhat. A broken foot was tiring as well as painful. Steve would need as much rest as humanly possible. A bodyguard also had to be hired, somebody big and strong who could conceivably carry Steve around. Nobody knew what the crowd's reactions might be, and Steve's broken foot might prove to be a problem. Mario was also in charge of renting cars for everyone, and most important of all, Mario had to make sure there were motor homes available for Steve and Peter where they could hang out and shower any time they wanted to. As it turned out, the event, the accommodations, and all the arrangements couldn't have been better had they been planned by Napoleon.

While Steve was out on the course during the race, Mario and I sat in the pit area and talked about Le Mans. I wanted Mario to come with us to France because I wanted to have a friend there whom I could rely on just in case things got touchy. I thought I would approach Steve about the Mario idea as the time drew closer. And so when Steve wanted to get Mario a present for a job particularly well done, I suggested, "Why don't we take him to France? It'll be a great present for the kid, and he certainly will be useful to you and Solar."

Steve took the bait and Mario was on his way to France.

After Steve's triumphant return to California we were back to where we were before—only worse. Now Steve seemed to be totally confused. He came to the Castle one afternoon to try to define his feelings and his desires as far as our marriage was concerned and left possibly more disconcerted than when he arrived.

He had brought me out to the gardens in the back where he started going around in circles before he opened the conversation with, "Look, baby, I'm having a terrible time functioning. I can't breathe!" Circle, circle. "You feel like a chain around my neck!" Circle, circle.

"Steve, goddamn it! Will you stand still and tell me exactly what you're talking about? Just what is it you want from me?" I was having a difficult time keeping my cool. These were not exactly the words one likes to hear from one's husband.

"Christ, baby, half my life is over and I wanna fly! I wanna go!" he said with intensity as once more he circled.

I stood there staring at him in disbelief. He was having a difficult time looking me in the eyes. When I was finally able to speak, I asked him exactly what it was he wanted.

"Do you want a divorce? Is that what you're saying?"

"*No!*" he said rather forcefully, which surprised me.

The more I pressed, the more agitated and tormented he looked. And the more he circled.

I remember thinking, This is the way marriages end. Just like this. Out in the sunlight, with the birds chirping, and the sound of children laughing. (Terry and Chad were playing in the nearby pool with their friends.) How inappropriate somehow. How absolutely bizarre.

In the end nothing had been settled. Steve went to the pool area and asked Terry to have our housekeeper fix him lunch.

I ran upstairs to the bedroom, not wanting Terry to see me upset. I stood behind the upstairs screen door and watched the happy scene at the pool down below.

I had to unscramble my brain and get organized. June wasn't so terribly far away. The children, the animals (now numbering three schnauzers and a cat), and I were booked on the SS *France,* scheduled to sail for Le Havre on June 17, 1970. (In those days airplanes frightened me, although I flew without hesitating. But whenever possible, I would quietly avoid them.) Steve was scheduled to leave two weeks before us with the Solar group (plus Elmer Valentine, who wanted to play in Europe) to see the twenty-four-hour Le Mans race and to supervise the camera car that was entered in the race. The 908 Porsche Spyder that Steve had driven to victory at Sebring had been equipped with three cameras and was to be driven by two alternating grand prix drivers to acquire footage for the film.

Chad, who was now ten years old, had been doing poorly in school, and in order to stimulate his motivation I had threatened to leave him behind in California while Terry and I spent the summer with Dad. Chad, who idolized his father and had inherited Steve's love for machinery, was not about to be left behind while his sister watched all the racing action in France! No way, José! It didn't take long for Chad to apply himself in school and bring up his grades.

And, of course, now I found myself stuck. How do I renege on my promise to Chad?

You have to go, Neile, I said to myself. There's no way out. "Ho' on bes' you can!" Binoy's wife used to say to me an eternity ago any time I was upset. Well, I would have to hold on. There was no doubt about that!

Steve went back to Palm Springs. Before he left the Oakmont house I handed him a book called *Papillon* which decorator Peter Shore had made me aware of. Peter had asked me to read it because he thought it might be something for Steve in the future. Peter was right. I thought it an absolutely terrific vehicle for Steve. So I bought the book and gave it to him to read.

It's interesting to note that my piles of scrapbooks of my life with Steve end abruptly in June 1969. It's as if a life had suddenly ended. There had been mounds and mounds of notes and cards and letters and magazine articles and newspaper clippings accumulated over the years, and then suddenly—nothing. The energy I had had to record our lives together for our children and posterity just wasn't there. I stopped pasting. Instead I shoved clippings and such in envelopes and uninterestedly laid them aside. Besides, Steve's interviews toward the end of 1969 were far removed from us. Their focus now was solely on his pompous assessment of himself as filmmaker-star-racer and saver of youth.

I was amazed at how convincing he was when he would advocate a "no-drugs" stance with the press, as if he were as straight as an arrow.

Through Mario I knew John Sturges was spending time at Southridge with Steve trying to lick the story problem for *Le Mans*. John wanted a story clearly defined, while Steve was pushing the idea of a two-hour movie that would be more or less a docu-

mentary on racing. His win at Sebring had reinforced this feeling, and he lost sight of the fact that
the world at large was not as enamored of car racing
as he was.

No matter how darling he was to look at.

On June 22, 1970, the SS *France* entered the port
of Le Havre as a passenger ship for the last time.
The French government could no longer support its
upkeep, and so the ship had proudly made its final
voyage as a luxury liner.

It had been a wonderful trip for Terry and Chad
and me. The children had been thrilled to see the
Statue of Liberty as we sailed past her into the open
sea. On board we swam, we watched movies, we took
our dogs for walks around the ship (Kitty Kat remained in our stateroom throughout the voyage. I
came well supplied with kitty litter), we ate ourselves
silly, we danced, we stayed up late, we visited with
friend Dixie Jewison and her brood (they were joining Norman in London), and whenever I picked up
a book to read, the children would find their friends
and explore the mysteries of the ship.

While on board, Dixie told me a funny story about
Steve. For some reason, Europeans occasionally mis-
took Steve and Paul Newman for one another. This
was possibly because they're both American, have
baby-blue eyes, are athletes, and basically play the
same types of roles (although I think Paul has the
wider range as an actor). Paul had been visiting
Norman and Dixie in Switzerland, and he and Norman had just finished skiing for the afternoon when
a little comedy occurred. A Swiss girl approached
Paul, offered him a piece of paper, and beamed
ecstatically. "Oh, Mr. McQueen," she chirped in broken English, "I have waited this afternoon for you.
Will you honor me with your signature?"

Paul never signs autographs, but on this day he

impishly consented. The words he wrote down were "Fuck you. Best, Steve McQueen."

As the Jewisons left the ship at Southampton, the first port of call, I had a sudden premonition that sadness soon would engulf me. I watched them from the top deck until they became little specks in the distance. Le Havre was still a few sailing hours away and the seas had become choppy. I wondered whether I'd survive the Channel crossing.

An uncharacteristically subdued Mario Iscovich was there to meet us. His left arm was in a cast. I inquired about the arm, and Mario nonchalantly waved it off with, "Oh, I was in a car accident a few days ago."

Mario, ever the extrovert, generally described everything that happened to him with relish, and so his behavior was a little puzzling to me. He was genuinely glad to see me and the children, yet his demeanor had changed. Gone was the cheerful cherubic boy and in his place was a man who looked as though he had experienced life too soon.

While we waited to get our luggage together, I took my three little schnauzers, Annie, Katey, and Bullitt, off the ship for a walk. Photographers moved in—very polite. They had heard we were on board and wanted to take pictures. We obliged and they left.

Solar had chartered a light plane to take us all from Le Havre to Le Mans. During the short flight I tried to extract from Mario the story behind his broken arm. No dice. It was years later, after his wounds had healed, before I was able to ply the truth out of Mario.

Mario had arrived in Le Mans exhausted from his long journey. As soon as he arrived at the château where Steve was staying, he tried without success to get some sleep. Soon, he heard Steve come down the stairs and ask for him. He also heard the voice of one of the film's crew members, who told Steve he was going back to his hotel in town.

"No, hang on," Steve had said. "Get Mario. I'll be right down. I gotta drop somebody off."

The somebody was a blond "Puff of Hair" whom Steve ushered into the car with the two men.

Recognizing Steve's dilated eyes, both men tried to dissuade him from driving. He was hyper and couldn't stop talking. As soon as Steve pulled out of the driveway, it was clear that this was an accident waiting to happen. It was raining and Mario begged Steve to slow down.

"Cool it, Mario. We're gonna have us a great time! Ooooweee!"

Shortly, as they were going around a curve, Mario heard Steve yell "Shit!" and he knew they were in trouble. Steve lost the car and they spun. They went through the kilometer cement bunkers on the road and became airborne. The car went down and headed for a grove of trees—more specifically, a big tree.

When they hit it Mario saw his arm snap. Everything was eerily silent for several minutes before he realized that Steve and Puff of Hair were over the windshield and the crew member wasn't moving.

The next thing Mario remembered was being in the middle of the country road with the girl stretched out cold, and Steve was saying over and over again, "Oooh shit! Oh, fuck, man! I've had it! I've really done it this time. Fuck! What're we gonna do, man? I'll lose everything now. For sure. Oh, fuck! Mario, do you think she's dead?"

Mario turned to Steve and said, "I don't know if she's dead, but I don't think we should move her."

After what seemed to be an eternity, Puff of Hair began to stir. She groaned and shivered involuntarily and her teeth began to chatter as she lay freezing on the road with the rain pouring on her.

As soon as Steve realized the girl was alive, he quickly pulled her up and placed one arm under her armpit and propped her against him, then wrapped her other arm around his neck. Steve didn't want to waste any more time. They began walking and soon the girl seemed to get better. Steve kept repeating, "It's not too far. It's not too far. Come on, let's keep going."

They walked in the starless night. Only Steve was familiar with the road, busy as he had been in the last few days picking up girls and driving them back and forth. Mario was beyond the point of pain and exhaustion, and the crew member, too, was obviously hurt. Miraculously, in the ink-black night, they spotted a farmhouse that was recessed about fifty yards from the road. Steve pointed and whispered, "Look, there's a car. We'll steal it!"

Mario looked at Steve and said, "You're crazy, Steve! You're not playing a movie role!"

"Shut the fuck up, man. You'll wake everybody up. Now, come with me!"

Steve tried jump-starting the car, and then the dogs barked and the lights went on in the farmhouse. Both Steve and Mario ran back toward the road with a "mad-as-hornet" farmer in pursuit. Fortunately the farmer gave up the chase, and the four of them arrived in Loué at two in the morning. Steve and the girl made themselves scarce, while Mario and the crew member got themselves to the hospital.

By midafternoon of the following day, when Mario, who had passed out—finally getting his much needed rest—woke up, he felt abandoned. He hadn't seen or heard from anyone, and here he was in a strange country in a strange hospital.

As he lay there feeling sorry for himself, he thought he heard a man speaking with an American accent. He prayed he wasn't dreaming and he prayed that God himself would come through his door.

He did. In the person of Stan Kamen.

"Hi, how are you, kid? I'm Stan Kamen," he said as he shook Mario's hand. "Now, don't you worry. I want you to relax. You're O.K. and I'm getting you out of here. All right?"

Stan took Mario back to Solar Village, the company compound, and gently warned Mario, "Nobody knows anything."

Mario acted accordingly and kept his mouth shut. At Solar Village Mario soon discovered he had taken the fall for Steve. Only Stan had expressed any concern about his present circumstances.

Steve, for his part, didn't show up until the next day. He was warm toward Mario and the other man (whose injuries were two broken ribs), yet very guarded.

"How ya doin', guys?" he asked, uncomfortably aware they shared a secret together. "Mario, how long are you planning to relax here? I need you to help me, you know."

Mario couldn't believe what he'd just heard, but he tried to keep calm and before Mario could answer, Steve had him out in the hallway. Grabbing Mario's right arm, Steve asked him if he was going to sue.

Mario was aghast and assured Steve he wouldn't. When Steve was satisfied the kid meant it, he told him to "hurry up and get out of here! It's time you earned your living!"

Within a few days Mario was back at the château with Steve, and within a few days Steve was back to his old ways. Mario found it all appalling. He reminded Steve the children and I were due from the States soon. "Why don't you stop this craziness, Steve?"

"Hey, kid, what for? Look at me. I'm the biggest star in the world. The number one sex symbol! All those women wanna fuck me, man!" And then, in an apparent effort to pacify Mario, Steve reminded him that he was tough and that Mario shouldn't worry about him.

Mario found Steve's behavior too painful to watch. All Steve seemed to have on his mind was girls. Preferably American girls and preferably very young. Girls and drugs. He would pick them up at bars and off the streets. Anything and anyone.

Sometimes it was even two or three anyones.

The little plane bearing the McQueen party flew over the beautiful countryside, and although the day was a smoky gray, France was still visible through the haze. I was happy for the children. And especially happy for Chad, who had worked doggedly to bring up his grades so he could be part of this racing world with its powerful cars and share it all with his father. But I was apprehensive. The last time I had spoken to Steve was five days earlier, just prior to our sailing from New York, and we had said very little of substance to each other.

We landed not too far from the race course, and while our baggage and our animals headed for our new home in Vire-en-Champagne, Mario took us in the opposite direction. Steve had instructed him to bring us immediately to the set. But Steve had decided at the last minute that his reunion with his family would best be carried out in the privacy and protection of Solar Village.

I spotted him right away resplendent in his white racing suit. His blond hair was longer than it had been in *The Reivers*, and his wiry, muscular frame was leaning against a Peugeot that was to be my car. It was obvious he was waiting for us.

I pointed him out to the children, and they started screeching in concert, "Daddy! Daddy! Hi, Dad! We're here! We're here!" *Bonjour,* Dad-dee! *Bonjour!*" Terry and Chad hopped out of the car just as soon as Mario stopped and ran toward him, then jumped into his arms. I stood by quietly, watching the happy reunion, not knowing how I was going to act when my turn came.

He had a wide smile as he caught my eye. "I'm happy you're here." He disengaged himself from the children, came over to me, gave me a kiss, and enveloped me in his arms.

"Welcome to Le Mans, baby. Wait till you see our

place. You'll like it. It's really somethin'!" I felt no pretense and I felt he meant it sincerely. And stirrings of hope for our marriage were renewed.

We drove back to the set briefly so I could greet John Sturges and Bob Relyea and the rest of the group, and take a peek at the million-dollar racing stable constructed for the movie. Little Chad was thrilled and Terry, who had just turned eleven, was trying to act blasé about it all.

I inquired about the script.

"What about the script?" Steve was obviously annoyed with my question.

"You know what I mean. Have you got one yet?" Innocently I had strayed into forbidden country.

I hadn't been around and was therefore unaware of John Sturges's growing disillusionment with the project. John insisted on finding a story he and Steve could both be happy with—a perfectly reasonable request. Steve, however seemed more concerned with the grandiose idea of "leaving some scratch marks on the history of filmmaking." In addition to the script problems, Steve apparently had been overstepping his bounds and going over John's head, which hadn't sat at all well with a professional like John. It surely must have been annoying to John to hear Steve refer to himself, over and over again, as a man who was wearing three hats in this production. "I'm a driver, an actor, and a filmmaker." To the press around the world yet.

Now he had adopted a new attitude with his fans. No autographs. No exceptions. This had been Paul Newman's edict for many years. It was a policy that worked for him and he stuck to it. Steve's sudden embracing of this no-autograph business had more to do with his ego than with anything else. It was part of a conscious posturing to be "the Boss."

Boy, oh boy!

Changes were coming fast and furious with Steve. I could hardly keep up with them, and was completely unprepared for what was waiting for me around the corner. These last several months of casual indifference and verbal hurts had been nothing but a dress rehearsal, baby!

The nightmare was about to begin.

The Château Lornay, where we would live until the filming was over, was forty-five minutes away from the Solar Village in Le Mans. It was an honest-to-goodness castle. Built in the fourteenth century and modernized after the Second World War, it made an imposing presence amidst the wine fields of Vire-en-Champagne. And yet sometimes, in the middle of the night, we'd hear creaking noises coming from the attic. No one in the château was ever able to identify just what these sounds were, so we disregarded them and all nervous imaginings that the castle was haunted. We felt our little dogs were sufficient guards. So long as Annie, Katey, and Bullitt remained oblivious to the sounds, we would have to assume they were harmless.

Our first evening at the château was a quiet one. We had dinner in the medieval dining room and the conversation, thank goodness, revolved around the children's activities. Steve seemed distant and contained; no doubt, my presence was irritating to him. He tried to make the best of it just as I did. We had agreed that we would meet to have lunch the following day in the mess hall at Solar Village. The children and I would come early to watch some of the filming. I was anxious to get Chad to the race course. It was his reward, and he was entitled to it.

That same night I asked Steve how he was handling the dope. He said, "Well, I obviously have to stay away from it when I'm filming the race sequence. But it's O.K. at night. Don't you worry your pretty little head. I can handle myself." He had plenty of grass, but I was pleased his coke supply was almost nil. But then I supposed it was only a matter of

time before he'd find himself a connection. Being a
movie star almost guaranteed it, although he at least
had the sense to be cautious about finding a supply
in a foreign country; foreign governments, he knew,
did not take kindly to either users or suppliers.

As soon as I was satisfied the children were comfortable in their new house, I kissed them good
night. Then I went to my room and slipped quietly
under the covers beside Steve. Steve had gone to bed
an hour earlier, exhausted from riding around in
those cars all day. The night was black, but I could
see the stars through the windows. There was a
warm summer breeze and the little white curtains in
our bedroom were flapping gently. I began to think
how much better it would have been to have stayed
in California this summer. I kept asking myself
whether I could have avoided France. Then quite
suddenly, I began hearing a noise here; a sound
there; now a flapping here, on my left.

I thought, That's the curtain. But then I realized
the windows and the curtains were on my right.
Then I thought it was Steve snoring. I inched myself
closer to Steve. He was breathing heavily, but he
wasn't snoring. The noises continued all around the
room and I decided they were real. My imagination
wasn't working overtime.

But what the hell were they?

I reached over and switched the bedside light on.

What I saw made me gasp! I grabbed the covers
and pulled them over me as quickly as possible. Our
bedroom had been invaded by bats! My God, there
had to be at least two dozen of them flying around in
the room and bumping into walls and into each
other.

I yelled to Steve to get under the covers. He had
been sleeping in the nude and I had visions of a bat
diving at him as it looked for a way out! When Steve
saw what was going on his reaction was one of horror, just as mine had been. But from under the

covers he yelled, "Shit, baby, somebody's put the evil eye on me! Get some candles!"

"Candles?" God! The man must be hallucinating! Candles! I'm slithering out of bed to find Kitty Kat and he's thinking candles! Could he be planning to burn the house down? I stayed close to the floor to find the cat. I remembered that from my days in the Philippines. Cats just sit there, just as calm as can be, and slap away at those bats with their paws. They bring them down one at a time, methodically. Which is exactly what Kitty Kat did.

The count was Kitty Kat 16 and Bats 0.

We found out the next day the "bat path" was right next to our house. Sometimes there would be a mix-up in their radar signals, and then they'd find themselves in the Château Lornay scaring the hell out of everyone.

Eventually we got used to the critters. They weren't as frightening as they were that first night.

But then Kitty Kat was always there to see us through each new trauma.

The next day was hot. Steve had left for the set early in the morning and so had Mario. The children and I were taking our time. No need to hurry, I thought. We had a good three hours before we were to meet Steve.

Joe McCormack, a young man who worked for us and whom I had brought along to help keep an eye on the children, had just informed me my car was all gassed up and ready to go. I wanted to unpack first and take a walk around some of the land that surrounded our château. Chad was impatient to get to those race cars, so I asked Joe to take him onto the set. Terry preferred to wait for me. From what I could determine this was primarily a farming region. A bull and a few cows grazed the fields that faced our bedroom windows. There were horses on the next hill. My cat had quietly positioned herself on a branch and was lazily eyeing the birds. She was in no mood to exert herself today. It had been a tiring night. My three dogs were happily romping around the gardens.

I took a deep breath of the fresh, fragrant air and I set aside the premonition I had had on the ship. Instead I crossed my fingers.

"Maybe we'll make it yet," I said out loud to no one in particular. For the first time in a while the load on my shoulders seemed lighter. Foreign locations had been good to us in the past. If we were lucky history would repeat itself.

And it was in this hopeful vein that Terry and I drove to the set.

They were filming at the Mulsanne Straight, a particularly treacherous piece of road on the Le Mans circuit. A short delay due to a mechanical problem with one of the cars gave us an opportunity to greet everyone. Husband and father, co-workers and friends. I took an immediate liking to Siegfried (Sigi) Rauch, a German actor who was playing Steve's antagonist. There were many grand prix drivers present that day, as well as a huge group of onlookers and groupies gathered behind the fences. The girls were dressed to the nines, false eyelashes and all. There were also a number of them on the hills around the course, mixed in with the male fans, all of them eager to catch a glimpse of the American movie star. The women thrilled to being waved to and smiled at by Steve McQueen.

The European groupie, I was to observe, was a much more aggressive type than her U.S. counterpart. Or maybe I had not seen the U.S. groupie up close.

Terry had found Chad and Joe McCormack, and together they went to the carnival site behind the grandstands. After that they went about exploring the countryside and the race course itself. When lunch was called we would meet in the mess hall at Solar Village.

As things happened, lunch break came sooner than expected. The mechanical problem was taking more time than anticipated to fix. Steve and I started walking toward his car. He seemed preoccupied. I caught his eye and he stopped walking, took my hand, and sat me on the guard rail. I expected the news wouldn't be good, whatever it was. There was too much hemming and hawing, and that was always an ominous sign. I waited. And soon the words came spilling out.

"Look, ah, I should tell you. There'll be women coming from all over the world to visit me this summer and—"

"Wait. Wait!" I covered his mouth with my hand. I took a deep breath. Slowly I took my hand away. "What women are you talking about?" I knew in my heart, but I wanted to hear him tell me.

"They're friends of mine." Oddly enough he looked stricken as he told me. I laughed at myself for even feeling a twinge for his pain at this moment. God! Why? Why do I care how he feels? I brushed this aside and it took several minutes, I think, before I felt I could even say anything coherent. My head felt as though it were being gripped by a vise.

"Well, we are kinda separated, right?" he continued.

"Leave me here, please." I was frantically searching for a place to run to. I felt I was hyperventilating and wanted to be left alone. "Have lunch with the children and tell them I've gone shopping. I'll see them later. I need some time to pull myself together." By now tears were streaming down my face.

Although the company had dispersed for lunch, there was still a mob of people hanging about the race course, reluctant to give up their prime location. They had brought their own lunches and were waiting for filming to resume.

I walked as fast as I could in the opposite direction. Away from Steve and away from the crowd. By the way they had smiled at me earlier that morning I was aware they knew I was the movie star's wife. I couldn't show the world anything but a smiling face. I wanted to find a tree, a hill, a bush. Anything that could shield me from those curious eyes until I could pull myself together.

I found a car that was parked behind the cameras and the big lights. Undoubtedly it belonged to a crew member. I pulled at the door and it was unlocked. I let myself in and laid down in the backseat and cried my heart out. I thought, I need Steve to hold me and comfort my breaking heart. Until I realized it was Steve himself who was causing me all this grief. He was putting me into conflict with my self-respect.

I had to handle it by myself. There was no one I could confide in. My support system was back in the United States.

I wandered around for the rest of the day. I have no recollection of how I got back to the château except I found myself at dinner with the children, Mario, and Steve.

In bed that night as I lay there exhausted from the day's emotional shredder, Steve reached over and cradled me in his arms.

"I'm sorry I hurt you, baby. I really don't mean to. I want you to know I love you. But I gotta do what I gotta do."

I was too tired to disengage myself away from him. Given a little more energy, I probably would have hit him with whatever was handy. This time around I was able to hold my tears in check.

And then quietly and gently, in an almost fatherly way, he asked whether I'd ever had an affair.

"No, of course not." I was glad he'd asked me in the dark. I'm not a good liar and I was afraid he might have seen through me. But just now I wanted nothing more than to fall asleep. I wanted to forget the day. Even temporarily.

Steve pressed on. "Why not? I wouldn't blame you. I've certainly given you enough provocation."

"I just never felt the need to." I wanted to get away from this line of questioning. It was the first time he had ever broached the subject with me, and it was making me feel uneasy. It seemed obvious that he was asking me only as a way to deal with his own guilts. At this very moment, he seemed like a man who was willing to take his punishment for sins committed against his wife. No more, no less.

I was not tempted to admit to my single indiscretion. My common sense told me it was unwise. It had been committed in anger and it was best left alone.

But he wouldn't leave it be.

In a lighthearted manner he again offered the opinion that "It's really amazing that you haven't even been tempted to have an affair."

"Steve, I didn't say I was never tempted. I said I've never had an affair. Now, please, I've taken a sleeping pill and I can't keep my eyes open. And you have to drive all day tomorrow."

I guess what he really wanted at this point was the reassurance from me that no matter how bad and no matter how abusive he might be, I would still love him and take no retaliatory measures. His macho code could never in a million years allow him to forgive me. He had to be positive he was right in his assessment. And so he prodded once more, to be one hundred percent sure.

And he lost.

"Steve, please, give me a break! I'm really so tired and I don't want to talk anymore." Steve simply couldn't comprehend that the day's revelation had left me numb—that and the medication coursing through my body, making it almost impossible to keep my eyes open.

He suddenly jumped out of bed and started rummaging through his dresser drawer. Even in the dark I could tell he had found what he was looking for. His movements were precise and sure. In a moment he was beside me. "Here, I want you to take this."

My eyes opened wide. Take what? I suddenly felt my heart fluttering. What the hell does he want me to take? Then all too soon I realized what it was. He was having a "toot," which he wanted to share with me. "It'll do you good, baby. You'll feel better!"

"Steve, you know I don't do that stuff. Have a good time. I'll see you around. Good night."

I wish I could say the night had ended there, but it had just begun.

"What do you mean, you'll see me around?" he demanded.

I was now thoroughly annoyed. I shoved the covers down and sat up. "Well, what the hell do you suppose it means?" I kept my voice down to a minimum. "I—Will—See—You—Around. Even the dogs know what that means. It means I'll see you when I see you. It means I'll see you if you come home for dinner. It means I'll see you if you sleep here. In other words—from time to time, from place to place, here and there and everywhere, with no set plans. If we run into each other, fine. If we don't, so be it. I doubt the children will know what's going on."

The tears came again and I hated myself for having so little control. "God, Steve, I really don't know any other way to handle this. I'm trapped! I can't disappoint Chad. He's so happy to be here with you! And I can't leave them. I wish I could." I reached for a tissue to dry my tears and blow my nose. "For my sanity—please—try to be cool. Try to show me some respect when your little chickies drop down from the sky to visit you. I am in town and I am sharing a house with you. If nothing else, show Terry and Chad the respect they're entitled to."

Steve had gotten up to look for a cigarette and once again I wanted nothing more than to blacken out the memory of the last few hours. "I don't think there's anything more to say. So if you don't mind I'm going to bed."

Instead of the cigarette he was looking for, he came back to bed with a joint. "Here, take a drag."

"Steve, *no!* You know grass does nothing for me but make me sleepy. I've already taken a sleeping pill. Good night!"

"You know what?" he started again.

"What!" God! There was no sleeping tonight. I could see that.

Very gently Steve said, "I wish you wouldn't fight me on this. I promise you a little coke will make you feel better. I don't want you feeling bad, baby! No matter what's happened you're still my baby."

I can't possibly be hearing this. I'm going insane! I've got to shut him up, I decided. In my emotional state it looked like the only way to stop him from talking was to give in to his wishes. Share the damn coke and then say good night. My nose was all stopped up from crying. I'd always heard him say it clears up one's sinuses. So what the hell, why not?

"O.K. Give it to me. Show me how to do it."

He couldn't have been more pleased. He turned the light on and looked for a nail file. "I'm just giving you a little bit, baby. Not to worry." I wasn't worried. I wanted it over and done with so I could go back to bed. He had dipped the tip of the nail file into his silver box and he showed me how to "suck up" the little mounds when he said "go." I couldn't breathe normally over these teeny piles of white dust or it would disappear into the air. Just like my talcum powder, he said.

"Can I go to sleep now?" I figured now that I had experienced what he seemed so desperate to share with me, I would be given my reward. Please, God. Make him shut up. I'm so tired.

He reached for the light switch to flick it off. "Well, what do you think? Isn't it great?"

"It's O.K., Steve." I nodded my head in agreement. "It's cleared up my sinuses."

And I giggled. Which was unexpected and which surprised me.

Actually it had done more than improve my sinuses. I had felt a sudden rush and for a moment I liked my husband again and I had the feeling I could handle whatever cards were dealt me. I felt stronger and braver and felt there was nothing I couldn't face. And when the next question came I was more than ready to answer it. With aplomb.

He was now in a lighthearted mood and he affectionately said how it had always amazed him that I had managed to escape romantic entanglements of sorts, especially given his example.

"I mean this with all my heart. I certainly would have understood. No shit, baby. You're the best."

"You really would have understood, honey?" Unbelievably, I had fallen for it.

"Sure, baby." Silence. "Did you?"

I was lying on my back with my arms under my head staring up at the ceiling, thinking how astounding it was I was no longer sleepy or tired. My thoughts floated sadly to those few days at the Beverly Hills Hotel when life seemed empty. What a laugh! Those were great days compared to now! But c'est la fucking vie, I said. I'm strong. I'll survive anything.

"Well?" Steve asked.

"Well, what?"

Steve slowly repeated the question. "Did you ever have an affair?"

I thought for a second. "Well, yes, as a matter of fact, I did."

I can only attribute the great courage that had come over me to the coke I had inhaled. I turned onto my stomach and looked at him with a big smile on my face. I felt daring enough to tweak his nose gently.

"Honey bunny, yours is not the only golden cock in the west, you know." As the first torrent of words came tumbling out of my mouth I became helpless in controlling the tide of anger and resentment that had been accumulating all these months. I was on a roll and it felt good and I meant to keep going.

"You know what, honey? He has an Academy Award, too. Now, if you're a good boy, someday you might win one." And as an afterthought, I pounded the last nail in the coffin. "Maybe, he might even present it to you!"

God, that felt fabulous, I thought. All the way to the bottom of my soul. Maybe we can call ourselves even now and start over from scratch. Starting now.

Silly girl.

Dumb, stupid girl.

Steve excused himself and went into the next room. He was back in a few seconds. He took me by surprise as he quickly grabbed my arm and roughly pulled me to a sitting position on the bed. My legs were ensnarled in the bed clothing and I couldn't get my feet on the floor.

He had a gun and pointed it to my head. "Who was he?"

I was struck dumb. No sound came out of my mouth.

This time he cocked the gun and pushed the barrel against my temple. "Who was the motherfucker?"

I could see his face twitching from the light that was streaming in from the room next door.

"You'd better tell me now or you're not going to live to see him die! And I promise you I'll find out who the motherfucker is! Make no mistake about that!" This time he yelled. "Who is he!"

And this time the name exploded from my lips involuntarily.

14

THERE WAS no sleeping that night—not for Steve and not for me. The "two free spirits who were free as the wind," as John Sturges had once referred to us, were free no more. Too many boundaries had been crossed—boundaries that should have remained sacrosanct. The "lovable kooks" who had complemented each other by their very differences had succumbed to the foibles of fame and fortune.

Infidelity on my part had never entered his mind. His vanity would never have allowed it. After all, I was his wife, I was Mrs. Steve McQueen. Could anyone ask for more? And the fact that I had picked another movie star to betray him with was unforgivable; and that the star was a man who also had the reputation of being a ladies' man was even more incomprehensible!

The truth was that when Steve entered the fast lane, he thought he would be immune to the consequences. He had rearranged the order of his priorities and had paid the price. The emotional security he had searched for so frantically in his youth and had finally found with me over the years had vanished into the night with just a few sentences.

And it devastated him.

We were both silent for a long time, there in the dark. Every once in a while my throat would emit a spasm out of fright, I think, as he stared at me menacingly. He had laid the gun down but I was suddenly mindful of the violent and lonely life that had spawned him.

Thoughts kept circling round and round my brain. Is he capable of killing me? And if he was, would it be considered a crime of passion and would he get off scot-free? And the children. What about them? Could they survive the emotional trauma? They're such good kids and we love them so much. Who would take care of them with me dead? Steve wouldn't be good with them without me. He was not a day-to-day parent. Terry was the apple of his eye. She was the mirror image of him. Chad was his son. The boy he always wanted. He loved them unequivocally and yet he was impatient with the ordinary demands of parenthood. We all understood and accepted that. But with me gone, who would take over that daily looking-after that the children required? Please, God, don't let him do anything stupid. It isn't right that it should end this way.

I was watching him closely. I was terrified of the gun that was only an arm's length away from him. The gun that had come into the country, undetected, with the movie props—the P.38 automatic he had gotten after the Tate murders. I could see his torment; every once in a while he'd close his eyes tightly and hold his face in his hands, as if he were trying to block out images that were flying around in his imagination.

And then unexpectedly he grabbed me again by the shoulder straps of my nightgown and with one swift motion pushed me onto a chair by the window. Miraculously, the straps had stayed intact. "Now let's talk. And I want straight answers."

He was as relentless as I imagine the Gestapo must have been. He was a fast and articulate interrogator, and when the answers didn't come swiftly enough for him there would be jabs to the arms, a slap across the face—not hard, just enough to let me know he meant business—or a pulling of my head back by a handful of my hair while he hissed at me, his face only inches away from mine.

"Where'd you meet him?"

"On a plane coming home from New York."

"Did you tell him your name?"

"I introduced myself."

"Did he talk to you first or you talk to him first?"

"I don't know, Steve. I don't remember."

Jab. "Try."

"I don't know. He probably did. I think he said hello to me first."

Jab. "Try again. I don't want 'thinks.' I want 'knows.' Got that?" Jab. "Huh?"

I was sobbing and barely able to catch my breath. I was being terrorized and yet I could see tears streaming down his cheeks.

"I'm sorry, honey. I didn't mean for it to happen, but you'd been so awful to me. He came along and he was nice and he made me feel desirable."

He had grabbed hold of my hair and had tilted my head backwards. "Desirable." Slap. "Desirable, my ass!" He smirked. "Listen, you stupid bitch! He romanced you because of me. *Me!* Not you! Men get their jollies off fucking other men's wives. Don't you know that?"

"Honey, I'm sorry. I never meant to hurt you."

"And what did you mean to do with that little number you pulled? Tell me that!" Jab. "What!"

"I don't know."

"Oh. You don't know! Who'll know? Shall I call up the motherfucker? Hm?" Jab. And then another jab.

"Please stop hitting me, Steve. I can't stand it."

"Well, that's too fuckin' bad, baby. You're in the big time now. You're playing with the big boys. You play, you pay."

I was feeling weak and nauseated and told him so.

But he was compelled to continue. "Tell me something. Did you enjoy yourself? Did you have a good time?"

"No, I didn't, honey. Please stop."

Slap. "I want an answer!'

"I answered you already."

"I want the truth! Did you have a good time?"

"No."

Slap. "The truth, goddamn it!"

"It's the truth, so help me God!"

"I'll ask you again. Did you have a good time?" He looked so sinister in the glow of the light coming from the other room.

"No, honey. I swear I didn't!"

Slap. Slap. "One more time. Did—you—have—a—good—time?"

And finally, exhausted from the emotional shock, I uttered a low, guttural, animal "Yes!"

He needed that "yes." He needed it so he could unleash the furies that were consuming him. He felt the final "yes" would give him the excuse necessary to haul off and punch me, which is what I was expecting. Surprisingly and thankfully, he slowly straightened himself up and gave me a look of such hatred that I cringed. He, too, by now, was emotionally spent. He turned around and walked out the bedroom door.

A few minutes later I heard his Porsche start up. He would try to drive the rage he felt out of his system.

As I stood at the window watching his car go out the drive, perversely, regardless of the harrowing experience I had just gone through, regardless of the torment I knew he was feeling, all I could think was, We're even now. Maybe he'll think twice before he fucks around again.

He drove around all night. It was six thirty in the morning when Steve came back to the château. His eyes looked haunted. My heart went out to him. I put my arms around him and hoped we could put it all behind us. "I'm so sorry, honey, forgive me." The pain, the tears and the humiliating loss of self-respect, didn't seem important anymore. I only wanted to get back to that place where we once were. I now felt as if I were totally responsible for our deeply scarred relationship.

He looked as if he'd been crying a good part of the night. Just as I had. "Take a good look at what you've done, baby. I hope you're happy. Nobody's ever reached me like you have. You've burned my soul and I'll be a long time forgetting that. If ever." Then abruptly he changed the subject. "I've got a lot of heavy driving to do today. I need some good strong coffee. Get it for me, will you?" All this was said in almost a monotone. I started getting panicky. I had knocked the wind out of his sails and he needed a tremendous amount of energy to carry him through the day's shooting.

I brought him his coffee in the bathroom, and as I turned to leave, he grabbed my arm and spun me around. "Tell me. Why'd you do it? Why another actor? Why somebody in my industry? Why?"

I could see the anger rising and I pleaded with him. "Please, Steve, let's talk about it later. I know you have to leave."

He gave me his cold hard blue stare and let go of my arm.

I stayed home and slept away most of the day. I was bone weary and if this morning was any indication, there would be another hard night ahead.

As it turned out there were hard nights and hard days ahead. Every one was a repeat of what had occurred that first night. He was relentless, he was unforgiving, and he pressed hard. And I know he tried to get it behind us, but he was incapable of doing so. That macho code was firmly implanted in his soul. He struck at all hours of the day, able to control himself only when company was present. This surprised me. And so I learned to stay close to either

Mario or Joe, and I never left the children's side unless it was absolutely necessary.

I prayed every day and every hour. God, did I pray. "Please, God, hold back the night. Just this once. I need a reprieve."

But night always fell. And, always, in the sanctuary of our bedroom, Steve would bring it all up again during those few hours before sleep claimed us both.

When I look back on those days I understand that by not leaving I obviously must have been punishing myself for the pain and sorrow I had inflicted on Steve (forgetting all that he had done to me). Yet I also still loved him and somehow I kept hoping this all would pass and the nightmare would end.

But a week after I arrived from the States, Steve and I agreed to separate—publicly for the first time.

It was a peculiar separation in that we still shared the same house and the same bed. Nothing had changed except we'd given notice to the world at large that all was not well between the McQueens. I thought going public with it might alleviate my plight. It did no such thing. Every man I came in contact with, every man I said "hello" to, every man who smiled and looked at me came under Steve's suspicion. My closets and drawers were rummaged through; my mail was censored and I was prohibited from going into town by myself. What the announcement did was compound the problem. I was under orders to appear at the village every day. And I timed it to coincide with the end of the lunch break. Which would mean Steve was on the set.

Steve, surreptitiously, asked Bob Relyea to inquire into Casanova's availability. He wanted Bob to offer him a part in *Le Mans* as a way to get him on Steve's turf. It had to look legitimate or, he reasoned, he might hesitate, and Steve wanted desperately to "beat the shit out of him." I believe Steve would have seriously hurt him had he innocently accepted this offer.

But it turned out Casanova was busy on another project and was unavailable to join *Le Mans*.

Thank you, God.

Steve now took to cross-examining Mario about me every day. The poor kid's loyalty was being tested because Mario and I were good friends. Mario had no idea of the reason behind the heavy interrogation, except that he was painfully aware of Steve's increasing paranoia.

On the Fourth of July, in an effort to give the children a bit of fun, we had a little party that consisted of Terry, Chad, Mario, Joe, Steve, and me. Tension was heavy in the air although we tried to maintain some sort of sanity in front of the children—in front of everybody, for that matter.

Firecrackers, long a favorite of Steve's, were our main form of diversion that day. The men had a great time placing cherry bombs in the middle of the cow dung scattered all over the fields in front of the house. They'd light it, then run like mad for cover! The children loved every minute of it! "Madame," our cook, had obliged us by preparing a variation of a Yankee Doodle turkey dinner with as many of the trimmings as she could muster. For dessert she had proudly produced a scrumptious *île flotant* in honor of the upcoming Bastille Day.

In the dark, narrow corridor leading to the dining room Steve cornered Mario just before we went in to dinner. "Who do you work for, Mario? Answer me that."

Mario thought it was a joke and he laughed. "You, of course." It was a ridiculous question until he heard the next three sentences.

"You remember that, kid. She may be my wife, but your loyalty is to me! You do understand that, don't you?"

Mario assumed Steve was concerned about Puff of Hair and the car accident that had happened twenty-two days before. Mario reassured Steve he had no intention of telling me anything about his extracurricular activities. Mario, frankly, wanted to spare me the pain and the embarrassment. He may not have been a sophisticated young man, but he was wise beyond his years. And he was loyal, despite the fact that he was dealing with Steve's Jekyll and Hyde personalities now on a daily basis. Then one day there was an incident that totally rocked Steve's faith in Mario, and Mario's in Steve.

Betsy Cox, Steve's secretary, had stayed behind at the Solar offices in Hollywood to handle the daily chores that related to Steve and to the production. Betsy was crazy about Steve and tried to do everything to please him, no matter how odd his requests were. She was the anchor in town.

Every once in a while Steve would get a craving for real American hamburgers. Betsy would have a box of three dozen hamburgers and cheeseburgers with everything on them sent via Air France. On those days everybody waited for the car to come bearing those wonderful hamburgers!

One day three boxes arrived from the U.S. filled with Fruit of the Loom T-shirts. Betsy had sent them at Steve's request. He was now buying clothes in bulk. He was into blue jeans, cords, and chambray shirts and T-shirts. The blue jeans were bought three or four dozen at a time, washed many times over for shrinkage, and then especially bleached by the studio's wardrobe department to make them look well worn. They were tailored to his form afterwards. The great clothes Steve had accumulated through the years from his movies and shopping forays were mothballed, thanks to the newly raised consciousness of the young and the spaced-out hippies. In his effort to keep up with them he became the epitome of the adult afraid to grow old. He seemed more lost than the kids who envied his position.

At Solar Village was a young, hippie type who had been hanging around the compound for the last three weeks. People just knew her as a "friend of Steve's," and she was left alone. Nobody could remember her name, although it was known she was an American (probably picked up while hitchhiking, since that had been Steve's modus operandi). She always looked as if she needed a bath and some clean clothes. Mario didn't know whether Steve was "carrying on" with her. He seriously doubted it, but there was a lot of whispering going on between the two and about the two. I don't have a specific recollection of her since there were so many groupies about. One face melded into the other.

"My God, she was dirty," Mario recalled. "I mean, it is hard to imagine. But then who knows? He was a little weird, too."

She was there when Mario began putting away the boxes of T-shirts in Steve's office—in the corner behind his desk. Because of Mario's difficulty with his broken left arm, he had dropped a box, which split open, spilling the T-shirts on the floor. Mario saw the girl eyeing the shirts and felt sorry for her.

"What the hell—" Mario shrugged. "Here!" and he threw one to her. "You look like you can use a new T-shirt. I'm sure Steve won't mind." The girl's eyes lit up, and as she expressed her thanks, in walked Steve.

The difficulties the film was experiencing had intensified in the last few days. Nothing seemed to be going right. John Sturges was unhappy about the absence of story. He had no desire to make a documentary even if it did feature Steve McQueen, and Steve was being stubborn in his refusal to see that a race is a race is a race.

"Where is the human story?" was John's lament. For the time being, cameras ground away recording for posterity the swift and dangerous machinery driven by fabulous drivers going around and around the course, stopping at the pit areas, getting gassed up, having accidents, etc., etc. On top of that, cars were breaking down almost daily.

Mario was well aware of the problems on the set and he became uneasy as soon as Steve walked into the room. He hadn't looked pleased and became less so when the girl opened her mouth.

"Steve! He's the nicest man!" Mario smiled when it dawned on him she most likely didn't know his name. "Look! He just gave me this T-shirt!"

Steve asked the girl to leave the office, giving the excuse that he and Mario had important business.

No sooner had the girl stepped out the door than Steve slammed it closed just as hard as he could, causing the little building's structure to shake.

"You fat little fucker! How dare you fuck with my women!" Steve started advancing toward Mario. "I told you once! You can have my food, you can have my money, but who the hell gave you permission to give her that T-shirt! *Huh?* That T-shirt is bought with my hard-earned money. How dare you fuck around with her?"

Mario was stupefied! "Steve, look at me! Look! I'm fat. She doesn't want me! What the hell would she want with me?"

"Shut up when I'm talking to you, you little fuckin' asshole! How could you do it? *Huh?* How could you do it?" There was no reasoning with Steve. He was giving the performance of his life. It was Academy Award time. It would have been funny had Mario not been on the receiving end.

Steve grabbed Mario by the lapels and yanked hard and started hitting him on the arms. Then he threw him against the wall and slammed him into the couch.

And with that, Steve went to his desk and poured himself some coffee, sat down, and with a smile quietly asked, "So, what have you got to say for yourself?"

Mario was eerily reminded of the two faces of drama. The mask of tragedy and the mask of comedy. He sincerely believed that Steve's mind had snapped. When he was able to, Mario stood up and slowly walked to the door. "I don't know, man, but I think you're fucking crazy. I quit."

"What do you mean, you quit?"

"I quit! I can't handle this, Steve."

Steve watched him silently open the door. "O.K. I can't hold you back, but I hope you know what you're throwing away. You will never work in this industry again."

Mario had one foot out the door and Steve tried another tactic. "I don't want you to go, Mario."

Mario looked at Steve sadly and told him how he felt—for the last time. "Steve, my arm is killing me and I can't handle you anymore."

Knowing now that he was not going to get his way, Steve angrily jumped up from behind his desk. "What did I ever do to you?"

Mario closed the door behind him.

That night as we were having dinner, Mario quietly packed his bags and asked Joe McCormack to take him to the train station. The train would get him into Paris at a ghastly hour, but he didn't care. In effect he was running away from Steve. He had hoped to say good-bye to me and give me some sort of explanation for his departure, but he had to get away from Steve first. He'd get word to me somehow.

A month later, Mario received a nice apologetic letter from Steve. Mario suspected the motive behind the letter was Steve's fear of a lawsuit. People at home had been urging him to sue for injuries sustained in the accident and Steve had got wind of it. However, Mario was not vindictive. Frankly, all he wanted was his freedom from Steve. Nothing in the world could convince him to do battle with Steve in court.

For Mario it was good riddance and good-bye.

See you around, Steve. Preferably not in the near future.

*   *   *

Everything around *Le Mans* was disintegrating.

Throughout that summer, Steve's outbursts toward me continued, usually without warning. They would start with an innocuous question like "What car did you drive that day?" and then he would be transformed into a raging bull.

The nights were frightening, made more so by the fact that the château was so private. And because of the gun, which he would wave around and point at me on occasion. Sometimes I'd wake up in the middle of the night and see Steve sitting by my side just staring at me.

There were times when he'd be feeling mellow after having smoked a joint and he'd catch me off guard as the relentless interrogation began again.

And I stayed, although I wanted to run away. But where to? Home? What about Terry and Chad? I had never broken a promise to them. And the thought of leaving the children behind was unthinkable.

By then I had also begun to believe it was all my fault. Steve was right. It was me! It had to be me! I would look at the man and I would see a man shaken to his very roots. If I hadn't been unfaithful, maybe the picture wouldn't be in the mess it was in. My God! Could it be my fault? How could I leave him now?

And, of course, no one knew of his suffering except me.

One day he told me he had wanted to kill himself and had purposely precipitated an accident on the track. He had escaped injury at the last minute when his survival instinct had taken over. As I stood there, faint with guilt while he recounted the story, I saw the glazed look come over his eyes and I immediately looked for cover.

"You fucking bitch! You see what you've done?" Slap. Then he pushed me hard against the wall and held me against it as he tried to control himself from demolishing me altogether. By some miracle he was able to resist the impulse. Instead he released me and told me to go away.

His head knew and understood why my fling had come to pass, but his heart found it impossible to forgive me.

On the set, John Sturges had nearly reached the point of throwing in the towel. He had become increasingly frustrated. Not only did he have his reputation to protect, but his star—who coincidentally was head of the production company—was so indecisive that nothing worthwhile was being accomplished. Thousands and thousands of feet of film had already been wasted, and still there was no story. What they had in the can so far consisted merely of cars, cars, cars and Steve, Steve, Steve and no dialogue.

Tempers reached the boiling point. One day mild-mannered Bob Relyea, executive producer, walked into his office, slammed the door, and in exasperation threw an ashtray against the wall and dejectedly announced, "We'll never finish this picture. It is out of control!"

Having heard Relyea's pronouncement, Bob Rosen, whose responsibility it was to protect the financial investment of Cinema Center Films, put in a call to the studio in California. The very next day the CCF heavyweights were on their way to Le Mans, and the day after that, on the next plane in, arrived the William Morris agents and lawyers, headed by Stan Kamen.

A big meeting was held at the Château Lornay, and it ended with the setting of a shutdown date. CCF had taken control and had told Solar, "Decide on whatever script you want, then shoot it! You have two weeks."

Steve's overt reaction was a nonplussed "My old lady and I are going to Morocco. I'll come back and shoot whatever it is you want me to shoot." Internally, however, Steve blamed Bob Relyea for having said the picture was out of control. He stopped talking to Bob and now considered him "the enemy." Steve also saw the William Morris people and Stan as ineffectual for having been unable to stop the CCF takeover action.

As soon as everybody had left the château, Steve's first words to me were, "I'm going to let Stan go. I need a barracuda and he can't hack it." He glowered at no one in particular. "He's too nice. Shit! They're all too goddamn nice!" After I recovered from the shock, I asked him to reconsider. But he was determined. "I want new people around me. People who aren't afraid to take chances." It took me a few seconds to recover. Stan had been with us for so long and had guided Steve's career so brilliantly, it was going to be difficult working with somebody else.

I needn't have concerned myself.

My days, too, were numbered.

"I need someone who isn't afraid to play dirty. Someone like Freddie Fields. I just can't help feeling that Stan and the rest of those guys from William Morris are working for CBS. Fuckers! Let's face it. CBS is bigger than Steve McQueen."

"Steve, honey, that's a little paranoid, don't you think? Whether you want to admit it or not, Bob was right. The picture is out of control!" He sat there with the chair tilted against the window. He was formulating his thoughts as he took a drag on a joint. Oddly enough, since the disclosure of my indiscretion, Steve was smoking very little grass now. He was down to nighttime indulging only. And he'd given up coke entirely. I think he was so busy keeping an eye on me that he didn't have the energy or the inclination to get high—lest something escape him. "Yup." He looked at me. "What do you think of Freddie?"

"If you're positive you don't want Stan [God, it pained me to say it], then you're right. Freddie is a barracuda. He's creative and aggressive, and I think he'll do very well by you. Call him. And then please call Stan and inform him of your decision. I feel very strongly he should hear it from you directly. There've been many great years together. All right, honey?"

Stan did hear from Steve directly. Only it was by way of a cablegram that read, DEAR STAN, YOU'RE FIRED. LETTER FOLLOWS. STEVE. He couldn't have done it more crassly. But he did write Stan a handwritten note about a month later. Big deal.

Freddie arrived shortly after that, and Steve gave him the rundown on what had occurred. Freddie Fields immediately assumed control and tried to alleviate as many problems as possible, and Steve and I went to Morocco on the invitation of the Princess Lalla Nezha.

A few days later Bob Relyea was on the telephone in his office when John Sturges knocked on the door. "Come on in, John. I'll be right with you."

"No, no, thanks. I just wanted to stop by to tell you I'm going home."

A few minutes into the conversation, Relyea realized John was referring to home in California! Not Loué, where the crew was staying.

John's reasoning couldn't be faulted. "If Steve was out of town and the script isn't written in conjunction with his input, I would just as soon go home. There's gonna be trouble along the way, and I don't see any point in staying."

Within a few days, Cinema Center Films had hired a new director, without consulting with either Steve or Bob Relyea.

So CCF had established new ground rules. No more Mr. Nice Guy.

By the time we got back to Le Mans a couple of weeks later, Bill Maher, who was now our business manager, was there with his findings. If Steve wanted to get his finances in order again, both Solars as they were presently structured had to be disbanded. In fact, we would be in a better position without those encumbrances. Agreed. Steve gave Bill the go-ahead to start dismantling the empire.

David Foster, who was just then getting into production, gave me a copy of a book entitled *The Getaway*. He hoped I'd like it well enough to convince Steve to do it. I hoped so, too, since David had been part of the team that had helped build Steve's career. While in the process of reading the material one afternoon in Steve's office on the set, I opened his desk drawer, looking for pen and paper. Realizing I was completely alone, I started reading the bits and pieces of paper that had caught my eye. What I saw was so hurtful it was enough to make me kill. I saw a starlet's name typed neatly on a memo pad next to her phone number. Beside the name and phone number was a little notation (not Steve's) that said, "On a scale of 1-10, I'd say she's a 9." Then on another piece of paper was a *Playboy* centerfold's name and phone number. And there were some other names. Strange names. But the one that upset me most was a letter written by an English duchess, asking Steve to come spend a weekend and she would make sure that so-and-so was present since Steve seemed so keen on her the last time he was in town.

What is it, I wondered, that drives generally decent people to rummage through their lover's private belongings in search of damning sexual evidence? I hadn't wanted to particularly, but once begun, I found it impossible to close the drawer and leave it be. Much as Steve, I knew, went through my drawers, my purses, and my luggage to see if he could come up with any more incriminating evidence. For as soon as I had confessed my affair, Steve was certain there were many more that he would uncover.

I had a feeling that Steve had cooled his straying nature because I had surprised and hurt him so. And I saw no point in confronting him with the information in his desk drawer since he was still so busy confronting me with what he thought was the most unthinkable act a woman could do to a man.

The daily confrontations were now taking their

toll on me. I was becoming deeply depressed, although I tried to keep up a good front. Sister Bridget, the nurse on the set, became my confidante and she comforted me a great deal. But she was helpless to do anything to protect me from Steve. All she could do was pray for us.

To make things worse, two weeks after shooting resumed, I began to feel poorly. When I fainted in Sister Bridget's hut, she made an appointment for me to see a doctor, which I resisted bitterly, saying it was only the heat. I reluctantly kept the appointment, fearing the worst. Two days later, I received the results of the tests. I was pregnant.

I couldn't bring myself to tell Steve. I had fallen off my pedestal with such a loud thud there was no question his reaction would be more one of suspicion than joy. I had visions of him growling at me for my carelessness and of him telling me a new baby would not a happy marriage make.

I wanted to be ready to act in case Steve's reaction to my condition was negative, as I expected it to be. As much as I would have wanted to have a new baby, there was no way I could withstand both the continuing physical and mental abuse and a pregnancy. I had to find out what the procedure would be. If any.

"No, madame. It is not possible to have an abortion in France," the doctor at the American Hospital in Paris said. But he was understanding and sympathetic and could put me in touch with a doctor in London. "Abortions are legal in England. But the sooner the better," I was told. "Please do not delay."

It took me three weeks to gather enough courage to face the issue with Steve. I made my announcement.

Steve looked at me disbelievingly. "What am I supposed to say? Hey, groovy, baby? You got some nerve, you know that?" And swiftly, before I could react to his words, he had pulled me by my T-shirt and had sat me on the bed.

"Whose is it, woman?" he taunted. "Are you gonna tell me or are you gonna sit there and lie?"

Tears started to well up in my eyes and Steve became more abusive.

"Oh, don't give me that shit! How am I supposed to believe it's mine!" His words were dagger thrusts. He raised his hand to slap me, but instead he took a deep breath and abruptly released me, then marched quickly out of the bedroom.

A shroud of melancholy descended upon me. God! Will it ever end? Would it ever be possible to be happy again? Would it ever be possible to live with each other in peace and in laughter? My mental state had deteriorated to such a point that holding my body up straight was debilitating. I spent as much time as I could in bed. I had to force myself to function. Our individual responsibilities were keeping us going. Mine to the children, Steve's to his work.

The children had to be back in school by mid-September. Steve had already decided I was to take them back, get them settled, and then immediately head back to Le Mans to stay with him until the end of the picture. Joe McCormack would go home with the animals a week before the children's departure to alert the couple staying at the Oakmont Drive house of the children's impending arrival. This all meant I had to move quickly if an abortion was to take place. It was beginning to look more and more like Steve would make the decision for me.

I asked him one more time, hoping he might reconsider, if I should make the arrangements in London. "Yes!" came the unhesitating reply.

Phil Abramson, the imaginative set decorator on Steve's last three movies, offered to come with me and see me through my ordeal. Phil wasn't aware of anything much except I was pregnant and wanted an abortion. Period. As far as anyone was concerned, Steve couldn't come because of his shooting schedule and it was best left that way.

Except for bits and pieces here and there, I have very little recollection of our trip to London. I remember the kindly face of the surgeon who saw me the day before the procedure was to take place. I also remember it was a brilliant summer day and that all of London seemed to be out on the streets. And if my memory serves me right, Phil took me to Soho that night for Chinese food before depositing me at the London Clinic.

I do remember well the hospital bed where I tossed and turned that night, unable to sleep, wondering out loud why at thirty-six years of age I had to terminate this pregnancy. If I had the guts I'd say, "To hell with you, Steve. I'm keeping it." But I didn't have the guts. The last few months had taken their toll on my nerves, and my only thoughts now were of survival.

Sometime before I was wheeled into surgery I had called the Richard Attenboroughs, and that afternoon Sheila, gracious and charming lady that she is, came by to visit and brought me flowers to alleviate the sadness I was feeling. I tried acting nonchalant, pretending none of the morning's events had mattered, but Sheila could see through it. To cheer me up she offered to smuggle dinner into the hospital that night. I declined, telling her I only wanted to rest. Which was true. The experience had been traumatic, and now that it was over I wanted nothing more than to be enveloped by those four walls.

As soon as I was able to, I returned to France, packed the children, and we flew home to California, where I had to organize their lives before rejoining their father. I was glad for the opportunity to escape—even for just a little bit. I felt the tension fall away from my much maligned body. The children, too, were glad to be back at school with their friends. Three months in France had been enough for them.

Then it was time to tackle Le Mans, hoping to pick up the threads of my very fragile marriage.

We had given up the mammoth Château Lornay and moved to the Château de Segrais, a "retirement home" that was run like a hotel. I liked it much better than the château since the rooms were airier and brighter, and Steve and I hoped it would spell a new beginning for us. I knew he was trying hard to forget. But regrettably, he was having a hell of a time. The fact that I, too, had much to forget did not even enter my mind.

One afternoon after my return, David Piper, one of the older English grand prix drivers on the film, had a ghastly accident on the race course when he miscalculated how fast he could take a turn by La Petite Maison Blanche, the little white house used as a marker by the drivers. He struck the rail instead, sending him spinning round and round, with sparks shooting under and around the Porsche 917 as David struggled desperately to control the car.

David was rushed to the hospital in Le Mans with a badly fractured right leg, then quickly flown to London. The English doctors did everything they could to save his leg but were unable to. He was a courageous and gallant man. When we visited him at the hospital, I was impressed by the way he was able to accept his misfortune.

It's really too bad Steve had developed tunnel vision where *Le Mans* was concerned. His inability to concentrate on developing a strong story spelled doom for the movie from the very beginning. He had been blinded by those magnificent machines and had failed to come to terms with the rest of the world. The world needed the human element to identify with. Cars were secondary to human emotions. He knew that, but somehow he forgot.

But to everybody's credit, the film thrillingly and gloriously captured the race world. Unfortunately, there weren't enough people out there who cared, and the film was a major box office disaster.

* * *

There was no wrap party when *Le Mans* ended.

The civil war that had erupted during the Cinema Center Films takeover had pitted friend against friend and had abolished the good feelings that had characterized the start of the production. And a budding empire that had hoped to take wing managed to stay aloft only long enough to lose several million dollars.

Steve went to lick his wounds in Switzerland. We drove the gray Porsche to the Niehans Clinic, where we stayed for two weeks and were rejuvenated physically. But mentally he was despairing, whereas I had become totally accepting of the harassment he doled out to me each day because by now I was thoroughly convinced the fault was mine alone and that I deserved whatever punishment I got.

By the time we came back to California, I felt I had been ravaged. I was desperate and finally enlisted the aid of our doctor, who turned us over to a marriage counselor. After a few weeks of therapy our marriage counselor felt he would be unable to help us in view of Steve's unforgiving attitude. He suggested we see separate psychiatrists. God! Anything! Anything that could relieve the unremitting tension between us!

At least Steve had his grass and his beers and his motorcycles to turn to. I had nothing. I didn't have the energy to go to dance class, I didn't drink, and drugs were not my scene. Cigarettes probably kept me from becoming unstrung altogether. I went from a pack a day to two and a half packs a day.

For Christmas, German actor Siegfried Rauch and his wife, Karen, came to Palm Springs to spend the holidays with us. So did my mother, and so did George and Jolene Schlatter with their daughter, Maria. I was ecstatic. At least the presence of the group ensured Steve would exercise a modicum of restraint. The only place where danger existed was in our bedroom. And I did believe I was in danger. There were guns in this house just as there were guns at Oakmont. Steve, increasingly, was finding it harder to suppress his anger. He had gone a step beyond working out. It had been his way of letting off steam. Now he was working out on me. I thought of obtaining a restraining order, but I knew the press would get wind of it and I felt a strong sense of responsibility to protect his reputation—for everyone's sake. I was boxed in.

When the holidays were over and we were back at the Castle, Steve had a particularly violent day directed mostly at the wall sconces in the entry hall and my collection of perfume bottles and antique boxes on my dressing table. I called Dr. Arons, my psychiatrist, who consulted with Dr. Goodheart, Steve's psychiatrist. It was obvious things were getting out of hand and we had to separate or it was likely I would wind up dead. But what was more distressing to me was the effect it was having on the children. They were aware something awful was happening. Terry was almost twelve and Chad was ten—still impressionable ages. One day after school, Terry had been upstairs with me in my dressing room when Steve had pushed open the door hard, slamming it against the wall, then had pulled me by the arm and had dragged me down the stairs as he called to Terry to "close the door and stay in there until I call you!" He had grabbed me by the neck and had pushed me into the living room, all the while asking me, *"Why? Why?"* And when I hadn't answered he smacked me across the face and then, suddenly ashamed of what he had done, he had left hurriedly on his motorcycle for God knows where.

Steve loathed himself for his inability to control his violent episodes. He was always remorseful afterwards and would hold me and tell me how much he loved me. I believed him. I needed desperately to believe him. But I was also determined to follow the psychiatrists' advice. We had to separate. I was afraid for me and I was afraid for him. And we were both afraid for the children—how it might affect them in the long run.

Betsy found Steve a guest house in the Pacific Palisades. It was old and small and damp. The musty smell suggested it hadn't been aired in years. It depressed me so when I first saw it, I asked him to move back in with me.

"I can't, baby. God knows there's nothing I'd like better. But I've gotta get over this or we'll never make it."

He didn't want to move into a house with all the comforts of home. It would have meant putting a period on our relationship, and he was not ready for that yet. He wanted a feeling of impermanence so he could leave everything at the Oakmont house except for the bare necessities, thereby giving him a legitimate reason to come by. Also, he wanted to think and get himself together. He felt a small guest house would preclude the temptation to have overnight visitors. It was a time for being alone.

I think very few people are aware how hard divorces and separations are on men. As difficult as they are for women, we at least remain in our own familiar surroundings. We have the children, the animals, and the furniture. The man is totally displaced. He has to think of things he never thought of before. The laundry, the food in the refrigerator, and if he's lucky, the maid he has to contend with. For a man like Steve, there were a hundred and one details he found impossibly confusing to deal with.

We were allowed to date each other, which we found absurd, but we dared to hope that by following doctor's orders, we'd get better. He never met my psychiatrist, but Steve had developed a grudging admiration for his. He no longer thought it unmanly to seek their help as he once had.

There were times when I'd spend the night at his place and there were times when he'd spend the night at the Castle. It still wasn't possible to spend time together without Casanova's name being brought up. Steve's anger would make me flinch, as always, but he was becoming better at suppressing it. The violent outbursts had lessened, which made me a little more trusting and a little less scared.

On February 9, 1971, Southern California was rocked by a violent earthquake that registered 7.2 on the Richter scale. The earthquake had taken place in the early morning hours, and while it had been in progress, Steve and I had simultaneously sat up in bed and gaped at each other. The Castle was swaying as it moaned and groaned like a giant dinosaur fighting to keep extinction at bay.

"My God! Honey, the kids!" was all I managed to say as I tried to stand up.

"Fuck, man! I gotta get down there!" Steve, in his rush to get downstairs to the children's bedrooms, had sprung out of bed like a cat, deftly knocking me over and spraining my ankle severely (I was unable to dance for a whole year). As it turned out, the children had acted sensibly. They remembered what I had told them about earthquakes and had positioned themselves in a doorway and waited until Steve got to them. When it was all over we all looked at each other as if waiting for the next round—not knowing exactly what to do. Our housekeeper, who had come into the hallway to join us, received an even bigger shock than the earthquake's when she came face to face with Steve, sitting on the stairway without a stitch of clothing on.

After our nerves had stabilized, Steve drove me to the doctor's office to have my ankle looked at. It had turned an angry purple and red and was throbbing furiously. After it had been wrapped and after I had been given crutches to walk with, I turned to Steve and laughed. "And you said you loved me so much!"

15

By Steve's forty-first birthday on March 24, 1971, things were looking up. Our thrice weekly dates and our daily phone conversations had melded, unnoticed almost, into our total involvement in each other's lives, and once again we were together at the house on Oakmont Drive. Once again we were a family, although it was against my doctor's advice. He felt it was too soon. But I felt I knew better.

After all, I do know the man, doctor, we've been together for fifteen years!

I was well aware that Casanova was alive and well in Steve's head, but thanks to the intensive visits with his psychiatrist, the name nowadays elicited only mild contempt for the man and a baleful stare for me. Although this was still a daily occurrence, it was one I could easily live with.

Then early one evening a producer-friend called to ask if he could drop off a script for Steve to read. He had been an agent at William Morris, and he was a man Steve admired for his gentle approach to life.

"Sure, Phil. Anytime. We're in all evening."

"Oh, great, Steve. Say, would you mind if I bring along a friend? We won't bother to get out of the car. It'll just save me having to double back to the Beverly Hills Hotel if he comes with me now. You might even enjoy meeting him." It was "Him"!

"Of course, Phil." Click.

"Neile!" It had startled me. By the way he bellowed my name I thought one of the children had had an accident. But it came to me they were at a friend's house and staying the night. It was Friday.

I came running down the stairs as fast as I could, thinking he'd had an accident, just as he came bounding up the steps, taking them two at a time.

The man I met on the landing was not a normal man. His face was red and his veins were sticking out of his neck and his eyes revealed my deepest fear. He had lost control of himself, for whatever reason, and I was alone with him. Without losing his stride, he had caught me just right. He grabbed my right arm, put it behind me, proceeded to push me up the stairs and then began swinging at me wildly with his left hand. Mercifully he refrained from using a closed fist. As soon as we were in the bedroom he pushed the door shut with his foot and simultaneously shoved me hard onto the bed. When I turned around and saw him coming toward me I thought I'd had it.

All I remember saying was "Honey, please don't!"

He grabbed me by my sweater and started shaking me. "You see what you've done?" Slap. "Now I even have the son-of-a-bitch coming to my house." Slap. "You sure you wouldn't wanna fuck him here?" Slap. "You whore! How dare you!"

I had no idea what had precipitated the outburst. It stunned me. But in between the shakes, the slaps, and the jabs, the story came out.

An alarm rapidly spread through my body. He is going to be here soon. Steve will pounce on him most likely when he extends his hand in introduction. Phil probably won't even know how to react since everything will happen very quickly. What if Steve shoots him? Oh, my God! All I could think of was that I had to get out of here. I was acting like a coward and I didn't care. If Steve went after him, he would surely come after me too. God, Dr. Arons, why didn't I listen to you? Jesus Christ! How do I get out of here?

Very quickly, kid. Very quickly.

I waited till Steve was sufficiently calm before I told him I had to pick up the children. In the meantime I prayed that Phil wouldn't ring that gate buzzer. At least not until I was out of the house. It was a little before six o'clock now and I headed for the beach. I wanted to be alone to figure out what to do. I was still shaking and still a little hysterical as I parked my car on San Vicente and went across Ocean Avenue and sat on one of the park benches. The sun had already disappeared behind the dark Pacific, and to my wry amusement, I noticed the pink of my sweater almost matched the pink evening dusk. The air was chilly and I hoped I'd catch pneumonia and die. God! Would it ever get better? Or had I condemned myself to this way of life forever? I sat there for a long time in the cold night air, not knowing what to do with myself. One thing I was certain of—I had no desire to go home. And the other thing I was certain of—I couldn't possibly live with him and keep my sanity. We would have to separate again.

I went back to my car and headed for my friend Ann Smith's house. I knew I was always welcome there and I knew she'd never betray me to Steve.

She was waiting for me when I arrived. Steve had been looking for me. She promised him she'd call if I came by. Of course, she didn't and wouldn't. That's what friends are for. I hugged her and thanked her and then told her what had happened.

I stayed at Ann's house for three hours. Steve called every twenty minutes to ask about my whereabouts. "No," Ann said, "she hasn't come by." And after Steve's last call Ann turned to me and reported Steve had called the police.

"You'd best go back, Butterfly [her nickname for me]. He's really worried now."

I was tired, but I couldn't go back—not just yet, anyway. I was frightened by what I might find at Oakmont. I drove around and around, idly thinking I might drive to Palm Springs, but finally after an hour, I figured it was time to face the music. Whatever it might be. I stopped at a gas station and went to a phone booth.

He answered immediately. "Baby, where are you?"

"I don't know, honey. Somewhere." I paused for a moment and then I cried haltingly, "Can I come home now?"

When I pulled into the courtyard Steve pulled me gently out of the car and held me in his arms while I sobbed. He rocked me side to side telling me he was sorry. After all I'd been through the last few hours I found out the man hadn't shown after all.

I thought to myself perhaps Casanova had found himself a date. And then again, perhaps he might have thought it best not to come and tempt fate.

Memorial Day night, 1971, was a night I shall never forget to my dying day.

We were living separately again, seeing our respective shrinks and once more playing the dating game. He was back in that wretched guest house, and the children and I were in our beautiful Oakmont Drive house. I couldn't bear the thought of him living there, but he promised he'd move as soon as he returned from Prescott, Arizona, where he was starting a new movie called *Junior Bonner.*

We still both hoped we could work it out.

One of the more positive and constructive results of his time with Dr. Goodheart, he had informed me, was that he no longer had the need to use hard drugs as a way of making a statement.

However, on this night of Memorial Day, when he picked me up he was already high, which made me apprehensive.

"On grass, baby. That's all!" He had come in and

talked to Terry and Chad for a while and then kissed them good night and promised to take them to dinner the following night. They were also making plans for the Arizona location. We were painfully aware I was not going to be there this time. Sadly, we had learned that money and fame were not a guarantee against harm's way.

On the way to the restaurant, the coke came out.

"Ah, honey. I thought you said that was over with." I must be calm. Be cool, kid. I was very nervous. I could feel the hair on the back of my neck bristling.

He said a buddy of his had given it to him and he was just trying it out. "Don't you worry, baby. I'm fine. O.K.?"

What could I say? I was in the car. I would have to be on my toes tonight, I could see that. At Chez Jay's, we dined and talked while he drank three Carta Blancas. I was watching him carefully, knowing full well what to expect. Shit! Should I refuse to go home with him? For some reason I couldn't. On the way home, he smoked a roach and swallowed what he couldn't smoke.

As we turned right onto Bristol Circle North from Sunset Boulevard (the scenic route, as we used to refer to it), the questions began.

"How did you meet him?" "Were you scared?" How did you feel afterwards?" Ever so gently, so as not to frighten me, I presumed.

Oh, but I was frightened.

By the time we had approached the speed bumps on Oakmont Drive, the battery of questions had crescendoed to such a pitch that I remember considering jumping out of the car. The jabs were coming fast and furious on my left arm and I was becoming hysterical.

As we drove up the long driveway to the house, Steve had one hand on the wheel and the other hand was holding onto my hair, tightly pulling my head back. As soon as the car stopped, I tried to open my door, but he was quicker than I was. He rapidly jumped out of his side and his powerful arms grabbed me by my neck and arm and pulled me out over the gear box and across his seat. He kicked me from behind and I went sprawling on the courtyard. And he came at me again, asking me, "Why? Why did you do it, you whore?" This time he pulled me up and slapped me hard against the side of my head. I remember the explosion and the incredible sensation of not knowing where I was for a second. And then another one caught me on my ear. This one sent me on my knees.

And then silence. Just as I started praying.

I looked up and saw Steve as in a freeze frame, his eyes staring toward the servants' room, with his arm in a pulled-back position ready to strike.

I didn't know why he stopped and I didn't care. I crawled on all fours to the back door ready to pound as hard as I could so Ariel or Mary (our houseman and housekeeper) would open the door. To my surprise it was already open.

(The next day Ariel told me what happened. He had heard a commotion going on outside after Mr. McQueen's car came up the driveway. He looked out his window and witnessed the scene. He didn't know what to do. He didn't want to interfere and yet he knew he must stop it. Ariel had picked up the radio on his dresser and had smashed it against the wall. Which apparently is what jarred Steve out of his agitated state. Immediately Ariel had then quietly opened the door.)

Steve's energy was spent. I knew I was safe now. I was hanging on to the doorway as my head leaned against the doorjamb. I was weary and I ached in forty different places. Steve put his arms around me, shocked at what he had done.

"Oh, my God, baby. I'm sorry. So sorry." And I knew he was. He just couldn't help himself. But I could and I didn't intend to make any more mistakes.

"Honey, I'm going to have to leave you." Tears were running down my face. "I must because if I don't, someday you'll kill me. And my God, honey, what will happen to the children? I don't want that for them. Do you?"

My knees and hands were scraped and I had a gash on my thigh, apparently suffered during the slide across the car. My face felt all right although my head was pounding, and I had blood blisters on my right ear.

Steve helped me upstairs and put me to bed. He kissed me good night and we held each other tightly. Before he turned to go he said, "I love you and I will always love you." He smiled sadly. "Remember that, will you?"

I was quietly crying again and through the tears I nodded.

"Good-bye, my husband. I love you. Take care of yourself."

Junior Bonner and Prescott, Arizona, were notable to me for my personal lack of involvement in Steve's new movie. That had never happened before. For the first time in fifteen years I felt completely separate from him.

Junior Bonner was the story of an over-the-hill rodeo champion. Sam Peckinpah was signed to direct and the industry expected fireworks between McQueen and the volatile director. Instead the two got on famously and Steve wound up turning in one of his better performances. And he looked fabulous.

It was a time for adjusting to changing circumstances. I wasn't ready to file for divorce just yet. That seemed so final. I still wanted to hang on, hoping for the impossible to reverse itself. Yet when I put Terry and Chad on the plane to Arizona to visit Steve for two weeks that summer, I felt like an outsider. These were my children, going to see Daddy. Why isn't Mommy on the plane with them? It was very depressing. I went home and stayed in bed for two days.

Although Steve called me two or three times a week, something had died between us, and it would require a major miracle not yet invented to resurrect it. Our conversations were aimless. How's the weather? How're you doing? How's the movie coming? Feelings were never discussed. Emotions were still raw.

The children came home with a new dog Steve had found in the desert. We named him Junior and he became the instant star in the neighborhood. This dog, part shepherd and part collie, was very agile and became adept at jumping from the porch onto the garage roof. But once there, he couldn't figure his way back to the porch and neither could anyone else—with the exception of the fire department. A fireman would have to get on the roof with the dog, then push him down the yellow safety slide, while all the children in the neighborhood would cheer Junior on. It became a regular Happening—much to the displeasure of the Brentwood Fire Department.

When Steve came home from Prescott, he brought me two beautiful Navaho bracelets. He hadn't announced his arrival and he came through the door carrying a briefcase, wearing a green embroidered cowboy shirt, jeans, and cowboy boots. He looked gorgeous and I felt an immediate stab to the heart. Being away from each other for ten weeks had done him good. He looked rested and he no longer had that haunted look. I silently thanked God for that.

I was at a loss for words. We both were. It was as if we had never met. Or worse. It was as if we had forgotten how to talk to each other. We were both acting, trying to act "normal," both trying to suppress the pain we had suffered and were still suffering.

After having a reunion with the children, he hugged me and asked me to dinner the next night. To avoid the kind of drastic change in mood that had precipitated the Memorial Day episode, we had been advised to take separate cars when going out and we both thought it wise.

I met him at the Santa Ynez Inn in the Pacific Palisades, which was close to where he was staying. Throughout dinner as he drank beer after beer, we talked about our lives, what it would mean to be without each other. We were both frightened of being alone, and yet there was no denying that the anger he felt toward me was too terrible a threat. I cried and he drank. We closed the place up and because he was too inebriated to drive, I risked taking him home to his guest house in his car. There was no problem, for he was asleep the moment his head hit the pillow. I sat and stared at the sleeping face. We were in a place we hadn't wanted to be. There was no turning back. Divorce was only a matter of time.

Not long after, Steve found himself a new and terrific guest house on Coldwater Canyon. Now formally on the loose, he started dating other women while we still saw each other once or twice a week. He spent a great deal of time at the Oakmont house during the day, conducting his business and spending time with the children. Since the very real possibility existed I would be seeing an attorney sooner or later, he consulted with his to explore. What the possible legal alternatives might be. He definitely had no intension of filing. He was going to let matters stand.

That year (1971) he also joined First Artists Productions, a new company, in partnership with three other giants of the silver screen: Paul Newman, Barbra Streisand, and Sidney Poitier. This company had been masterminded by Freddie Fields and David Begelman and gave the individual artist control of his projects.

After much discussion I had convinced Steve he should go ahead and do *The Getaway*. He had been reluctant to do it because the main thrust of the story dealt with the wife's unfaithfulness.

"Look at it this way, honey. You've been through it, you know how it feels." I actually said that teasingly, but the immediate tenseness of his face and body promptly told me I should back off. "I'm sorry, honey. I was just kidding."

Anyway, since *The Getaway* was handy and since Steve wanted to test the effectiveness of First Artists, everything fell into place quite nicely for David Foster and Mitch Brower, a new team of producers.

And even as these events unfolded, somewhere in us was still the hope of reviving our marriage.

But finally, on the first Friday in October, I filed for its dissolution. Steve was angry and hurt, but I had to get on with my life. No matter what it brought. I couldn't bear to live it dangling in the air like a trapeze artist. Not anymore.

The time had come for some semblance of order.

Ali MacGraw's star seemed suddenly to burst on the Hollywood scene. Following her movie debut as the stylishly beautiful Brenda Patimkin in *Goodbye, Columbus,* she had married the successful and handsome Bob Evans, who was in charge of production at Paramount Studios. She seemed to have a fairy tale existence with him. Then he cast her in the enormously popular *Love Story* and shortly thereafter, as befits a king, she bore him a son, whom they named Joshua.

A new Paramount film called *The Godfather* directed by Francis Ford Coppola was creating a disturbance of sorts in the Evans household. The film was being touted as Paramount's next big hit, and as head of production, Bob Evans was doing everything possible to ensure its success—including, apparently, installing a bed for his bad back in his projection room at home so he could watch and supervise the film's editing at all hours of the day and night. While others found this obsession and dedication to his work admirable, Ali did not. She felt like the forgotten woman.

Steve and she chanced upon each other at the right time: she, the shunned wife, who had expressed her great admiration for Steve McQueen in interviews, even before their meeting; and he, the almost divorced man still experiencing the emotional upheaval brought about by a break in a deep involvement of long standing.

The Getaway began shooting in El Paso just three weeks before our divorce became final on April 26, 1972. We had been married for fifteen and a half years and as I left the Santa Monica courthouse in the company of my lawyer, I suddenly felt lost and alone.

The judge had congratulated me and Steve (in absentia) for the manner in which we had conducted our divorce proceedings. He was impressed that our custody agreement declared the children were free to come and go between our two houses according to *their* wishes, not ours. Their choices would be based on their needs. (We had agreed beforehand the children's welfare was of paramount importance. No games were to be played at their expense.)

Arriving at the Santa Monica courthouse had been disconcerting. As used as I was to photographers, I had been stunned to find them waiting for me curbside at eight thirty in the morning. I asked my lawyer why on earth they would be there. Surely they must know Steve was in El Paso with *The Getaway*. He said that was precisely why they were there—to record a possibly momentous occasion that might affect Steve, Ali McGraw, and Bob Evans.

As soon as I got home, I immediately placed a call to Steve, who was just as traumatized as I was upon learning that, after all those years, we were no longer man and wife. It was difficult for either one of us to carry on a rational conversation. Trying to discuss with one's ex-spouse what it meant to be free again was unnatural and unreal.

Suddenly, Steve interrupted our aimless conversation by asking me to come and join him in El Paso.

I almost choked on my cigarette. "My God, do you realize what you're saying?"

"No, I'm not sure, but I'll sort it out later. Anyway, come on down."

In spite of the situation I had to laugh. Possibly it was what the moment required. A little levity. When we recovered we agreed it wouldn't be a good idea for me to make a personal appearance on that particular location.

Before I hung up I said just think of me once in a while and he replied I always do.

And that ended that.

I have sometimes wondered what sort of pandemonium I might have caused the company (not to mention Ali) had I appeared on the set. I laugh as I write this now. The circumstances would have been tailor-made for Noel Coward.

In any event, Steve had informed me of his affair with Ali almost at its inception. He didn't want me to learn of it through the press and definitely not from the children. His concern was that I might hear about it at a possibly vulnerable moment. Steve said he was fascinated by her—by her quick mind and by her sophistication. He said she was a "heavy lady," which in Steve's parlance meant "really terrific."

My reaction to this affair with Ali was one of genuine alarm. I saw my alimony going out the window because of what was happening in El Paso! Alimony, after all, was only as good as a man's earning capacity. My God! Ali MacGraw was the wife of a big Hollywood mogul. I was suddenly envisioning a time when all work would cease for Steve because he had been labeled an untouchable. Something someone had said to me in jest kept coming back to me: "Hell hath no fury like a woman scorned—unless it's a man."

I had heard stories of producers' banding together to prevent certain actors from working. In fact, I knew of an actor, a friend, whose very promising career was ruined when he made the mistake of falling in love with the already married daughter of a movie magnate. It had been tough going for a few years for this fine talent—which had to have been an eternity for him—until mercifully, television and European films beckoned, saving him from oblivion. His Hollywood movie career was never able to reachieve the lost momentum.

Thus, my concern for Steve, who was now embarked on yet another phase (or so he thought) of his life. This one was called "I ain't hidin' no more"—in an obvious reference to me when he felt compelled to sneak around with his various lady friends during our marriage, causing a certain amount of paranoia in his personality. "Bull, McQueen!" had been my reply to that one when he discussed it with me. And I added, for good measure, "Your 'truth' and your 'letting it all hang out' was in large part the reason for the ruin of our marriage. So don't give me that. You can tell Ali that. Or another girl. But please, not me. I've been there. Remember?"

"O.K., O.K.! Jesus!" He had not anticipated my reaction. "Well, it sounds good anyway, don't it?" He laughed. And now he was back to being a bad boy.

An act I was very familiar with.

And even now, even while he was several hundred miles away, I could see his face break out into a wide smile, showing those wonderful teeth and those crinkly blue eyes.

Although Steve and Ali's affair was strongly hinted at, it was never directly acknowledged. It was there for everyone to see, yet the press people were treading lightly, I suspect more out of respect for Bob

Evans than for the principals involved. Then, too, the tabloids as they are today had not yet evolved.

The rumors, though, spread like wildfire in Hollywood, and the result was curious.

There was a good deal of resentment toward Ali. One could feel the undercurrent very strongly. But why? Certainly this was not a new phenomenon. Leading ladies have been falling in love with their leading men and vice versa since time immemorial. Ali, as if in the days of old Hollywood, was branded a *scarlet woman!* in the community. This was ironic, since we were in the era of a more permissive and enlightened "new" Hollywood. Moreover, Bob Evans, who was adored by the press, was fast becoming a martyr in their eyes. He was welcome anywhere in the world—except El Paso. Steve said when Bob Evans heard his wife had fallen in love with her leading man, he determined to launch a campaign to retrieve her. I think, from what Steve told me, Bob was caught betwixt and between. Bob had been instrumental in Ali's decision to join Steve in *The Getaway,* just as I had been instrumental in convincing Steve that Ali and he would be terrific together on the screen. (Although we were in the process of divorce—and even after our divorce—Steve almost always sought my advice.) Ali had told Bob she was content to stay home and play house, and Bob retorted that it's time you went back to work. He jokingly told her, "You're getting boring already!" He felt the chemistry between Steve and Ali would be sensational.

Finally Ali agreed to do the movie, and Bob recounted this story to me over dinner at agent Sue Menger's house as he looked lovingly at Ali, who was seated across the table from me. Bob was my dinner partner that night as I had already filed for divorce and had come alone. It was the first time I had met Ali, although Bob and I had met each other somewhere along our Hollywood years.

I recollect an incident although I don't remember

the exact details. Somebody from the company—I think it was Sam Peckinpah, the picture's director—met with Bob Evans in Mexico (how the meeting was arranged I don't know) and Sam asked Bob not to come to the location lest he upset the apple cart. Bob knew enough about producing movies to be sensitive to the possible budget deficit that could be brought about by a romantic upheaval by one of the performing artists.

It had to have been very difficult for Bob Evans to make the decision to stay away. On the one hand he wanted Ali back as his wife, and on the other hand there was his desire for her to do well in her first "grown-up" role, which he had selected for her. If he appeared in El Paso, she might become emotionally unhinged and thereby upset her performance. And yet, by electing not to appear, he risked permanently damaging their relationship as husband and wife. How he was able to reconcile all that in his heart with the events that were taking place is difficult to assess. It would be presumptuous of me to hazard a guess. But honoring the request to stay away had to have been painful. And I have to give Bob Evans enormous credit for being able to honor the status quo.

I think it was probably at this juncture that a compromise was reached. Ali was given time off to join her husband in New York to promote *The Godfather*. The picture that appeared in the newspapers all across the country following that picture's premiere in New York showed a glowing Mr. and Mrs. Evans laughing and dancing and looking into each other's eyes.

In truth, Ali wanted nothing better and nothing more than to be back in El Paso with Steve McQueen.

With reason.

She was mad about him and he about her.

During the period *The Getaway* was shooting in El

Paso, I started detecting a hoarseness in Steve's voice that seemed to come and go. At first I thought it was my imagination and then I began to think it was our telephone connection. I was wrong. He was being bothered by something in the air down there, he explained.

After a while, his hoarseness had advanced into an annoying, sort of throat-clearing exercise. Since we talked frequently—mostly about the children—I was able unconsciously to chart the progress of the cough. Finally, I asked him what in heaven's name was the matter? It didn't sound like an everyday cough. He wasn't sick and neither did he have a cold. He felt only as if there was something constantly caught in the back of his throat.

"So stop smoking cigarettes and grass, for God's sake!" I had pleaded.

"Don't be silly, woman! I need to wind down at night!"

Steve was unable to undergo a battery of tests that our doctor had advised until the completion of the movie. The results of the tests would determine the course of action.

I was uneasy. Ethically, since I was no longer his wife, I couldn't discuss my ex-husband's ailments with our good Dr. Kert. And yet, because of our long-standing relationship, I felt entitled to the information. I couldn't put Dr. Kert in a compromising position. I would have to be patient and wait until Steve himself filled me in when the tests were completed.

Within forty-eight hours after the conclusion of principal photography, Steve was wheeled into the operating room of Mt. Sinai (Cedars-Sinai today) for the removal of polyps in his throat. This was a direct result, I was told, of too much smoking.

Only a handful of people knew Steve was in the hospital. Freddie Fields and I waited in the coffee shop downstairs for Steve's return from the recovery room. During our conversation, I learned that Freddie was now being regularly subjected to the abusive irrationality that was so much a part of Steve's personality.

Freddie has since said, "He was suspicious of anything and everything, including himself! And I was his best friend at that time!" Freddie used the word "paranoid" about some of Steve's actions, much as Hilly Elkins long before, Stan Kamen, Mario Iscovich, and a host of other people had used it. The same description was applied to Steve for many years, but Freddie had been unaware how deeply rooted the problem was.

Steve had been withholding half of the agency commission he owed Freddie. Freddie felt it was Steve's way of testing their friendship and working relationship—that is, if I hold this from you, will you still work for me or will you like me as much? Steve never needed an actual reason to act against an imagined grievance. My feeling was that Freddie had most likely said something that Steve hadn't happened to agree with at the time. It didn't matter. I knew Freddie was entitled to those fees. I promised him I would talk to Steve as soon as I felt the timing was right. (Which I did eventually, and Freddie Fields did receive the full amount he was owed.)

In Steve's room a tub of flowers was sitting on the windowsill. They were from Ali. Steve was clearly disappointed that she had elected to stay away. And knowing him as well as I did, I knew he would forever hold it against her. Only the Lord knew when it would surface, but I was certain it would when she least expected it.

Ali's reasoning was well founded. I think she was not yet ready to tell the public a divorce was imminent and she was still living with her husband. As far as the world was concerned, a reconciliation between the Evanses was still possible, and to show up at the hospital would have created unnecessary gossip she neither needed nor wanted.

Plus their son, Joshua, had to have been a major consideration in Ali's thinking. Steve had already told me Bob Evans was bitterly opposed to Joshua's exposure to him, and I imagine Ali didn't want to test Bob's hurt feelings any more than necessary.

I stayed the afternoon as Steve fidgeted in his bed. What he had undergone was not major surgery, but Dr. Kert wanted to keep him in the hospital for observation for a few days nonetheless.

Steve had never been comfortable in hospitals. He detested them and feared them at the same time. When our children were much younger and Chad would have his yearly severe asthma attack, it was my responsibility alone to stay with our son at the hospital. Terry was hospitalized once with pneumonia and once with acute tracheitis, and neither time had Steve come to see his daughter, the apple of his eye. It wasn't that he hadn't cared—he was apprised of what went on at every moment. It was his own irrational fear. (This fear might have had something to do with his going to Mexico rather than an establishment hospital during his final illness. I don't know. He never discussed it with me.)

Now here he was, expressing through body language that he felt like a caged tiger. He was also very cranky because he wasn't allowed to utter a sound. He was never at his best writing anything down, and the slow process irritated him. Now he was being forced to. It incensed him.

And to top it all off, Ali wasn't there to see him through his convalescence. She, whom he thought he could count on. Her commitment couldn't be as complete as she had led him to believe, could it?

He could be so exasperatingly simplistic that sometimes one wanted to shake him and say, Grow up, Steve, for goodness' sake!

Then the morning after surgery, he dressed himself and calmly walked out of the hospital unnoticed and walked all the way to Freddie's office, which was only three blocks away. Using the voice he had been asked to pamper, he announced that if CMA wanted its commission, then, by golly, they'd best find someone to drive him home. Done!

The year was 1972 and it was the beginning of summer.

Steve was forty-two years old and in the prime of his life.

Today, I am convinced that this was the start of the insidious cancer that would in time destroy him. It was as if it had announced its presence to this almost perfect body and had said unceremoniously, "Beware. I am here."

16

AFTER GOING THROUGH the most turbulent, the most debilitating and the most excruciatingly painful two years of my life, there I was—alone, after fifteen and a half years. To say I felt lost is putting it mildly. I had pushed for the divorce because I saw no other way out. It was for my own survival. When we were together, Steve had me believing I was the cause of the mess our marriage was in. And yet when I was by myself and able to think clearly, the fact remained that his accelerating selfish and self-serving demands and behavior were so outrageous as to defy anyone's sense of decency and self-respect. Who knows? He might eventually have asked for a divorce anyway. We certainly seemed headed in that direction. I cried myself to sleep, night after night, over what should have been. I prayed for the pain to go away quickly or I was sure it would kill me.

And as time went by, I came to the conclusion there had to be an ending before there could be a new beginning for me.

I danced for hours until it was time for the children to come home from school. At night when the children went to bed I buried myself in needlepoint. I took classes at UCLA. I let my hair grow out. I lost an enormous amount of weight without noticing it. My cigarette smoking escalated to three packs a day.

298

And still the pain of our breakup would come rushing back at me with an intensity that would leave me breathless and limp. What I was going through, I understood later, was a period of mourning.

As always, Steve and I were in touch with each other. And I could tell how enthralled he was in this new relationship with Ali. It was shattering to me that he had found someone so quickly and someone so visible. Some days I would say, "Good. Better her than me." And then on some days I'd wallow in self-pity, unable to pick myself up off the floor. It had been a lifetime since I had been on my own. Could I manage again? My feelings of insecurity were powerful but my sanity had been at stake.

In the end I had come out with much less than I had been financially entitled to, but it hadn't mattered. I wanted no delays and I knew in my heart Steve would come to the rescue if the need ever arose. For now it was time to gather my own resources and concentrate on me—the new me, whoever that might be.

And as soon as I found her I resolved never to lose her again.

There is no doubt Steve's and Ali's relationship was a genuine love affair. And as long as it was an affair it was fine. In time, however, because of his basic hostility toward women, he would come to resent their marriage.

Steve had brought Ali and Joshua up to the Castle so we could all get reacquainted. It was somewhat awkward because here was the "king" come back to his abandoned castle, with the pretender to the throne and the now deposed queen. But we all survived. Sometime during that visit Ali took me to the side and said she hoped I hadn't resented her alliance with Steve. She said she never would have gotten involved with him had I still been married to him. I smiled because she was so earnest and so open and so direct. I had always liked her. I liked her that minute and I still do. Maybe it's the old school tie. She and I had both graduated from Rosemary Hall (a few years apart). The coincidence wasn't lost on either one of us, and we rather enjoyed the bond.

Ali had already filed for divorce from Bob Evans, and because Bob's ego had been painfully wounded, he had threatened to declare Ali an unfit mother because she was living with Steve. It was 1972 and such things were possible; although Steve felt it was an idle threat.

Luck had been with her when she found a house off Mulholland Drive that looked down on Steve's rented guest house on Coldwater Canyon. The easy access between the two houses (twenty-five yards on foot or a fifteen-minute drive by car) made it possible for Steve and Ali to live together quietly and undetected by a curious world.

Not too long after that Steve told me he'd decided to go ahead with *Papillon*. Earlier he had been concerned about the fact that the film's characters were French. My argument had been if all the actors involved spoke the same way, with no accents, and only alluded to themselves as Frenchmen, then problems wouldn't arise insofar as the public's accepting them in general, and Steve, as Henri Charriére, in particular. After thinking it over, he had agreed with me, and this time had hired himself out as an independently contracted actor. "Let the producer do his thing. I'll just act this time around."

As a little footnote on the making of *Papillon*, ever since Steve had seen Eli Wallach wear a gold tooth as an extension of his character in *The Magnificent Seven*, Steve couldn't wait for the day when he'd be able to do the same. *Papillon* gave him the chance. He thanked his lucky stars he had remembered the gold tooth as soon as Dustin Hoffman walked onto the set with his little wire glasses. Steve never did take kindly to being bested, even by a little prop.

* * *

The children were delighted with Ali—until the phenomenon of divorce hit them.

As much as he worshiped his father, Chad couldn't bring himself to go to Jamaica, where *Papillon* was being shot. Not yet. Although he couldn't articulate his feelings then, he couldn't leave Mommy behind. We agreed with the suggestion of a psychologist that nothing would be gained by forcing Chad to Jamaica. Terry, on the other hand, couldn't wait to get on that plane with Ali to see her dad. It was a little different for my thirteen-year-old daughter. She was more sophisticated than her brother. There was Ali's own movie star allure, there was Jamaica, and of course, there was Dad, love of her life, whom she would have all to herself.

It didn't quite turn out that way. Terry had a wonderful time, but by week's end her feelings for Ali had done a turnaround. No longer was she the "nice lady" Dad was seeing. She was serious competition. Terry would have to back off a little bit and think about this "nice lady" who had invaded her father's life.

For Steve, the stabilizing life patterns had been jerked loose. Fifteen and a half years' worth. He was grateful to Ali for filling the emptiness and rootlessness he again felt acutely. So as the phoenix rose from the ashes, a new Steve began evolving and emerging.

Because she was so in love with him, Ali failed to recognize the dark side looming at her. All she allowed herself to see was the facade. This personality he had cultivated and perfected over a lifetime—the very thing that had made him, at that time, the highest paid movie star in the world. He projected honesty as if he had invented it, when in fact he was a master at psychological manipulation.

Ali would get more than she bargained for. She thought she had a charming, adorable, handsome, and passionate man, and what she discovered later was that she had a charming, adorable, handsome, passionate, and disturbed man.

By the end of June, Steve had pretty much decided he and Ali should marry. His sense of honor dictated he do so for Joshua Evans' sake.

Unwittingly, I feel, Bob Evans himself had precipitated the events he would have preferred preventing. Respectable and decent human beings are strange animals when cornered and entangled in a marital mess. They often find it difficult to control their anger and a most unfortunate consequence is often the child custody battle. In this case, however, cooler heads prevailed.

Steve told me of his plans over dinner. And although I expected it, I felt as if a left hook had been delivered to my chin. I had to have a drink (which is rare) to collect my wits about me. I certainly was not about to show him, of all people, how I felt. Then he asked me what I thought was a strange question. "Ali told me that she'll give up working. What do you think?"

"Think about what?" At first I thought it was none of my business. Let them figure it out. But he'd asked me. I had to give him my advice, didn't I?

"Personally, honey, I think you're making a big mistake asking Ali to give up working. Right now she's riding the crest. She's a big movie star. How can you ask her to give that up? It's not like giving up a secretarial post. If I were her, within a few months' time, I'd be flashing my social security card. But then, I'm not her. If she promised you, then believe her. What choice have you got?"

Ali kept her son and gave up her work, and on July 13, 1973, with Terry, Chad, and Joshua as witnesses, Ali also won her man.

The failure of love has a curious effect on different individuals in this very strange little commune called Hollywood. Supposed friends arbitrarily drop you as soon as they are certain "the powerful one" is really out of the picture. The attention and interest ceases overnight. I did come, however, to admire people like Sue Mengers, who told me up front, "Hey, babe, I go where the power is!"

After a few months of frenzied activity—from dance classes to musical theater classes, to my social appearances, to my shopping sprees, to my children's need for me and my need for them, to doing the SHARE show, to caring for my animals, to quietly putting the Castle on the market, to looking at other houses—I found I had been running so fast I had become fatigued. My brain and my body had simultaneously said, "Enough!" It was time to take a deep breath and slow down.

I took a good look at myself and asked myself what was missing from my life (besides a husband). Not much, to tell the truth. My good friends were still my good friends. The peripheral friends didn't matter. They were fawning over Steve and Ali now. As they would fawn over the next Mrs. McQueen. I had a sneaking suspicion, given Steve's personality and what I perceived Ali's to be, that their marriage would not live happily ever after. I was already hearing less than loving stories here and there from the children. Ali was giving as good as she got, which delighted me. When one day a picnic had been planned—they were going to the motorcycle races and Ali had overextended herself to make the day a memorable one for everybody—Steve looked at the chicken on the big plate and glanced at Ali disapprovingly and insensitively said, "Hey, Ali, you gotta learn how to make fried chicken like the maid."

Ali was incensed and threw the plate of chicken at him. "Here, cook it yourself!" Ali had regretted the incident later on because she had broken an antique plate of hers.

My idea now was to go back to work. That shouldn't

be too hard, I reasoned. I did it once. I can do it again. And, for good measure, I decided to go back to my name—Neile Adams. So there. I had had enough of Neile McQueen.

It didn't work out as I'd hoped. As good and supportive as the press were to me, Neile Adams' reappearance on the employment scene did not create mass hysteria at agents' offices as I thought it would. Stan Kamen, who had remained a good friend through the years, tried to be helpful. But despite his efforts, I realized that I'd simply been gone from the scene too many years. Not only that, but the name Neile Adams meant nothing to the new young producers and directors doing the hiring. They generally responded with a slow, "Ohhhh, yeahhh. She was a—uh—dancer, wasn't she?"

On the other hand, when the name Neile McQueen was mentioned, they immediately connected my face to the name.

So there was that dilemma to wrestle with.

It took four years of nonsensical name-game playing to realize finally that Neile McQueen was who I was. Period.

I was never going to set the world on fire and I surely was never going to win any acting honors. For that matter, I wasn't counting on winning any dancing awards either. Certainly, if my daughter's generation didn't know who Esther Williams and Rita Hayworth were, what could it possibly matter what name I used? I had been a minor celebrity as Neile Adams in the mid-fifties and early sixties. So what? Who knew, who remembered, who cared?

And so Neile McQueen it was.

Terry and Chad were living with me and, on the surface, seemed to be adjusting to our situation rather nicely. But Terry was being affected by our divorce in more ways than I could have ever imagined.

She loved her father, yet was unable to control her

rage toward him. She blamed him and Ali for having wrecked her home life. I think Terry harbored the feeling that if Ali hadn't come along Mom and Dad would still be together. It was an irrational and erroneous conclusion, but a child has a hard time seeing facts. She retaliated by tormenting him in ways only a daughter can. She would be rude and uncooperative and deliberately upset him whenever she could, especially when she was not within his reach. She and Steve were soul mates and she knew instinctively just what buttons to push. Here was Steve, who hadn't forgiven the entire female population for what his mother had done to him, and here was Terry, his beloved daughter, the apple of his eye, growing up to be a woman. Terry was just as stubborn and fearless as Steve was. And together they made quite a team. Poor Ali was caught in the middle. She saw the problem and understood it well, but she had no control over the matter. What is there to do when a stepchild resents you just because you're there? I could see it so clearly. When Steve and Terry had words—which was often in those days—I knew Steve would take it out on Ali. And in order to protect herself, her only recourse was to try to keep the father-daughter relationship down to a minimum during those particularly trying days. I know Terry once called her father to apologize for something she had done. It was a good hour after their fight, and Ali must have already felt the brunt of Steve's anger, for when Terry's call came, Ali was upset and told Terry Steve was out, when in fact he was there. And there were times when Ali wouldn't give him the message that Terry had called. I stayed out of the way, neither giving nor withholding advice. This was something they would all have to weather through. I knew I would have reacted exactly the way Ali did. (Terry and Ali have since reconciled their differences and are now good friends.)

Chad was a different matter altogether. He had

been reluctant to leave me, although he had this great need for his father. As soon as I became involved with another man, however, Chad immediately took flight and went to live with Steve and Ali. She couldn't have been nicer to him. Ali chauffeured him everywhere—to school, to doctors, to the orthodontist. Anywhere he needed to be driven. She took care of him as I would have. She tried guiding him toward more artistic endeavors, like music and art. In the end, though, Chad, too, began to resent Ali, and he refused to do his assigned chores around the house. Unfortunately, when Chad bucked and went to Steve, the inclination was to side with his son, rendering Ali helpless.

But as everyone knows, not one event breaks up a marriage. The accumulation of little annoyances eventually mushrooms into a giant cloud.

The temporary new man in my life rankled both Steve and Chad. For a while Chad refused to come and see me; but I discovered after a time that Chad's real concern was about reconciling his feelings for his mother, whom he was crazy about, and his stepmother, who was married to his father. I was finding out how truly complicated a divorce is for children. I tried to make it as easy on Chad as I could. I never demanded he see me. I was confident that with the help of a psychologist and the solid foundation he had under him, he'd be able to sort out his feelings without the burden of guilt.

Steve, despite the way he had fired Stan Kamen after the Le Mans fiasco, still felt a strong attachment, and when he was in the neighborhood would occasionally pop into Stan's office at William Morris. On one of these occasions, Steve, who obviously needed to talk to someone, sat down and opened the conversation with, "Hey, have you seen that guy Neile is living with?" Stan nodded in the affirmative. "Did you notice he looks like me?"

Stan started to laugh. "I never thought about it,

Steve. But did you notice that Neile and Ali are not dissimilar in looks?"

Steve stared at Stan incredulously. There was a bit of silence, then Steve jumped up. "I gotta go." He shook Stan's hand and left.

As for me, I had made a decision to reign supreme in my household this time. Economically I had the upper hand and I called the shots. The nicer the man was to me the more contemptuous I became, until finally I could bear it no more. After two years I asked him to move out. We had served each other well and I was grateful he had come along when he did. But by 1976 it was time to regroup. I wanted out and I wanted to be alone.

I had worked here and there. I had had a small role in a film called *Fuzz*. I played Burt Reynolds's deaf-mute wife and was lucky to have the only tender scene in the whole movie. I also had done *Women in Chains,* a run-of-the-mill TV movie starring Ida Lupino. I played a mean murderess serving time in a women's prison. Steve sent me a present on the first day of filming. In a brown paper bag was a carton of cigarettes with a small saw inside.

Indeed one way or another there had always been an interchange between us. And now following our meeting at the Beverly Wilshire Hotel we had become good friends and frequently spoke to each other. There were times when I'd meet him for dinner at the Golden Bull, a restaurant he liked in Malibu. Our relationship by now had moved on to another plateau. We had become two old friends who had weathered much. Although he claimed he hated all "that Hollywood gossip," he enjoyed hearing about who was doing what to whom. He would at times feel fatherly toward me and give me advice regarding my love life, although I felt he resented whatever life it was I had without him. I stayed clear of his. Knowing what a recluse he'd become, the less I knew the better. I didn't want to be accused of spreading any rumors. Especially since I was the ex-wife. It would be a "lose-lose" situation. I could appear bitter to other people, and more important to me, I didn't wish to incur his wrath.

He enjoyed coming to my parties at my new house on Amalfi Drive. Sometimes he and Chad would come together. One night he was moved to ask, "Why can't I move in with you? I like it here."

"No, my darling. You have your own house and I am not your wife anymore."

His reply had been a very definite "You will always be my wife."

My mother, who lived in New York, came down with cancer in the fall of 1976, and my friends Amy and Milton Greene generously turned over their guest room to me so I could be near her at Lenox Hill Hospital. Steve brought the children to New York to visit their grandmother, and he spent a great deal of time with her, consoling her and giving her hope— the kind of hope a dying mother likes to hear: that her daughter and ex-husband might patch things up.

As far as I was concerned, it was nothing more than talk. We had belonged together in another time and in another place.

I liked where we were now. Independent of each other, yet in a sense together and crazy about each other.

My mother died on March 1, 1977.

The night before she died, she told me she would keep an eye on me, the children, and Steve. Always. "I'll be your guardian angel."

It wasn't too long after my mother's death and my arrival back at my house on Amalfi Drive in Pacific Palisades that I received my early morning phone call. Steve had developed the maddening habit of waking the world up as soon as he opened his eyes. With a cup of coffee at his side and a cigarette or a joint accompanying it, he would proceed to conduct his business regardless of the time. Six o'clock or six thirty in the morning was his usual calling hour. I had voiced my objections loud enough so that we had reached a compromise whereby the calls to me were to be made after his business calls. I did feel sorry for his agents and his press agents and whomever else he had any business dealings with. The greeting most always started with the disheartening words, "Hello. It's Steve."

I say disheartening because none of these people looked forward to his calls, which were seldom pleasant. He was hyped up in the early mornings, having plotted his attacks on his "enemies" in the middle of the night before while they went innocently about their normal business, which was sleeping. The advantage of these confrontations was their surprise. The verbal abuses heaped on those who worked for him were so devastating that they would acquiesce immediately to whatever requests Steve would subsequently make. Good or bad. Unreasonable or not. Anything to get this madman off their back.

I, on the other hand, now had only family matters to discuss with him. Sometimes, just to irritate him, I would have a gentleman friend answer his call and tell him that "I'm sorry, Neile can't come to the phone right now. Can she call you back?" The answer would invariably be a loud click.

I generally did look forward to his calls. In many ways, we were still two kids who had shared a lifetime together and still enjoyed hearing and gossiping about each other's adventures.

Now something unusual was afoot if the messages on my answering machine from the previous night were any indication. Steve had called about a dozen times at fifteen-minute and half-hour intervals. Finally he said he was going to bed and would catch up with me in the morning. So whatever it was could wait and could not have been too important. Besides,

his voice did not have the sort of urgency that por-
tends an emergency. If nothing else, he sounded
positively gleeful, although I detected a sheepish un-
dertone. I wondered if he were stoned at the time of
the calls.

Well, whatever it was, it would be interesting.

I looked at the clock when the phone rang. It was
ten after six in the morning. (Son-of-a-bitch! He just
refuses to operate on anybody else's schedule but his
own!)

"What?" was my hostile greeting.

"Hey, baby," he started. "That wasn't really true
about your matinee idol, was it? You know, Don
Juan?" This was more of a statement than a question. What the hell was he talking about now? *Oh!
Oh!* (Light bulb popping!)

"Oh, well—ah—ah well—ah—no—oo—ooo. Not
really."

"Jesus Christ!! I had a feeling it wasn't!" He started
chuckling in spite of himself. "You really shouldn't
make up stories like that! Christ! I almost killed the
guy!"

"What do you mean? What happened?" I was suddenly alert and I sat up on the bed.

"Well, you're not going to believe this."

Oh, yes I would. I was afraid of what I was about
to hear, but I certainly would believe it.

Back in 1972, after I had divorced Steve but when
the wounds were still raw, through Sue Mengers I
had met a matinee idol I will call Don Juan. We had
gotten along well at this party, and he and I had
agreed to have dinner the following weekend. It did
not take long for us to discover that we were not
suited to each other. As charming as he is, the man
exasperated me with his orders. I was a smoker then,
and he absolutely forbade me to smoke in his car.
That was strike one. Strike two was no garlic bread
for dinner. He claimed to have an aversion to women
whose breath reeked of garlic. Strike three was im-

personal. I had plainly forgotten what dating was all about. I realized I hated it. I wasn't ready. It was as simple as that. So the man took me home, kissed me good night, and vanished from my life.

Shortly after this encounter, when Steve and I were going through division of properties, I had asked Steve to come and pick out what he wanted in the way of furniture and art. He had made his choices from the upstairs section of the house. No problem. Now he was downstairs eyeing the pool table. He wanted that and the lamp fixture over it and the antique cue stick holder.

I said, "No, you can't have that."

He asked why not. I said because the children use that table quite a bit, especially when they have their friends around.

"Not to worry. I'll have the kids on the weekends anyway."

"I don't care, Steve. I don't want a big empty space in that area of the living room."

"Now, look"—he was getting irritated now—"Marty Ransohoff gave me that table for *The Cincinnati Kid*, if you'll remember, and I want it."

Because he was being stubborn, I determined this pool table was the thing I wanted most in the world!

"I beg your pardon, sweetheart. Marty Ransohoff gave *us* that table in appreciation for me making life easier for him during the filming of *Cincinnati Kid*."

It wasn't true, but it sounded good as I was saying it. I was rolling now and I didn't want him to get the upper hand or I'd lose the damn table. The idea was to keep going once I had his attention. Since I was on the offensive, I continued boldly.

"Besides, you really wouldn't want that table anyway. Don Juan and I made love on that table the other night!"

His manner, which had been reserved to begin with because he was participating in the disintegration of his household, became icy cold. He stopped and stared at me through slitty blue eyes. I held my breath. My heart stopped and I stood as still as I possibly could. If I don't make a sound, this moment will pass, please God. I thought, now he's really going to kill me and all for that lousy pool table, which I couldn't care less about. And over an actor whom I'd kissed good night once!

The unexpected happened. He stared me down for several seconds—and they seemed like hours.

"You're right. I don't want it." Then he turned and went out the door.

I credit his romance with Ali, which at this time was still new and obviously wondrous, for his keeping himself under control.

Now it was five years later, and the actor was being talked about by a divorced couple at 6:10 in the morning.

Knowing my ex-husband as well as I did, I expected the worst. I just crossed my fingers and prayed the Don's handsome face was intact!

It seems that the previous evening, while Steve was at the El Padrino Room of the Beverly Wilshire Hotel engaged in a phone conversation with a girl friend, an out-of-towner who had had one too many recognized Steve behind the beard and proceeded to harass him verbally.

"Hey, big movie star! How come you're big and ugly?"

"Hey, big movie star! You think you're tough, don't ya?" etc., etc.

Steve had tried to stare the man down, and when this tactic failed, he turned his back on the jerk.

Still the abusive onslaught continued, even after the maître d' tried to quiet the man down.

Eventually Steve's short fuse erupted. He calmly laid the receiver down and with lightning speed, even with the extra poundage he was carrying, crossed to the table where the stranger was sitting, jerked him up, and knocked him down. The waiters quietly and efficiently picked the man up, slapped him ever so lightly to revive him, then escorted him out the door. Good riddance! Quite aside from the ill manners the man had been exhibiting, Steve now had an apartment in the hotel and was a good customer. He was a movie star besides. They were going to protect him at all costs.

Steve went back to the phone and continued his conversation with his lady friend. Within a matter of seconds he felt somebody tapping him on the shoulder. When he turned, Steve saw a handsome, smiling, and vaguely familiar face. As the man proffered his hand, the good-looking face said admiringly, "Hi, I'm Don Juan. I just want to congratulate you for what you did. I think it's great! It's about time a jerk like that got his due!"

Steve, hearing the magic word "Don Juan," was transfixed. Lucky Steve, who mentally filed away grudges like a computer bank. As luck would have it, here was one of those grudges standing innocently before him. All he wanted to do was to commend Steve for his effort.

Steve coolly dismissed the lady on the other end of the line with a cold "Later." He hung up the phone and turned to face the Don.

Steve had been waiting for the appropriate moment to settle this particular score all these years. As though in a trance the key words swam around his head. Pool table . . . my old lady . . . made love . . .

What better time than now?

A sudden commotion at the front door interrupted the confrontation between Steve and Don Juan. The stupid animal who had earlier incurred Steve's wrath had come charging back through the room like a crazed bull rushing a red flag. Don Juan immediately rallied to Steve's defense by thrusting his arm out toward the man in the hope of stopping him. At this same instant, as chance would have it, Don Juan's face accidentally positioned itself right next to the animal's face.

Steve, in his infinite wisdom, immediately saw the possibility of throwing a punch and getting two for one. He never was one to resist a bargain. Simultaneously, as he let the punch fly toward the two men, he hissed at Don Juan, "You son-of-a-bitch! You fucked my old lady on my pool table!"

The astonished and uncomprehending look in Don Juan's eyes in that one flash of a second convinced Steve that the man didn't know what the hell Steve was wild-eyed about.

But it was too late. The punch had left home plate and was headed for a home run.

How it was settled with the other man I forgot to ask.

Apparently Steve extended profuse apologies to Don Juan, who graciously accepted. Thank goodness.

Once, while taking an old-fashioned walk in Palm Springs, a fan recognized Ali and ran up to her excitedly asking for her autograph. Ali smiled and was ready to oblige when a voice beside her said, "No, sorry. We don't sign autographs." Steve hadn't been recognized because of a beard he had started to grow, and he hadn't appreciated the unintentional snub. The incident reinforced my feeling that Steve would have a hard time accepting Ali's celebrity; I was willing to bet that Ali would never get to do a film without Steve. It would be O.K. if they worked together, but if she did, trouble would be sure to follow. My feeling is that Steve systematically went about destroying Ali's career because of his need to have her in his hip pocket at all times. He wanted her at the house because his mother hadn't been there when he had needed her.

For the unsuspecting Ali all this was very well and good when the marriage was fresh. Life was exciting then and she decided to devote herself to her new

husband and their life together. They bought a house
on the beach at Trancas and Ali threw herself into
remodeling it.

The Towering Inferno had provided Steve with the
vehicle to catch up with Paul Newman. After eighteen years he finally had first billing over Paul, although Paul's name was slightly higher on the right
hand side. It was the same deal offered to Steve
when Paul had wanted him for *Butch Cassidy and the
Sundance Kid* five years earlier. As if the effort to
catch up had been exhausting, Steve now wanted to
take 1975 off and just drop out of sight. Which he
did. He busied himself in front of the television set
all day long. He drank beer and smoked grass from
morning till night and gained weight. A lot of it. He
grew an unruly and unattractive beard.

Ali said it frightened her to see him lead an entirely different life than she was leading. By the time
she came downstairs at 8:30 in the morning, Steve
would already have been up for two hours, flopping
around in the Jacuzzi and smoking cigarettes and
joints. One after the other.

There had been a great deal of discussion about
Fancy Hardware as a vehicle for Steve and Ali. But
Steve was in no mood to work, though Ali needed a
movie. It had been three years since *The Getaway*.
Steve feigned interest in the project and led everybody on. He removed his mailbox from his house
and made a deal with the gas station at Trancas to
accept his mail and his scripts. As far as the world
was concerned, Steve and Ali's house didn't exist.

Also, Steve instructed his agents to alert producers
that for him even to read a script, a million dollars
had to be put in escrow and the script delivered to
the gas station. I assumed he was testing them (Let's
see how much you really love me!). Surprisingly
enough, scripts came regardless of his outrageous
demands.

Ali had become increasingly restless, and fights

had become commonplace. Plates and glasses and
other objects flying and breaking at the house were
not an unusual occurrence. Both Steve and Ali had
volatile personalities, and when they clashed, anything was bound to happen.

Chad told me that one night in Palm Springs he,
Terry, Steve, and Ali went out to dinner and something was said that he didn't catch. But by the time
they reached the house, Steve and Ali's bickering
had grown into a full-blown argument. Terry and
Chad were sitting in front of the TV watching a
show, trying to wait out the argument. Then he
heard Steve angrily say, "Ali, you need to cool off,
goddamn it!" and a second later, he saw something
come flying past the window from above and into
the pool down below. It was not a small object. Chad
looked at Terry, and Terry looked at Chad, and they
asked each other, "What was that?" Then Terry said,
"I think it's Ali. I think Dad just threw her off the
porch!" And he had! Ali just kept swimming around,
in her nice dress, trying to figure out what to do.
Chad told me he could see she was really angry. It
took her a while to get out of the pool. Steve called
to the children and told them to get to bed. And by
the time they woke up the next day, everything was
all right again.

But not for long. Sometime toward the end of
1976, Steve was ensconced in his new apartment at
the Beverly Wilshire, ostensibly because his house
was too far away from the studio where he was
working on *An Enemy of the People*, when he opened a
fashion magazine and saw a pretty young girl staring
at him from the pages. It wasn't too hard to track
her down. He found out that her name was Barbara
Minty and yes, she would have a drink with him.

Barbara has told Terry and me that when she
came to Steve's hotel room on the appointed day,
she discovered him there with two beautiful blondes
in very tight jeans and gold chains, one sitting on

either side of him on the couch. Steve and Barbara
hit it off, nonetheless, and began seeing a good deal
of one another. Coincidentally, she had a small ranch
just outside Ketchum, Idaho, not too far from where
Steve was planning to build a log cabin.

Meanwhile, when the movie *Convoy* was offered to
Ali, Steve was incensed that she would even think
about doing it. He wanted her home. Ali asked him,
"What if I were to enroll in a pottery class in Venice
for two days a week? What would you say to that?"

"I still wouldn't like it."

To which Ali's calm reply was, "Then I might as
well do the movie. At least I'll get paid for it."

A short time after that—in November 1977—Steve
filed for divorce.

Because I felt a certain kinship toward Ali, and
because I was a little older and a little wiser perhaps,
I purposely asked him if he had taken proper care
of Ali financially.

"No, alimony there ain't none. But don't worry
about her. She's fine. I bought a beach lot from her
for three times the amount she paid for it." The way
he delivered the pronouncement made it sound as if
he had been fair.

But Ali never got a dime. In fact, he even reduced
her to negotiating for the tribal rugs she had loved
and had bought for her home with Steve.

It was a bitter divorce and Steve hadn't shown any
sensitivity to the situation. He left Ali to fend for
herself while he moved Barbara into the Trancas
house even as Joshua was still there and Ali's clothes
were still in the closet.

It was not one of his shining moments.

In June of 1977, we celebrated Terry's eighteenth
birthday with a big party at my house. Besides Terry's friends, we invited friends who had been with us
through the years. Stan, the Jim Garners, the David
Fosters, Bill Maher, Sherry and George Peppard, the

Rick Ingersolls, Rupert Allan, Jim Coburn, among them. Steve and Chad brought little Joshua Evans along, and because of the troubled circumstances surrounding their marriage, I left it to Steve to bring Ali or not. Ali didn't come.

I thought Steve looked awful. He had swelled up like a giant balloon. He also seemed to be coming down with another in a succession of colds—he constantly had either the flu, the runs, or a head cold. I jokingly told him his extra fat couldn't fight off those germs invading his body.

That summer Terry and I took off for Europe and went backpacking through France and Italy. We had a glorious time together. As soon as we hit town at the end of summer, Steve carted me off to MGM to see *An Enemy of the People*, a film that originated from his disenchantment with First Artists, who kept asking for his second film. (Each star was committed to do three.) As a way of retaliating he had randomly pointed to one of Ali's books and up came *An Enemy*.

"That's what I'm gonna do," he said. "That one!" Now it was still a rough cut, but he was anxious for my opinion. I sat through the first five minutes looking at the film and the man emoting up there before it finally dawned on me the person I was looking at was Steve! I turned to him aghast! "Honey, that is you, isn't it?"

"Yes, that's me," he answered, rather annoyed.

I almost yelled. "Forget it, kid! It'll never sell. Not in a million years! First of all, there are a lot of people out there who don't even know who Ibsen is, you know what I mean? *An Enemy of the People* sounds like a western. They're gonna come into the movie house looking to see Steve McQueen and what they're gonna see instead is this big, hairy slob! You're crazy!"

"Shut up, goddamn it. Talk to me after it's over!"

Perhaps it's unfair to say the movie was terrible. It just wasn't Steve's métier. I hated seeing him looking plain ugly. Unfortunately, my take on the movie was colored by the way I saw him. He was a man more at home with emotions than words; this attempt to do Ibsen seemed as though he were deliberately trying to destroy the image he had carefully cultivated over the years. I thought to myself, Words have become his windmill now. He had given up car racing a while back and motorcycles had lost their charm for him, mostly due to the *Le Mans* fiasco, except as objects to collect. Maybe he had to give this a shot. This enigmatic man was an experience unto himself.

My reaction was a disappointment to him. I knew that pained him. He had worked long and hard on the character and he thought he could pull it off.

At about this time I started performing on the dinner theater and stadium circuit. It's not the kind of work that does much for one's career, but it kept me busy. I also appeared in a succession of episodic television shows, and when each one aired, Steve and I would have dinner and watch the shows.

In late March of 1978 I opened in *Can Can* in Las Vegas. I was doing two shows a night and by the end of the eighth week was exhausted and missing my family and friends. Steve called me one day and on a whim I asked him to come and spend a couple of days with me if he had nothing better to do. "I need a friendly face!"

I wasn't too concerned about the public recognizing him. He looked like a well-dressed bag man at this point.

Sure enough, a few days later, I received a call late in the afternoon. Steve was somewhere on the outskirts of town. Would I pick him up?

He couldn't have found a seedier motel to stay in and "crap out" if he had tried. He was on his way back to Los Angeles from Idaho, where he had been working on his next film project, *Tom Horn,* the story of a man out of step with the approaching new century. He'd been hiring and rehiring writers and finally he decided he wanted to take a crack at the script himself. Now he was in need of a breather, so the timing had been perfect.

That afternoon in that seedy motel in Las Vegas was the last time he and I ever made love.

When we got to my apartment he asked to be fed. As he was gobbling down the tuna fish salad I made him, he asked rather matter-of-factly whether he and I could make it back together again.

There was no question we couldn't and it was no more than a rhetorical question. But I answered it anyway.

"Honey, too much time has elapsed. We love each other. And that's forever. So there's no need to live together. I couldn't put up with you anymore. No adult woman could. You need a young girl who is still malleable enough and can run with the tide. I'm too set in my ways and you know what? I like not having to answer to anyone."

He understood that. He laughed and reached for my hand across the table. "We're gettin' old, you and me, baby. I'm building me a log cabin in Idaho. You'll come see it when it's done. Maybe you'll change your mind."

And then as an afterthought he asked, "Hey, why can't you and me and Ali and Barbara all live together under one roof?" I just shook my head and he laughed at the thought as if he were telling a joke on himself. "Can you imagine that? Ooooweee!"

17

SOMETIME AFTER Steve arrived back at Trancas, he came down with the flu. And then the flu turned into walking pneumonia. And there it stayed for a very long time. Despite all the medication. Despite all the care. The doctors were baffled; they had given him every conceivable test.

Throughout all this, neither Steve nor Chad had made Terry or me aware of his illness. Chad was told Steve had bronchitis and that it was flu-related. Steve was confident he'd get over it, whatever it was. He gave orders not to have a big deal made out of it. After several weeks, the doctors had come to the conclusion he had a fungus in his lung, most likely picked up in the desert during his biking days. So they began treatment with a sulfa drug.

And it worked. He began to recover and feel better.

Except his strength was a long time coming back. He tired easily, walked slowly, and used a cane to help him around.

And because he was his usual ornery self, Barbara Minty (now solidly entrenched in the house) and Chad thought soon he'd be back to normal.

I came home in July and started making plans to sell the Amalfi house. Terry, who was now nineteen years old, felt the need to move out from under Mom's wing. She and a girl friend moved into an apartment, and Terry began her trip to independence. I was delighted although I missed her very much. My house had become too big for me to live in by myself.

One day in October Steve asked me to come and visit. When I drove down the beach road to his house, I saw him at the bottom of the incline giving orders to Chad and his friends about moving some cars and trucks around. He seemed his usual self—deploying his forces like a general and yelling as if a battle were in progress.

With one difference. The general standing there was wrapped in a maroon bathrobe and leaning on a cane.

And when we walked toward each other, I noticed one shoulder was lower than the other. "Sometime it just aches from the dampness around here." My heart went out to him. I wasn't used to seeing this man weak or sick. As I put my arms around him I told him, "I know I'm always going to keep a room for you to come to in case there's nobody to take care of you."

His face looked drawn under the beard but he was in good spirits. He described what had happened the last few months and added that the doctors wanted him to leave Trancas. It was too damp and apparently not agreeing with him. He had instructed real estate brokers to search actively for land that was reminiscent of the farm he remembered from his early youth with Uncle Claude.

I met Barbara Minty for the first time. (She told Steve after I left she was so nervous about meeting me that she changed outfits three times.) I was taken aback at how young she looked. And then I found out she was only four years older than Terry (whom she hadn't met yet), which would have made her twenty-three years old then. Actually, the first thought that crossed my mind when we were introduced was, She looks like she could be Ali's daughter, for God's sake! I found her to be very sweet, very shy, very pretty, with very little to say. I most likely intimidated her. I was, after all, the mother of his children and I was older (probably as old as her mother, I wryly thought). And I also was the woman to whom Steve said "I love you" at the end of phone conversations. I knew she must have been sitting or standing beside him. But Steve said she understood that. For this I gave her credit: it would have been a hell of a lot more than I would have understood.

As I observed her and Steve together, I thought they had a pretty good thing going. She certainly seemed to care for him. Also she and Chad had become friends—which was important—and as children do, they played games together. Chad recounted the story of the time he and Barbara were playing tag when Steve came through the door. His reaction had been immediate. He ordered Chad to sweep the deck around the house and ordered Barbara to cook him some chicken. That settled that.

By Christmastime, Steve was feeling pretty good. He was looking at ranches in the Santa Paula area and had put the Trancas house on the market. When it sold, he had plans for Barbara, Chad, and him to live in a sixty-foot motor home. I thought it was an awful idea. "Listen to this scenario, Steve, and listen good. Barbara and Chad are much closer in age than you and she are. His hormones are working overtime right now. You wanna tempt fate?"

Silence. "You have a dirty mind, you know that?"

But the next day, after thinking it over, Steve called to tell me he would rent two trailers when the time came. One for him and Barbara and one for Chad.

On December 28, 1978, we were all together again for Chad's eighteenth birthday. The party consisted of the same grown-ups who had attended Terry's party the year before and, naturally, Chad's friends. This time Joshua Evans wasn't present and Barbara Minty was.

It was the last time the camera caught us as a happy family group and also that last time the four of us would be together under such happy circumstances.

If proof ever was needed that Steve couldn't handle being a filmmaker, as he would like to have been known, then *Le Mans* in 1970 and *Tom Horn* almost a decade later would have to be the perfect examples.

Steve's biggest problem was his inability to trust someone else's judgment. He'd delegate a responsibility and then he would take it away. He referred to this same tendency in another person's personality as "doing a 360." Oddly enough, it was the very same trait he failed to recognize in himself.

As an actor, when he worked with strong directors and/or strong producers, his contributions to the success of his movies could be enormous. Left to fend for himself as the chief executive of his own movie, charged with making all the final decisions, his 360s were in great part to blame for his failures.

Tom Horn suffered from too many writers and too many directors. By the time the final shot was completed, four directors had been on the movie, not counting Steve, who personally had taken over at one point. The Directors Guild of America had intervened and had insisted the company bring in a card-carrying member of the guild.

Steve was a stickler for details in all his movies. Unfortunately, he carried it to such an extreme the films suffered under the weight of all that detailing. The gold tooth gimmick was revived for this picture. Only we saw it protruding from Linda Evans' mouth. In addition to this, Steve also insisted she not wear makeup. I thought he went out of his way to make this gorgeous woman look quite plain.

Tom Horn began principal photography in the cold wintry desert of Tucson, Arizona, in February 1979. Even with having to battle snow, sleet, and ice, Steve,

Chad, and Barbara were back home by Easter of that year. Chad had worked as a production assistant and as an extra. Our precocious and gorgeous dog Junior had vanished in the wilds of the desert, which had upset me when Steve called to inform me.

Upon his arrival back in town, Steve complained to me about the couple I had found to house-sit at Trancas. Steve discovered through casual conversation that this wonderful French couple had had the temerity to invite another couple over to play gin. I couldn't take him seriously.

"Hey, why don't you just thank me for getting you a first-class and responsible couple? Don't complain so much."

I couldn't put my finger on it, but he didn't seem like himself. I was familiar with the nuances of his personality and his mood changes. But there was something else. The blue eyes were dull and tired. The sparkle was gone.

Easter Sunday of 1979 found Ali egg hunting on the beach with Joshua and other children. After she and Steve split up, Ali had found a house to rent a short distance from Steve's. Although Ali hadn't seen Steve in a year, Steve and little Joshua, who were fond of each other, were able to keep in touch.

That Sunday the Easter egg hunt went as far as Steve's part of the beach. As Ali looked up, she saw him moving about on the porch. After hesitating for a few seconds, Ali thought to herself, Hell, why not? I can't hide from him forever. I'll go up and say "hello" and "no hard feelings." After that it might even be possible to communicate with each other like normal humans.

She walked up to the house and called to him.

"Hi! I thought I'd drop by and wish you a Happy Easter."

"Hi." He looked at her appreciatively. "You're lookin' good. How ya been?"

"O.K. I thought it's about time I met the lady

who's living in my house, don't you think?" She smiled to show the bad feelings were gone. "Where is she?"

Without hesitation Steve snarled, "She's down below where she belongs!"

Ali laughed, relieved as she was finally to have confronted the ghost.

Ali never did meet Barbara that day. Their introduction to each other had to wait until the following year when all of us would be in mourning.

A few weeks later Princess Grace of Monaco was in town for one of her board meetings at Twentieth Century-Fox. Rupert Allan was having a small luncheon for her, and as always, Rupert included me in the group.

Having arrived early and being very nervy, I started scanning the tables to see with whom I had been paired. The name Alvin Toffel stared at me from the place card next to mine. Alvin Toffel. What kind of a name was that?

I called to Rupert. "Rupert, who is the man sitting next to me?"

Rupert smiled. "Oh, you'll like him. He's the president of the Norton Simon Museum."

"Oh, Rupert," I whined. "Why do you always put me next to the old folks?"

"Don't worry. He's nice. Oh, by the way, he's just gotten divorced."

"Oh, that's terrific, Rupert." I was now petulant. "Not only do I have an old man with a strange name, but he's also getting a divorce! Isn't that terrific!"

"Now behave yourself. Grace will be here momentarily."

I walked toward the buffet table and ran head-on into the Cary Grants, who were talking to a good-looking man—not a flashy kind of handsome, but handsome nonetheless. We talked, but although introductions were made, I missed the man's name.

When we sat down to lunch, he came over to my table and sat down. I wondered what had happened to Alvin What's-his-name. No matter. I liked this one next to me. Al Something. We mostly talked only to each other throughout lunch and after lunch. So as not to appear rude, we would occasionally join in the conversation around the table and then concentrate on each other again. It finally dawned on me this might be Alvin Toffel. "Are you?" I asked.

Of course he was.

The man was so interesting. Rupert said he was brilliant. He had originally been an air force fighter pilot and had been in the Strategic Air Command. He had been well on his way to a career as a pilot in the air force when the opportunity to participate in the engineering management of the Gemini and Apollo space programs had intervened.

His reputation for handling the management problems of complex aerospace programs eventually led him to be loaned to the White House staff to help set up President Nixon's Office of Management and Budget. Later Norton Simon persuaded him to return to Southern California, and after working at Simon's side for a period, he became president of Simon's several foundations and the Norton Simon Museum of Art.

Alvin Toffel's personality, I discovered as the afternoon wore on, had its own romantic undertow which I was finding hard to resist.

It's amazing how one meets the right person when one isn't looking.

In the parking lot, I heard someone say when Al went to retrieve his car, "He's very attractive. He'll make a wonderful extra man at a dinner party."

"Aha." I smiled innocently at the woman. But I knew she was out of luck. This one was mine!

In July of 1979, Steve purchased a fifteen-acre ranch in Santa Paula. He also bought a hangar a hop and a skip away from the ranch to store his various collections of American memorabilia. Antique toys, old gas pumps, cars of years gone by, and antique motorcycles. He had become an avid collector, and when time allowed, he and Barbara went to swap meets all over the state and country. At one point he seriously considered buying a Peterbilt so he could go from swap meet to swap meet, load up and even sleep in the truck when necessary.

On my forty-fifth birthday, a few days after Steve closed on the Santa Paula ranch, I received the last gift I was ever to get from him. It was a unique antique brass pepper mill. Set in a square box with intricate designs on all four sides, the mill also had a little drawer at the bottom to catch the pepper when the handle was turned around. The handle is much like an old Victrola handle.

When I called to thank him, Steve told me the Trancas house had finally been sold and he and Barbara had moved into the hangar while the ranch was being readied. Chad had found himself an apartment and the problem of the living accommodations had been solved.

Steve had discovered airplanes and had become all enthused about flying. (He was impressed when I told him Al had been a jet fighter pilot.) But Steve was into antique airplanes. As was generally the case, when Steve chose to do something, he threw himself wholeheartedly into the project. It was the same with flying. He kept buying one after the other, until he had five antique airplanes. The money from *The Towering Inferno* was pouring in and it kept him happy. And as soon as he got his license to fly, he insisted on taking Terry up—against my nervous objections. Airplanes still frightened me. But she had a great time and hadn't been the least bit frightened.

I had sold my house on Amalfi Drive and bought a smaller house in Beverly Hills, which I was busy remodeling. I needed the cash to complete it and Steve loaned me $40,000 in order to bridge the gap. He only asked that I return the money after the closing on my Amalfi house.

Life seldom flashes a cue card announcing that a change in one's life is imminent.

I fell madly in love with Al Toffel and became engaged to him the night of my birthday. This unusual man had caught me totally by surprise. The more time I spent with him, the more enamored I became. He was all the good things I had ever known—the real thing, a man of substance in a town generally inhabited by superficial people. Fortunately, Al agreed we could make the not yet lived-in Beverly Hills house our new home. I didn't have the energy to move again.

Shortly after we moved to Beverly Hills, Steve made one of his typical early morning calls. This time, Al answered it. Although Steve had been aware of my deepening relationship with Al, it had irritated him to be confronted by it unexpectedly. (I had been tickled. Steve was so predictable.) When I got on the phone, he immediately went into a tirade about how he desperately needed the money he had lent me and wanted it back right now. He said he was broke (which was absurd). Luckily, the Amalfi house was to close in a few days and I told Steve to hold on. When I told Al about it, he offered to give me the money to give to Steve, which I thought was an extraordinary gesture. He also asked that no more financial arrangements be made with my ex-husband.

It had been the men's first encounter with each other, and neither had been happy about their early morning introduction over the phone. From then on, Steve called at more respectable hours out of deference to Al's wishes.

That summer I worked at the St. Louis Muni Opera and Kansas City's Starlite Theatre in *The Desert Song*. Al flew cross-country after work to be with me.

Life was really good.

Steve left for Chicago that September to begin *The Hunter.* I thought the script was so-so and that he deserved better and could do better if he would only bother to read a few of the scripts sent to him. To me it read more like a TV movie than a feature film. For the moment, he said, it was the only decent script available to him.

He had a whole different team now. Freddie Fields had sold his agency and had gone on to become a producer. Steve was now being handled by ICM and Marvin Josephson, a man I had never met.

Bill Maher and Steve had had a falling out. It was the same old problem, Steve's abusiveness and insensitivity to people who worked for him. But even through all that, Bill still made himself available to Steve when the necessity arose. Bill felt he owed Steve that.

Steve felt he should go ahead with his film. He understood there was a whole audience out there who had forgotten or never knew what he looked like. His last film as Steve McQueen, superstar, had been *The Towering Inferno,* five years earlier. Hardly anybody had gone to see *Tom Horn* and *An Enemy of the People.* As it was, by the time *The Hunter* made its appearance in the movie theaters, it would be the latter half of 1980. Six years is a long time away from the screen. Audiences are fickle. They change allegiance at the bat of an eyelash. In fact, he had all but disappeared from the box office list of stars.

So although we talked often, he and I didn't see each other again until a few days before Christmas. When I spoke to him after he had finally finished with *The Hunter,* Steve informed me he was checking into Cedars-Sinai because of a low-grade temperature he'd had for two weeks running. He had had a persistent cough and was generally pretty tired. The strain of the location in Chicago had taken its toll on him.

Al and I had already made our plans to marry

when the holidays were over. We had picked a date:
January 19, 1980. I had told Steve over the phone
that he was not going to be invited to the wedding
because "I intend to be the star at this wedding. Not
you, my darling. The focus will be on Al and me."
He had understood completely and we had laughed
over our circumstances.

And now here we were, Al and I, in this hospital
room with Steve, five days before Christmas, where
the two men met formally for the first time. Airplanes was their commonality for the moment, but
their communication deepened. I could tell they liked
each other.

Steve seemed subdued, extraordinarily so. Barbara was usually quiet so that meant nothing to me.
One usually couldn't read her face.

What I didn't know at the time was that Steve's
X-rays showed there was a major problem with half
of his right lung. What it meant exactly wasn't clear
yet. Not until the tests were completed.

Little did we all know that three days before Christmas would bring the most disastrous news Steve had
ever encountered in his entire life.

Chad called me the following Saturday evening.
"Mom, Dad was operated on this afternoon and he's
in intensive care. I thought you'd want to know."

My God, I thought, they've done surgery on him.
Not just a little biopsy like he said they would.

When Steve came out of surgery, Terry and Barbara found themselves facing each other in the recovery room. The first time they had met had been
in Sun Valley many months before when Steve had
called Terry asking her to join them for a bit of
skiing. Their second meeting, in the recovery room
at Cedars-Sinai Hospital, was ominous. The doctor
had slowly articulated for Steve what they had found.

It was cancer and it was inoperable.

Mesothelioma was the medical term for the tu-

mors found in the lining of his body, and his were
malignant. It was a very rare form of cancer, probably caused by asbestos. (Steve could scarcely pro-
nounce the word and when I found out about it, I
thought of all those times he had worn those flame-
proof racing uniforms treated with asbestos. Then I
remembered his smoking, and the operation for the
removal of polyps eight years before, and the times
he had wrapped an asbestos-treated rag around his
nose and mouth, tying it on before he had put on his
helmet; had all these elements caught up with him?
But then, what about all those other drivers throughout the years who had done the same thing?)

It became apparent to Terry her father had been
so groggy at the time he had been told of his condition that he had no recollection of her presence in
the recovery room. After he had been brought back
to his hospital room, Steve, wanting to spare his
children any unnecessary pain, had told them a bald-
faced lie.

"Guess what? It isn't cancer. I'm gonna be fine."

Terry, who has the same temperament as her father, lied to him as expertly as he had lied to her.
"That's great, Dad. Let's go skiing as soon as you
recover from whatever it is you have. O.K.?"

Chad chose to deny what he had learned and was
comforted to know Dad would be well soon and was
all smiles.

On Monday afternoon, Christmas Eve, I stepped
into Room 8501 at Cedars-Sinai to find Steve sitting
in bed while Terry fiddled with a small Christmas
tree. Gaily wrapped boxes in different sizes spilled
over onto the floor from the desk where the little
tree sat. From what Steve had said, Barbara had
gone to do some last-minute shopping and Terry
was keeping him company.

I was anxious to see him. I had already learned
what was wrong with him. Naively, I had thought
the strength of his spirit and his belief in himself

would show me if he could conquer this new reversal. So many events that had occurred in his life would have broken a lesser man, but not him. I expected this wouldn't either. He sent Terry to get him a soda, then without mentioning the dreaded word, he made me promise—on our children's lives—that all I would say to anyone if questioned was that he had an unidentified fungus of the desert variety. Then he added, "I am gonna make it, you know. Barbara is heavy into this health stuff, and she's putting me on all these vitamins and feeding me healthy foods. I've already stopped smoking and I'm gonna work out and lead a real healthy life in general. Not to worry, baby. I'll be just fine." I promised to keep the secret and left—with a lingering doubt.

In the afterlight, I think how courageous Steve was to be able to carry all that off in the way he did—even later, when the *National Enquirer* reported in a sensational manner that he was dying of cancer. I also think how dastardly one of the nurse's aides and her boyfriend were to slip the story to the *Enquirer.* And what an absolutely first-class lady Barbara Walters was for having turned them down when approached and for immediately informing Steve's press agents, who attempted to get the story killed. Another reporter who showed her true colors as far as we were concerned was Rona Barrett. She handled everything with taste and never resorted to sensationalism. Actually she kept a very tight rein on what she reported with regard to Steve. And for that we thank her.

The *National Enquirer* story has an equally unsavory footnote. There was a coffee shop at Santa Paula, not far from Steve's hangar, that he used to frequent. One day a young man (a college kid, Steve said) turned up at the coffee shop and struck up a conversation with him. Steve felt relaxed in that setting. They knew him well there, and he wasn't bothered by any of the regulars. Steve, who had an affinity for young people trying to make it in this world, took a liking to the kid. It wasn't long before Steve had this kid to his hangar showing him his planes and his various collections of memorabilia. The point is, later, Steve let his guard down. Not too long after the kid had Steve's confidence, the trusty young man showed up with an innocuous camera. Steve first saw him take a picture of Barbara, then of Barbara's plane, then of Steve's plane. A litle warning light had gone on in Steve's head. But not big enough. Steve questioned the boy about the camera. The reply had been perfectly rehearsed.

"Oh, I'm sorry about that. I hope you don't mind. One of my subjects at UC Santa Barbara is photography. I just thought those old planes might be really interesting. But if you'd prefer I didn't, then I won't. I apologize." Steve said he had been struck by how sincere this boy was.

I suppose we all get taken in at one time or another. Steve told me he felt foolish after the kid's long speech.

"Hey, don't worry about it. Take all the pictures you want. Makes no big never mind if it'll help you."

It sure helped the kid. Steve said those were the very pictures that turned up in the *Enquirer* accompanying the horrid and insensitive article.

By the end of the first week in January of 1980, the soreness under Steve's right arm where they had cut him to do the exploratory surgery had eased considerably. Terry said his mood vacillated from lightheartedness to depression. And still nothing was mentioned about cancer.

For the next several days his main concern, according to Terry, was the date of my wedding to Al. He kept asking her when Mom would get married. Terry, in her effort to throw him off, would hem and haw, saying she wasn't exactly sure.

"Come on, Terry. Tell your ole dad here when

your mom is gettin' married. I know damn well you know when!"

Terry would laugh, amused as she was over Steve's transparent motives. And still she wouldn't say. Chad was no help to Steve, since this darling son of ours remembers no dates except his own birth date. (This kid is going to make some woman very unhappy over this some day.)

Because she suspected something imminent, Terry called me early one evening. "Mom, it's nothing Dad has said to me. It's more because of all the questions he's been asking. You know how he is. When he asks too many questions he's usually poised for action. Well, he's been asking me repeatedly about the date of your wedding. So I would assume he's going to try and beat you to the altar."

"I'll just wait until he calls me. Then we'll really know for sure what he's up to!" There was no question but he'd call to tell me.

On the Tuesday before my Saturday wedding, the phone rang and intuitively I knew it was Steve.

"Hey, Nellie! How you doin'?" He was in good spirits on this day. I was happy to hear that. We went round and round, talking about everything in creation without actually coming to the point I knew he wanted to cover. Finally I told him I had to leave. It was then he blurted it out. "I'm getting married tomorrow."

"I beg your pardon?"

"I'mgettingmarriedtomorrow!"

"You're getting married tomorrow? Is that what you just said, you son-of-a-bitch! You couldn't wait till after Saturday?"

"No!" He was petulant now. "If I wait until after you get married, they'll say I got married because you did!"

"They'll say that anyway, you old fool!"

"I don't care. I'm still gonna do it before you!"

Actually, it really didn't matter one way or another

who got married first. It was a game. And it was fun giving each other a hard time. I couldn't resist one last parting shot.

"Tell me one thing. What do you have in common with her besides her youth and beauty?"

"You're bad, baby. You know that, don't ya?" He took a breath as if preparing to extol all her virtues. "She loves me, you know, honey? She says she would live anywhere with me, including pitching a tent out in the desert. Plus she takes care of me."

And so on January 16, 1980, Barbara Minty became Steve's third wife. Our children weren't present. From my recollection of what Steve told me, the minister from his new church in Ventura (he had become a born-again Christian) married them in his house, with Sammy Mason, his flying instructor, who had reintroduced him to the Lord Jesus, and Sammy's wife as the only witnesses.

On the Saturday afternoon of January 19, 1980, Ali MacGraw called me up to wish Al and me a happy life together. She had decided against coming to our wedding that evening because she was concerned about the media's reaction. She was afraid the concentration would shift from Al and me to her and me and Steve's absence. I admired her for her foresight but still wished she would come. I liked Ali enormously and always felt that her marriage to Steve didn't get the chance it deserved because of all the outside forces.

Ali at one point offered to design my wedding dress. We had a great giggle over that one. "Can you imagine what ideas that would engender in the minds of these crazy people?"

When I shared with Ali that my live-in boyfriend of long ago was planning to get married the weekend after I did, she was moved to joke, "What you should do is pull out of your wedding, and then Steve and the other one will most surely hang themselves!"

Obviously I ignored Ali's advice!

My wedding to Alvin E. Toffel, given to us by very close friends Sandy and Jerry Moss, was the sort of grand affair I had always dreamed of. The wedding ceremony itself, held in the Mosses' living room, was small. Jerry Moss gave me away and Terry was my maid of honor. Chad was there and so were Al's three daughters. And when Jerry turned me over to Al during the ceremony I said to myself, In this cosmic life, this is what I'm here for. For this man.

The guest list for the reception, by contrast, was large. Sandy had the tennis court tented and I felt like a first-time bride, except that my surrogate mom and dad were of my generation. There was wine, food, and dancing, and I felt like Cinderella. It was a wonderful night!

Thank you, Sandy.

Thank you, Jerry.

And thank you, Al, for being the best husband a woman could ever hope to have.

After Steve and Barbara were married, Mario Iscovich received a call from Steve. Would he come to Santa Paula?

Mario agreed unhesitatingly. Steve had tracked him down while *The Hunter* had been filming on the Paramount lot. They had had lunch together and it was then Steve first told Mario he hadn't been feeling well.

It was ten years after Le Mans and Mario was doing quite nicely. He was writing screenplays now and was at present working for Stanley Kramer. Steve seriously suggested Mario write a script about flying. Steve said he'd star and Mario could produce. Mario loved the idea, but he also knew the man too well. Steve could change his mind by the time Mario walked out the door.

Steve had started methodically to say his good-byes while he still had the strength and while he still looked good.

When Mario came to Santa Paula, Steve had wasted no time. He took Mario aside and without warning and almost without emotion sat him down gently and said, "Mario, I don't think I'm going to make it."

Mario had seen the tabloids and had heard the rumors. He had also seen the way Steve looked. Not great, but not bad either. And so he had refused to believe any of it until this very moment as Steve stood there telling him what was in store for him. Mario said he wanted to run! To hug Steve! To make it all go away! But he sat there rooted to his chair, unable to utter a word. Unable even to lift his arm to push himself up from the chair.

Steve was bidding the kid (who was now almost thirty years old) farewell. He hadn't treated him well a long time ago and he wanted to make amends. Steve continued, "Is everything all right between you and me? You're not mad at me anymore, are you, kid?"

With enormous force, Mario pushed off from the chair and gave Steve a hug. "No, Steve. I was only mad at you for a little bit. But I put it all aside many years ago."

And for Mario that was his last glimpse of Steve.

Elmer Valentine was part-owner and manager of a new club called the Roxy, on the Sunset Strip. One afternoon Steve showed up to talk to Elmer. As it had with Mario, Le Mans had put the whammy on that friendship, too. Steve claimed that Elmer had left him abruptly to manage his business affairs at the Whisky A GO-GO. Since then, they'd phoned each other here and there and shared an occasional lunch, but that's all. This afternoon Steve had come bursting into the Roxy to make sure Elmer didn't believe any of those ludicrous rumors. They told each other jokes and laughed together as in the old days. Steve said he couldn't stay long as he had a few errands to do. "But I'll call you real soon. We'll break some bread together."

As they said good-bye, Elmer put his arms around

Steve and immediately perceived Steve was indeed a very sick man. "He felt so thin under all that layered clothing. It just wasn't the same Steve and I knew, man. I knew."

Bud Ekins and Steve went to Boston to look at a collection of antique motorcycles. During the flight Bud could see Steve wasn't feeling up to par. He also saw a Steve who would get lost in thought and would seem depressed for short periods. He'd snap out of it as soon as Bud said something, but then off he'd go again to that place where no one was allowed.

In Boston, Steve bought $65,000 worth of antique motorcycles. Bud said they were the kind one would kill for. On the flight back to L.A., Steve had said he would leave Bud his entire motorcycle collection if anything were to happen to him. Bud had replied, "Don't be ridiculous, Steve. Leave them to your kids. I certainly wouldn't do the same for you!" The two friends laughed and Steve had agreed with Bud.

However, as a compromise, Steve had told Bud, "I'll tell you what; in case of anything, I want you to pick out a couple for yourself."

As a result, Bud wound up with the two best motorcycles in the entire collection.

As Steve would have wished.

One early evening Steve called and Al answered the phone. Steve had recently taken one of his first cross-country flights from Santa Paula to Santa Monica in an antique Stearman biplane, and he was still feeling proud of the accomplishment. He was extolling the virtues of flying to Al and imagined "my type of flying was simple compared to the complex jobs you used to fly."

"Not so, Steve. The old 'taildraggers' are more challenging in some ways. Next time you're up to it, I'll go up with you."

This discussion went on to be the longest conversation the two ever had, and Steve confided to Al that the unrelenting back pains at night found him sleeping on the floor to get some relief. Sometimes he'd have Chad pound on his back to help loosen the congestion plaguing him.

Sometime during this talk the subject of the tabloid stories and the cancer rumors had come up. (Al is too smart a man not to have detected what was going on even though I had kept the real nature of Steve's illness to myself.) It was the first time Al had heard any bitterness coming from Steve.

"Suppose it's true? Just suppose? Why do I have to do anything? Doesn't a man have a right to die any way he wants?"

Al thought Steve's attitude and control were profound and noble and touching, and he wanted very much to help this man in any way he could—this man who was the father of my children and who my husband knew meant a great deal to me.

Al agreed with Steve. "Yes, he does have a right to handle it any way he wants. But, just supposing, if he knew he was dying and if he had a chance to help influence his children, what would he want done?"

Steve sighed audibly. This was exactly what had been troubling him. "I'm not sure. I think they'll both be O.K., but I'm a bit concerned about Chad. I think he'll have tougher problems than Terry."

Al tried to ease his mind. "I will watch out for both of them. I can see they're both fine kids and you're proud of them both."

"I am."

So there it was. The unspoken had been spoken. There was no doubt left in Al's mind that Steve was dying. And as if to break the solemnity of the moment, Steve said, "Sorry about getting married before you did!"

"No sweat. It caused me no problems at all! Take care of yourself, Steve. When you're feeling better, you can show me what a Stearman can really do."

"Yeah. You'll show me!" They laughed and said their good-byes.

Once in a while I would try to put myself in Steve's shoes. What would I do, how would I act, if I were told I was dying and the only reprieve from pain would be death itself? I don't think I could have acted as admirably as he.

And so when I'd talk to him and he'd be excited and looking forward to a plan he had just made, I had to summon all the strength I had in order to be just as enthused as he was about his plans.

He was excited about a trip he had promised Barbara. Steve's favorite show on the tube was "The Love Boat." He never failed to watch the damn thing. And although I tried and my agents tried, I could never get cast in one of the shows. I had wanted desperately to surprise Steve. In any case, Barbara was doing a modeling assignment in Acapulco some time in early May, and Steve thought going on one of the Princess cruises would be great. He went about outfitting himself at J.C. Penney's, which he had nicknamed Jacques Penay. He chose Bermuda shorts (never had he worn those), shirts that matched, and picked out all the leisure suit outfits he thought he would need. For good measure, he also threw in a straw hat and white deck shoes for himself. It had been an absolute joy for him to go from rack to rack unrecognized and undisturbed. He said Jacques Penay was all he had hoped it would be. Something out of his childhood in the midwest.

A month before his departure for Acapulco on the Princess cruise, the papers had carried a picture of Steve and Barbara at a press screening of *Tom Horn*. The picture showed a very changed Steve. His face was gaunt and his eyes just weren't the same. Even his smile was different.

And so when he called me after they arrived back from Mexico with the news that he had contracted

the turistas over there, I was afraid to ask him a
question but I did anyway, hoping against hope.

"Did you lose any weight?"

"Yeah, baby. I'm afraid I did. Twenty pounds'
worth."

Oh, God, here it starts, I thought. Only three
years ago it was my mother and Steve had gone to
New York to comfort her, unaware he was already a
marked man.

And now his turn had come.

The death sentence had been handed down and it
was irreversible.

Steve's odyssey for a cure for his terminal illness
began almost as soon as the news had been delivered
to him. He found a doctor in the San Fernando
Valley who convinced him that several weeks of in-
travenous feeding of mega-doses of vitamins and a
new diet might possibly retard the progress of the
disease. These were administered in a camper Steve
rented, on a parking lot just outside the doctor's
medical offices.

After the end of the treatment, which was sometime in July, Steve went back to Cedars for a blood
test and transfusion. There he received the news
that the treatments, which had been painful, had
been for naught. There was no improvement. In
fact, in order to make him feel comfortable, his
abdomen had to be drained.

I had been in Seattle for six weeks performing in
Where's Charley? at a dinner theater and fortunately
Al, even with his rapidly developing new business,
had been able to arrange his affairs to be with me.

Terry called regularly with information regarding
her father's health.

Steve refused to give up. After he checked out of
the hospital he and Barbara vanished. And so did
my daughter. Their departure had been so sudden
that even Chad had no idea where they were. Sev-

eral days later, Terry called to say they were in Mexico. Steve had found another doctor, who was into alternative methods of curing cancer. Terry said Steve had checked into a clinic on Rosarito Beach and had investigated the doctor (a dentist whose license to practice had been suspended) and his methods thoroughly and had decided "to go for it." Steve felt he had no choice. His own doctors held no hope for him, while these doctors were giving him hope. For a lot of cash on the line.

Terry now began a routine. She drove down to Mexico on Thursdays, stayed through the weekend to keep her father company, then drove home on Mondays. During the week Steve had her doing errands for him he couldn't handle while in Mexico.

Every now and then when the coast was clear—that is, no photographers lurking about—he would go into town for ice cream and other junk foods.

The tabloids were relentless. As soon as they found out where Steve was, they went to incredible lengths to get pictures of him, which by now would have revealed a desperately sick man. When I was there they even had a helicopter flying overhead in the hopes of catching Steve walking around. One of the guards told me that one tabloid had offered $50,000 for pictures of Steve. If that story is true, I give those guards enormous credit. The temptation had to be tremendous.

Sensing the end was coming closer, I notified Bill Maher Steve was dying. The very next day Bill called to tell me Steve had sent a note asking him please to come and see him. The meeting between the two men had been a very emotional one. Bill had had no inkling of Steve's condition and had been appalled at Steve's physical appearance. It was a new Steve who asked that bygones be bygones and it was the old Bill who accepted Steve's apology without hesitation.

18

WHEN THE CALL came for us to come to Mexico, we were ready.

Al knew it would be the first time I'd be seeing Steve in his serious cancer stage, and he wanted to be with me to give me the emotional support he was sure I would need. But he was also mindful of granting me, Chad, and Steve the privacy we required. He drove us down in the morning and arranged to disappear while Chad and I stayed with Steve, and to pick us up toward evening.

Terry was in Los Angeles running errands (picking up money, picking up medicine). The cash Terry was picking up was necessary for Steve to have since everything at the clinic was cash on delivery.

Barbara, on this day, was in Los Angeles. She had checked in at the L'Hermitage for a change of scenery. Steve, although sick and weak, was still feisty and ornery, as always. My daughter had told me there were many times when Steve would tell Barbara to leave the room. Terry attributed it to nothing more than a sick person's irrationality. I think Barbara did too, but I'm sure it was hard to take at times. Especially when she was there all the time and was so easy to pick on.

I wonder if he could have lived a little longer had he not gone to Mexico? Maybe not. Who knows? I'm convinced the treatment did nothing for him at all except cause him to bear unnecessary pain. And, of course, it gave him hope. The "clinic" wouldn't (or couldn't) prescribe painkilling drugs to him. They were said to be "incompatible" with the treatment. To ease the pain, morphine would have been offered to him, I'm certain. It must have been frustrating to him not to be allowed his beloved pot, just when he needed it most.

I somehow wish he'd opted for interferon. It was an experimental drug and the culture done by his U.S. doctors to test the possible effectiveness of the drug showed very positive signs. The drug seemed to be compatible with his form of cancer. However, in order for interferon to be administered, three conditions had to be agreed to.

One: He would have to stop all other treatments. It was the only way doctors could tell whether the drug was working. Two: He would have to go to a Texas clinic for six weeks to be monitored. And three: The medication would cost Steve $900,000 for a six-week supply. But he was one of the few people who could have afforded it.

It certainly doesn't matter now. Steve refused to give up the Mexican treatment. He wanted them both. Unfortunately, in a cruel twist of fate, the unconventional treatment he had put his faith in even robbed him of his dignity ("I've sure learned how to be humble, baby").

The treatment, as far as I could see, consisted of several daily coffee enemas, tremendous amounts of vitamin and mineral pills, freshly squeezed juices, body shampoos, image therapy, and a revolting concoction of raw liver, chopped and blended with either apple juice or pineapple juice, which Steve drank every day. I remember the nurse gleefully saying she was planning to take movies while Steve drank the mixture because "he looks so cute and makes such funny faces." Chad and I had looked at each other in astonishment at the lack of taste and sensitivity this woman had exhibited. I shudder at the thought that somewhere there could be 8mm prints of Steve in that clinic at Rosarito Beach.

It was impossible to ask too many questions at the clinic. I could only observe. Steve had chosen this place and I couldn't show my disapproval, no matter what my opinions or my observations were.

These people at the clinic certainly kept him busy. He and I were able to talk during intervals of his daily regimen. And at that, the conversations were limited to ten to fifteen minutes at a time. He would either tire and fall asleep or a treatment would have to be administered by the nurse. I was struck by the vacant and pained look in his eyes. It was obvious he was suffering greatly; Terry told me one day the pain had been so great that Steve, out of despair, had picked up a table and had thrown it against the glass door.

Had Steve gone into cardiac arrest he might have been mercifully spared the pain he valiantly endured each day. I was told by a nurse this clinic had no equipment for any sort of emergency. Nor was there a laboratory or any X-ray equipment. The clinic offered only its own concept of health food care and hope.

Steve, like my mother before him, vacillated between denial and acceptance of what lay ahead. "Can you believe this? Me, of all people. The doctors in town gave me no hope at all, you know. And here . . . why, I'm actually feeling better. Praise the Lord. They say I'm gonna make it." His raspy voice, the shortness of breath, and the tumors that were visible on his body gave lie to that opinion. I was glad he had his newfound religion to hang on to.

Before I left the room after that first conversation, he had grabbed my arm and had pulled me toward him. "Frankly, I think they're all full of shit! I'm not gonna make it! If it weren't for the kids I would have given up a long time ago!" The hoarseness of his

voice and the weakness of his body couldn't hide the
anger he felt as he said those words. And then just as
suddenly we were back to the accepting person. "But
I've made my peace with the Lord." And again,
"Praise the Lord."

Throughout the day we talked, any time it was
possible for him. When he slept, Chad and I went
for short walks. And then we'd talk again. There was
so much ground to cover.

Ali, who had been sending notes to Steve all along
without getting a response in return, was desperate
to see Steve. I again asked him to see her. She had,
after all, spent five years of her life with him—four
of them married to him. His answer to my request
had been, "It'll make her feel better, but it's not
going to make me feel better."

I never understood the deep hostility he felt toward
Ali. Most especially at this time, when he was so
heavily involved with religion that he carried a Bible
everywhere he went. Even when dying, he still couldn't
find it in his heart to see this woman who had once
loved him. And all she wanted was to tell him she
would always be there for either of his children if
she was ever needed.

Steve had told me he had always felt a sense of
betrayal when Ali had refused to visit him at the
hospital eight years before. He felt her commitment
to him was not as complete as she had led him to
believe. His feelings were misplaced and convoluted,
but I know he never forgave Ali for that.

Unfortunately, there was a child involved, a little
boy named Joshua Evans, who worshiped Steve.
Weeks earlier, arrangements had been made for Chad
to pick up Joshua and to bring him to Santa Paula to
see Steve. It was July and Steve had just been through
the "camper treatment." The phone rang in Joshua's
room at five in the morning. Ali was annoyed. Who
could be calling this early in the goddamn morning,
she wondered. It was Steve.

"Chad can't pick Joshua up this morning. Can you drop him off?"

"Well, I don't know, Steve. I think I have something to do today." Ali wasn't being coy or playing games. It was, after all, five o'clock in the morning. What person has her wits about her when awakened at an ungodly hour? "I'll call you later, O.K.? But I really don't think I can."

"Fine," said Steve a little too curtly. "I'll be in all day."

Ali had no way of knowing that was good-bye. She called all day long and there was no answer, and Joshua never did get to see Steve again. Steve, in effect, "never cleaned up with Joshua," as Ali puts it. She feels, maybe it had to do with the way he felt about her. It is sad when one thinks that when they first married, Steve had even talked of adopting Joshua.

To give Steve the benefit of a doubt, it is possible that was the day he checked into Cedars to have his abdomen drained and get a blood transfusion. In the state he was in, everything, it seemed, was done at a moment's notice.

One incident occurred in Mexico that absolutely chilled my heart. I felt as if I had suddenly gone mad.

Chad and I were coming round the bend toward Steve's bungalow (it was nap time inside and Chad and I went for some fresh air) when we saw Steve's truck come to a stop right in front. There were two women in it. Chad identified the woman driving as Judy, the caretaker's wife at the Santa Paula ranch; he didn't recognize the other woman.

As they jumped out of the truck we quickened our steps and were directly behind them as they entered Steve's bungalow. I heard the unidentified one excitedly say to the nurse that her agent had booked her for another engagement later on in the evening. "It's imperative I see Steve right now!" she said.

Obviously this was no stranger. But my mind couldn't decipher it all. Not on the instant. The words "agent" and "booked" threw me in this somber atmosphere. Was this woman an actress? What would she be doing here? Could she be an entertainer? A singer, perhaps? Maybe Steve wanted some live entertainment after being shut off from the rest of the world. That wouldn't be too farfetched—not for Steve. Hell! Why not?

Then under my breath I said, "Holy Moses, the actors' strike must be over!" This insane bit of logic continued for a few more seconds. (Friend Leonard Goldberg had cast me in an episode of "Fantasy Island," and I had been in the middle of filming when the television series had been interrupted by the strike in 1980.) And then, as I again focused on the woman—whom I now surmised to be a nurse moonlighting as an entertainer or vice versa—the conversation between her and the nurse penetrated and began making sense. I realized, much to my dismay, the woman was in fact a "healer."

There to do her special brand of magic on Steve.

Where she came from or who found her is a matter of conjecture.

Her flip show-biz attitude and her "let's hurry up, I'm booked at another place" comment nauseated me. I headed for the door, followed closely by Chad. I ran as fast as I could to the wall facing the ocean. The ocean spray and the wind felt good on my face. I took a deep breath.

I stood there thinking silently as I surveyed the beautiful and peaceful scene around me, with my son standing next to me.

Life is so strange, I thought. A few years ago, when this very same place was a hotel welcoming travelers, I stayed here for a weekend trying to heal the wounds after the final split. Now here I am again. Only this time this place is a clinic welcoming travelers who are outward bound, and Steve is among them.

I had to calm down so as not to upset Chad any more than he was. Chad was in a bewildered state. He had clung to the hope that somehow Dad would beat this dread disease. He believed with all his heart his father was indestructible. But after our arrival in the morning, when he had seen his father through the window looking frail and with eyes sunken in, logic would no longer let him deny the inevitability of the ending.

I longed to spare my children the pain awaiting them. Steve was making plans for all of us to spend Christmas in Sun Valley. Terry, Chad, Steve, Barbara, Al, and me. The new log cabin had just been completed and Steve wanted to roast marshmallows in the open fire. I wanted Chad to face the possibility Steve wouldn't be with us come Thanksgiving. I wanted him to see that Steve's dream for Christmas with all of us together was, in a way, the hope he was buying in this place in Mexico.

It was late afternoon now and very soon the sun would begin its descent behind the ocean. I expected Al momentarily. I wondered out loud what the healer was doing. How did she perform miracles? Would Steve get up from his bed and be the perfect Steve I once knew? Would Steve's massive tumors be gone? Was she able to alleviate his pain? And was this healing business part of his born-again Christian religion?

We decided to head back, ambling along silently, mother and son holding hands, each lost in his own thoughts.

It was only a year ago that Steve's sentences became peppered with "Praise the Lord"—much to my amusement, at the time. The first time I heard him utter the phrase, my reaction was to laugh and ask, "I beg your pardon?" When he told me he was going to church one morning, my reaction had been the same. His response had been to change the subject. It was such incongruous behavior for him that none of us could accept it. And he felt most uncomfortable discussing this newly found philosophy with me.

He embraced this new religion with a fervor. He and Barbara attended church every Sunday, and the first time he insisted Chad join them, the devilish kid couldn't wait to get out and call me.

"Get ready, Mom. The next time you see Dad, he'll have a plastic Jesus sitting on his dashboard!"

We had made fun of him, I think, because he had shown no signs of having flown into a calmer and happier space. He was still the same Steve—rebellious and troubled and cocky. Chad was forced to take flying lessons and forced to go to church or "he'd have thrown me out of the house!" On the days Chad and Steve went to church, the first thing Steve would reach for in the truck, afterwards, was a joint, and then they'd stop and pick up two six-packs of beer before heading home. Chad has said, "I was generally cross-eyed on those Sunday mornings!"

Terry was never forced to do anything. His independent daughter had a mind of her own, and she was the only one who dared say "no" when she felt like it. Over the phone she would hang up on him when he became abusive. He admired her tremendously for that.

As we approached Steve's bungalow on our left, I caught sight of Steve coming toward us from the right. He was surrounded by the healer, the nurse, and one of the clinic's doctors. Steve told me, rather proudly, that with the help of the healer, he had been able to surmount his weakness long enough to take a swim in the pool.

We stood there talking for a bit while the healer handed me a brochure proclaiming the wonders of her art.

Steve was obviously tired and in pain. I tried to

help him back into the bungalow but he refused any help. He was determined to make it back on his own steam. And he did.

Before he went to bed and just as I was leaving, he said two things to me. "Would you bake me a chocolate cake for tomorrow? Bill Maher is coming to see me. He can bring it down." I felt as if I were being asked by a very sick child.

And the other was his way of asking me to forgive him for the pain he had caused me a long, long time ago.

In a hoarse voice and in between spasms of pain, he whispered in his own primitively poetic way, "I'm sorry I couldn't keep my pecker in my pants, baby. I never loved anyone more than I loved you. And that's the truth."

The one thing I had been able to accomplish in Mexico was the prevention of the complete exploitation of Steve McQueen. It was a minor victory, but a victory nonetheless.

During the course of a conversation Steve and I had had on the porch of his bungalow, he had explained the reasons why he felt he should permit *Life, Time,* and *Newsweek* magazines to photograph him. "I think I should hold a press conference with my doctors here from the clinic. I want to help them spread the word. So what if I look like a broken man? My spirit is whole. The fact is, I'm alive and they've helped me. I owe them that. People should know about this place." He told me the doctors running the clinic were pressing him to do this on the premise that it would help countless people who might otherwise be stuck with the conventional American treatment.

I had looked at him with horror. A press conference! It was insanity! In his present state it hadn't occurred to him to make sure there was real merit to the treatment before influencing others to come to

Mexico. "My God, Steve. Please. I beg of you. Don't let anyone con you into holding a press conference now. Wait till you get well. Then hold all the press conferences you want and parade around as much as you want. And above all, don't let anyone photograph you now. If you get well, you'll regret those pictures and if you don't, why not leave the world and your fans with the memory of the Steve McQueen they know! Don't you think that'll be kinder to everyone, including the children?"

That had reached him. He looked about him, his dull blue eyes darting back and forth. Slowly he said, "Yeah, maybe you're right."

"What about your biography? Did you and Chuck [Charles Champlin] ever get together?"

"No." He shook his head regretfully. "Bill [Maher] and his agent had a couple of meetings, but I couldn't hack it no more. I was just too tired." Steve was very fond of Chuck Champlin. He admired him and respected him and wanted very much for Chuck to write an "as told to" type of biography. I'm sorry it never came to pass. Chuck would have done him justice.

Shortly after our visit in Mexico I was stunned to hear Steve's voice on the radio praising and congratulating his doctors at the clinic for helping in his recovery from cancer. His shortness of breath was even more pronounced as the microphones amplified the sound. But the doctors were quick to explain that "Steve was just too close to the microphone."

I just prayed Steve had refused to be photographed. He had.

A few days after the radio interview, lo and behold, an "international press conference" had been arranged at the Los Angeles Press Club by Steve's clinic doctors to spread the word about how well he was doing in their care.

I thought of people out there, in the same desperate circumstance as Steve, frantically seeking the remedies that Steve had unwittingly endorsed—people with average resources mortgaging their homes or selling whatever they had to run to Mexico for their glimmer of hope. How unfair.

Around October 22, 1980, Terry called me to tell me that Dad was coming home. He was expected the following day. But the following day turned into a day later and another day later and one more day later. He had stopped at a hospital in Tijuana that had all the modern equipment for detecting cancer. He was given a CAT scan and the news was dire. There was cancer in places they never even thought of.

Knowing him as well as I did, his journey home by car could mean only one thing. Steve was coming home to die. By car, he could see and savor his beloved California one last time. Why else would he elect to come home by car? The bumps and jolts had to be painful.

Barbara told me she had driven slowly and had stopped when the pain had proved unbearable to Steve.

By Saturday they were safely home in Santa Paula.

On Sunday, Terry, Chad, and I went to the ranch. Steve was sequestered in the bedroom with one nurse standing guard just outside the room and another in the kitchen.

Before leaving the ranch to go into town to pick up some supplies, Barbara gave me the news that Steve was now being urged by the clinic doctors in charge of his case to go to another clinic in Juárez to have the tumors in his neck and his stomach removed. I was horrified because I had consulted with our doctors here and I knew there was no way Steve would survive much longer, no matter how strong his heart. There was no pulmonary function to support his system. But I could do nothing, legally or otherwise. I suspect, neither could Barbara. Steve still had his faculties and the decision would be his. There was nothing to do but wait.

While the kids busied themselves about the ranch, I snuck around the back of the house and climbed the stairs that led to the porch and Steve's bedroom. I tried the French door and to my surprise it was unlocked. I moved ever so gently so as not to startle Steve in case he awoke. I had seen him lying in bed with a blue T-shirt and nothing else and had correctly assumed he was asleep. The overhead fan was gently whirring. I stood at the foot of the brass bed and watched this emaciated man who had once been so strong and handsome. Except for his heavy breathing and the softly turning fan, everything was still inside this room.

It smelled of ... death. The same odor I had detected in my mother's room before she had passed away.

I must have been standing there for fifteen minutes before he opened his eyes. It took him a minute to focus on who I was.

"Is that you, Nellie?" His voice was barely audible.

"Yes, it's me, honey."

He smiled. "I thought I'd never see you again."

"Oh . . . I'll always be around."

"God, I'm so tired."

"Go to sleep, honey. I'll see you later."

I left as quietly as I had come in.

The irony of the day hadn't escaped me. It was November 2. On this day we would have been married for twenty-four years, had we been kinder to each other.

And this day, I knew for certain, would be the last day I would ever see Steve alive.

On Monday, Steve had decided to go ahead with the operation in Juárez. Why Juárez? As usual, everything was done in secrecy and on the spur of the moment. But, as usual, as soon as Steve reached his decision, there was no stopping him. This time what probably had gone through his mind was the inevitability of his death. (Let's do it now and make me comfortable, if that's at all possible. If I don't make it, then I don't. I'm not gonna, anyway.)

Evangelist Billy Graham, at Steve's request, had gone to the ranch to see him and spent about three hours with him, praying with him and talking of spiritual matters.

By late afternoon, Steve was ready to depart for Juárez in the rented Lear jet with his clinic doctor and the two nurses to submit to the unorthodox operation.

Barbara drove to Juárez by herself, Chad arrived at the hospital on Tuesday evening, and Terry arrived on Wednesday morning. The insistence on absolute secrecy had thrown everybody into a state of conspiracy. It was the left hand not knowing what the right hand was doing. Barbara had completely forgotten to inform Terry where her father had been taken to. My daughter was hysterical until Steve's office finally tracked Barbara down. Barbara sent word back to Terry that she would be calling within the hour, "but only if she promises not to get mad at me." My God, I thought. It's as if they're children!

Steve and Chad had the same blood type. So it was left to Chad to give his father the blood he so badly needed. Chad was told to eat steaks before he was transfused. At one point Steve had asked, "Does it hurt, son?"

Sometime Wednesday afternoon, Steve informed the children that as soon as he recovered from this operation, he intended to go to Germany to try a new treatment. He wanted both Terry and Chad to go with him.

The following morning, Thursday, November 6, both children, incredibly, in their effort to be closer to their father, watched the entire operation.

The vigil had begun.

I went about my business during the day waiting for the phone to bring me the bad news.

That night—another irony—Al and I had been invited to the Zubin Mehtas for dinner. I had sold the Oakmont Drive house to Nancy and Zubin six years earlier—the house I had lived in with Steve and the children for eleven years. So in my old house, with my new husband, I went through the motions of socializing with the nice group of people invited that evening.

Still the call didn't come.

We went to sleep that night hoping it would never come.

And then, in the middle of the night, the jarring sound of the telephone ringing awoke us. It was around four o'clock in the morning, and as Al handed me the phone, I held on tightly to his hand. "Hello?"

It was my daughter. Her voice was steady although it was obvious she had been crying.

"Mom . . . Dad's dead."

I called Ali as soon as I was able to pull myself together. I had made it a point to inform Ali all through those last weeks of Steve's rapidly deteriorating state. I knew how sad she felt over the alienation from Steve. I felt strongly that she deserved to feel a part of all of us.

In many ways I think it was a blessing for her not to have seen him. Sometimes I feel that unconsciously, Steve preferred her to remember him the way he was, whether he wanted to admit it or not.

As soon as I gave Ali the news of Steve's death, she told me she'd wake Joshua up to tell him. The one thing I remember clearly that early morning was bursting into dry sobs right after Ali's concerned "How are you, Neile? Are you all right?" I had answered "Yes," had put the phone back in its cradle quickly, then had been hit by dry spasms. Al's comforting arms were around me immediately.

We arrived at the ranch in Santa Paula a half hour before Terry, Chad, and Barbara arrived from Juárez. Chad couldn't sit still. He wanted to walk around the ranch and obviously needed someone to talk to. Al went outside with him while I stayed inside the house with Terry and Barbara, listening to these two young people make the funeral arrangements. I thought it inappropriate for me to say anything, so I didn't. I was concerned about Terry, who at critical times has a tendency to keep everything inside.

Chad, in the meantime, as he walked around the grounds of the ranch with Al, was reliving what had gone on the last few hours in Juárez.

"After the operation, when we were told Dad was responding well, we all went back to the hotel."

Then sometime in the middle of the night, Terry, whose room was right next to Barbara's, heard the phone ring. She jumped out of bed, opened the door, and waited to see whether Barbara would open her door. As soon as Terry saw her, she knew what the news was. Barbara then went to Chad's room to wake him up. Chad refused to believe the news.

"I want to see for myself."

With that, Chad woke Grady up and asked him to take him to the hospital. Grady was the ranch hand at Santa Paula and had arrived the day before to be of whatever help he could.

When Chad reached his father's room at the Santa Rosa Clinic, he didn't know what he'd find, but he knew he wanted to be alone in there. The room was dark and he groped for the light switch. When the light came on, he saw Steve still in his bed and his eyes were open. He thought, How blue they are! as he closed them gently with his fingertips.

He noticed Steve was clutching the Bible Billy Graham had given him.

"And then I felt his hands and they felt cold. Then I felt his feet. They, too, were cold. And then, you know? I touched his heart. And his heart was still warm. I was surprised. I leaned over and kissed his heart and then said, 'So long, Pop. I love you.' "

The funeral service itself was short, simple, and beautiful. It was held in the garden of the land he loved so much. Al held Ali's trembling hand on one side and my hand on the other. We were crying openly and copiously. Barbara stood in an Indian cloth dress with cowboy boots and stoically held herself together. She didn't show any emotion. I thought it was admirable and strange at the same time. Terry felt faint and went inside the house. Chad stood there with tears streaming down his face.

Many of Steve's friends from long ago wanted to come but hadn't been invited—people like Jim Garner, George Peppard, Bob Culp. Elmer Valentine and Bud Ekins were the only familiar faces. The rest were strangers to me.

Before our divorce, Steve had said to me, "When I die, I want you to have my body cremated, have a big memorial service for me with all of my buddies, and I want you to have my motorcycle in that church at the altar to represent me. Then I want everybody to have a big party!" That had been a while ago, and his friends and acquaintances had changed drastically in the last two years.

The most touching tribute to Steve that day was the "fly-by." Several planes in a cross formation flew overhead immediately after the pastor's final words as a farewell to Steve from his flying buddies at Santa Paula.

Earlier in the day, Ali and Barbara finally met. They had never set eyes on each other until then.

When the time came to say good-bye to my children and Barbara, I kept thinking how Steve used to say, "Life is a scam, baby." In the end, the greatest scam had been perpetrated on him in Mexico. He had unknowingly and bravely brought it about in his quest and fight for hope and life.

They put out a press release that said he died of a heart attack.

Technically, perhaps.

But there's no question he died of cancer.

Was it all just a dream?

It certainly seems so at times. And yet I have Terry and Chad as living proofs of what once was.

On occasion, at gatherings in familiar places with familiar people, I half expect to see Steve standing there with beer in hand, enjoying a joke and a laugh with some friends. And then, just as suddenly, I feel his absence keenly.

How could that body have been invaded by a speck of germ that had grown so unhesitatingly with total disregard for the person housing it? It had proceeded to destroy so silently for so long that its seemingly sudden appearance had taken everybody by surprise.

And now he was gone forever.

On the way home from Santa Paula, following the funeral service the Sunday after he died, memories of Steve came at me and flooded my senses in a series of montages. . . . Steve and Terry looking over his collection of cars and motorcycles. He had told her, "They love me so much that when I walk in the room they wag their fenders at me! But honey, you and Chad sell everything after I'm gone. You'll most likely need it for taxes.". . . . Steve chastising Elmer Valentine, who had a weight problem and couldn't keep away from the refrigerator, "You open that door one more time, Elmer, and you're gonna get frostbite!" . . . Steve showing the children, to their utter delight, how he could walk on water. He'd take a running start several yards from the pool, run furiously, then as he passed the edge of the pool, he would pump his feet back and forth like mad, giving the illusion he was walking on water for maybe three seconds. It made the children clap and shout. . . .

Terry and Steve (with full beard and lugging a bit of extra poundage) at the Bistro Gardens for lunch, standing in line while waiting for a table. Unable to stand not being recognized, he had gone over to the maitre d' and said, "Excuse me, you may not remember me, but my name is McQueen. I'm an actor." . . . The Ontario Raceway in 1971, when he had agreed to start the race only with the assurance a helicopter would pick us up, and his ire at the discovery that another couple had been assigned to the same helicopter with us. He had refused to leave until the Raceway had rented another helicopter for the other couple, leaving us with our own helicopter. And then his audacity at the races when he had wanted to change the words to something more to his liking than the time-honored, "Gentlemen, start your engines!" thereby ruffling the feathers of the officials. . . . Naming one of his cats Ruby in my honor. He thought that was too good to let go by! . . . Steve, wanting to give Chad lessons in the ways of the world, cavorting in the Jacuzzi with his son and three naked nymphs. . . . Elmer in need of $10,000 and able to borrow the amount from someone. Steve had asked Elmer why he hadn't come to him. "Because you wouldn't have given it to me," Elmer had replied. Steve thought for a second, then laughed. "You're right!" . . . The time Paramount Studios had given him Gary Cooper's old dressing room, and to bring him down a peg or two, I had sent him a cage full of pigeons and let them loose in his new dressing room. He had walked in with old friend David Resnick, who had rolled on the floor hysterically when he saw Steve's shocked face. Then both men had enjoyed a good laugh! . . . The time after our final parting that I first saw him walking down Rodeo Drive with a blonde. I had Terry in the car with me and I was able to curb my urge to step on the gas and run him down! . . . The new Ferrari I had given him which he had demolished within an hour of taking delivery. Driving down the Coast Highway, he had been stopped at a light admiring a pretty young thing in a brief bikini when a sailor doing the same thing had plowed into him . . .

My life and times with Steve had spanned twenty-four years. More than half my life at the time of his death. They were over now. Gone. Finished.

That he loved me and that I had been the most important person in his life I have no doubt.

That I loved him and that he had been the most influential person in mine cannot be denied.

Good-bye, my friend. You are missed.

It sure was one hell of a ride.

Epilogue

November 13, 1980

DEAR NEILE,

What I know is that marriages go on longer than marriages, and two people who've shared a lot of years can't become unrelated even if they want to, and often as not they don't want to.

This is a cumbersome way of saying I've thought of you for these last several weeks and these last few days in particular. I know they've been hard and sad (and, as an unwanted bonus, angering). I'm sorry; it really is a great loss and I send all good thoughts and deep sympathy to you and the children.

I wish you happiness in your new life and I'm pleased that things have gone well for you.

I'm sure our paths will cross; just wanted you to know that you had been much in my mind.

Best,
CHUCK

(Note sent by Charles Champlin a few days after Steve's death.)